# T H E
# FINANCIALLY
# CHALLENGED

# THE FINANCIALLY CHALLENGED

## WILSON J. HUMBER

**MOODY PRESS**

CHICAGO

ISBN: 0-8024-2737-5

1 3 5 7 9 10 8 6 4 2

*Printed in the United States of America*

*To the four special ladies in my life:*
   *My wife, Jeanie, the butterfly that can pull a plow,*
   *My mother, Barbara, my constant cheerleader,*
   *My mother-in-law, June, who jumps in wherever needed,*
   *My helper, faithful assistant, and friend, Candy Harris,*
*and the couples who prayed me through my greatest*
*financial challenge ever these last four years. May God*
*richly bless and reward their labor in prayer and faithfulness.*

# CONTENTS

Introduction                                              9

1. Attitude Is Paramount                                 19

2. Your Income                                           39

3. Giving                                                69

4. Your Reserves:                                        89
     Savings and Insurance

5. Spending Your Reserves:                              115
     Unemployment and Underemployment

6. Your Home                                            129

7. Your Car                                             149

8. Debt—The Black Hole                                  165

9. Spending Plans                                       189

10. Your Personal Plan                                  213

    Bibliography                                        229

# INTRODUCTION

If you feel increased financial pressure and stress in your life today, this book is for you. Perhaps you have, are, or will be changing jobs. How do you adjust to or plan for that period of unemployment or being in between jobs? Maybe you still have the same job, but due to a number of circumstances, you're working for 50 to 80 percent of what you earned two or three years ago. Maybe you are a two-income family expecting a child. You face the difficult decision of either adjusting your lifestyle to a lower standard of living or coping with the psychological and financial burden of child care and the stress of being both a full-time parent and a breadwinner. Toughest of all, perhaps, are those of you who are single trying to establish your own households. If you have children or other dependents, you are coping with both the loss of your mate to death or divorce and heavy financial pressures. If you are one of the fortunate ones whose life hasn't yet encountered these situations, you can avoid the problems others experience by taking preventative measures. The odds that you will experience financial difficulties in the future are almost 100 percent.

This book has two purposes. First, it will provide you with the necessary information to either prevent or cope with the problems that finances can bring to the uninformed. And second, it will encourage you as you live with the psychological, physical, emotional, and mental pressure all of us have or will experience. You will be exposed to almost everything you need to know about handling money and possessions. Once you act on the new information by adopting more appropriate behavior and habits, you will find your life less frantic. Once you grasp the fact that more than half of the problem isn't what happens, but how you respond, your pressure and stress will be replaced by peace, joy, contentment, and thankfulness.

## THE TOP TEN

Let's begin by examining ten sources of financial pressure to demonstrate that what you feel is caused by some very real forces and factors.

## 1 Declining Personal Income

We in America today are experiencing declining personal incomes. Even if you haven't increased your lifestyle in the last decade, inflation has probably increased the cost of most goods and services you purchase faster than your income has grown. I took my first job in 1959 at the then minimum wage of 75 cents per hour. My eighteen-year-old son, in his first job at $4.25 per hour, current minimum wage, tells me I was nuts for accepting such wages. Yet if you look at the facts, I was earning more then than he is today: With one hour's wage I could attend three movies because movies cost 25 cents. My son, with his hour's effort, can only afford to go once. He earns almost six times what I did, but most items cost ten to twelve times what they did when I was eighteen.

Perhaps you have heard the phrase "delayering of business"; many businesses are reducing costs by removing layers of employees between the top and the bottom. "Decentralization" also squeezes you as companies dismantle their monolithic headquarters to reduce costs and improve service and efficiency to their customers by spreading out geographically. There are only two ways to increase the bottom line in business—increasing prices (income) or reducing costs. Since raising prices often results in loss of volume, companies are concentrating on staying competitive or surviving by eliminating jobs, spreading out, and combining two jobs into one. All these factors contribute to America's declining personal income.

## 2 World Markets

For almost 200 years of our country's history we were the center of the world's market. In 1950, for example, America produced 90 percent of the world's automobiles. Today we are still a major producer, but we do not control the market. Examine America's traditional areas of manufacturing and you will find that in many areas we have lost our dominance in world markets. During the eighties,

19 million jobs were created in America, but most of these were in lower paying service industries rather than higher paying manufacturing jobs. Both in terms of the number of jobs available and the hourly wage, we have lost ground in today's global economy. Millions of jobs have been transported out of the U.S. The short-term price of free trade is pressure to those whose wages or jobs have been reduced or eliminated by world market forces. The bottom line again is less income for many Americans and greater financial stress on you.

## 3 Higher Taxes and More Regulation

Let's look at a little history so you can see the long-term trend and the resulting squeeze on your paycheck. Income taxes were enacted by Congress in 1913 as the sixteenth amendment to our Constitution. The concept was moral, noble, and logical: Take a very little from the very rich to give to the very poor. Initial income tax rates were 1 to 6 percent on incomes from $200,000 to $5,000,000 per year, in today's dollars. Those with incomes less than $200,000 paid no income taxes at all since government was financed primarily by tariffs and import duties. Social Security taxes, which were enacted in 1934, started at rates of 1 percent on wages up to $3,000/year. Every year since taxes started, they have consumed more and more of your income. Some of you may be thinking, *What about the fifties, sixties, seventies, and early eighties when the tax rates were much higher than they are today?* Both presidents Kennedy and Reagan enacted massive "tax cuts," and tax rates have fallen from a 93 percent top bracket of the early fifties to the lows of 1988—28 percent. That's true, but don't confuse tax rates with tax revenues. In 1950 Americans paid 27 percent of their personal income to taxes, whereas today taxes consume 42 percent of your wages. Tax rates have dropped, but deductions have been reduced or eliminated, and more sources of income are taxed. The bottom line is a greater and greater squeeze on your income from higher taxes.

What about the ever increasing cost of government rules and regulations?[1] A client of mine who owns a McDonald's hamburger franchise showed me a study which states that there are 39,000 regulations from more than 500 different government agencies that potentially affect him as a fast food operator. In constructing his third franchise in California he had to deal with thirty-nine agencies for water quality, thirty-eight agencies for waste management, seventeen agencies for air quality, and fourteen agencies responsible for regulating solid waste. Those 108 pieces of red tape were California only, not counting the vast array of federal bureaucracies' rules and regulations. Guess who pays for all those rules, regulations, and regulators? You the consumer. Both in terms of higher taxes and higher prices for your Big Mac, fries, and Coke.

Thousands of companies today are relocating facilities in states with lower tax rates and less regulation. Thousands more are choosing to relocate outside the U.S. for lower wages, lower taxes, less regulation, and pro-business climates. The effect on you is greater strain just to hold your ground financially.

# 4 Consumerism and Lawsuits

Our legal and political system today is becoming more and more anti-business. From the beginning of consumerism with Ralph Nader in the sixties to today, the trend is pro-consumer, pro big government and anti-business. I am not against protecting the rights of the individual, but I believe we need to examine the reality of the benefits, the cost of providing those benefits, and the potential loss when we give up our individual freedom of choice to the government in return for "potential" benefits. Automobiles, for example, will rise $1,500 in price during the next three years to comply with existing consumer-mandated requirements. The Freon you use in your cars and your home air conditioning will be shortly unavailable. All 1995 car and home air conditioning units now require a substitute for Freon, which was deemed harmful to the ozone layer. Even the EPA is currently reversing its original decision on the damage done to the environment by Freon and other CFCs, but unfortunately the law stands. Freon has doubled in price several times. When you have to replace your existing car or home air conditioning to comply with these new standards, guess who pays the thousand dollars it costs to convert your system?

Lawsuits are a particularly expensive component of the age of the consumer. Our courts hand out millions of dollars in judgments against businesses and organizations. That makes everything you buy more expensive. In January 1994, the family of a deceased cancer patient was awarded an $89 million judgment against an HMO who had denied her experimental treatment for cancer. The members of the HMO will all pay higher fees in the future to cover this and future potential awards. Since every type of health care provider is aware of these facts and potential future claims, you can count on your own health coverage costing you more. Every time a patient sues a hospital or doctor, you, the consumer, pay the claims over time in higher prices for medical care.

The fear and losses from lawsuits have eliminated hundreds of companies and jobs. Lawsuits have raised the cost of all goods and services in this country 10 to 15 percent. The result—still more difficulty maintaining your standard of living.

## 5 Declining Growth of Population & the Economy

Thirty years ago environmentalists predicted doom and gloom from the world's population explosion. Using the extrapolation of short-term demographics they told us it would be standing room only on our planet within a century. But extrapolation of data often leads to false conclusions. If I skip breakfast and lunch today, what happens? Normally I'll make up for it at dinner, but if you base your predictions on only two events (missing breakfast and lunch) I'll die of starvation within six weeks. Unfortunately, much of what we read, hear, and see is an erroneous extrapolation of short-term data to illogical conclusions.

Occasionally, watershed events do alter the course of our nation's finance as well as our own. One such event was the 1973 Roe v. Wade decision legalizing abortion. Everywhere in the Bible sin has its consequences. I honestly believe part of the consequence of sin as a nation is our financial burdens. Prior to 1973 our increasing population provided a greater number of taxpayers, a growing population, and a growing economy. Today's growing taxes fall on the same number of people, producing heavier tax burdens. Today's slower growing population results in a slower rate of economic growth. No longer can we grow out of our problems.

## 6 The Debt Explosion

We have a complete chapter on debt and its dangers later in the book, but that chapter is focused on you the individual, not our economic system. The trend of increasing debt is squeezing the life out of the individual. Look first at your government's debt and a little history. It took our nation more than 200 years, until 1981, to accumulate one trillion dollars of debt. In only twelve years, to the end of 1993, that number grew to $4.3 trillion, and even the most generous of predictors say we will add another $1.5 trillion to our national debt by the end of President Clinton's term. The problem is that those statistics grossly understate the problem.

The reported figures use smoke-and-mirrors accounting to persuade and mislead you. Three quick examples. First, the 1993 "deficit reduction—tax act" was inaccurately named. The spending cuts are three to four years in the future (subject to the whims of that Congress), but the tax increases are now. Net result, a debt that will grow $1.5 trillion in four years. Second, you read today that our country's deficit, the difference between income (taxes) and outgo (spending) is shrinking. That is untrue because "off balance sheet" financing doesn't report all debt; considering receipts for the Social Security "trust funds" as income is robbing Peter to pay Paul. The excess in contributions of taxes collected less claims paid is supposed to build reserves for the future when the baby boomers retire and demands on the Social Security trust fund increase dramatically. In actuality, our government replaced Social Security funds with government IOUs. We are sweeping a growing problem forward. Finally, our government's method of keeping books is misleading and deceptive. There are two methods of accounting—cash and accrual. Cash accounting, used by all individuals, considers income the year money is received and expenses the year an expense is paid. In cash accounting my promise to pay you a dollar next year is not income to you until it is received next year. Your promise to pay a bill next year is not an expense until it is paid next year. What you will owe and have to pay next year, like your mortgage, is not on this year's income statement, only what you paid the mortgage company this year. In accrual accounting, the realities of both future income and future expenses are considered in analyzing your current year's income statement. No company listed in Fortune magazine's 500 largest companies keeps books on a cash method. Only the U.S. government does, and by so doing, it dramatically understates its debt.

If our government kept books like General Electric, you would know that our government debt isn't $4.3 trillion but $17.5 trillion as reported by the National Taxpayers' Union. So what, who can relate to trillions of dollars? Let me make it personal. Your share of the government debt is more than $160,000! What's worse, your share of the debt is growing about $2,000/year since all we pay on the debt is interest, not principal, and we are still adding to your debt. Out of every $100 in taxes you pay the government, $20 is used to pay interest on a debt that is growing larger each year. Worse yet, as of this writing, interest rates are at twenty-year lows. When or if interest rates rise, it could easily take 100 percent of the taxes of all fifty states just to pay interest on the debt. Then you have major trauma to our country's financial survival. Remember 1981 when interest rates were triple today's rate? If interest rates rise dramatically and we eliminate all government spending other than the seven sacred cows (interest on debt, defense, Social Security, Medicare, Medicaid, veterans' benefits, and civil service) we are still deficit spending. The longer we delay the decision of balancing the budget the bigger the debt and more painful the solutions.

Besides the potential coronary to our government, we have the tremendous load of debt in most of America's great businesses. Examine the balance sheet of most large companies and you will find they are saddled with huge debt. Debt for our companies and our government has become a way of life. What happens if we have another hiccup in a segment of our economy like we experienced in the real estate or oil and gas market a few years back? You may find another potential crisis in the banking or insurance industry like we saw with the collapse of the Savings and Loan industry. Who got stuck with the S&L bailout? You, the taxpayer, of course. Spread $500 billion over twenty years and it only costs you $500 more per year in increased taxes.

# 7 Demographic Trends

Three more factors squeeze and financially challenge the consumer today. First is the aging population. With increased technology and improvements in medical science, people are living to older and older ages. A generation or two ago people who lived to age sixty-five retired, but most of them died within a five- to seven-year period. Today's retiree at age sixty-five can expect another twenty to twenty-five years of life. These longer life spans create a triple financial stress. First is the strain on Social Security. According to the *Kiplinger Tax Letter*, today's couple who retire at age sixty-five draws Social Security benefits of about $1,650/month if each has earned and paid in the maximum for Social Security benefits. In three-and-a-half years they will have received back every penny they paid into Social Security, but they will have another sixteen and one-half to twenty-one and one-half years during which they continue to collect Social Security benefits of $1,650/ month. Even if you ignore indexing of benefits for inflation that couple represents an economic liability of $326,700 to $425,700. The truth is that "Social Security" is really welfare.

The second squeeze of the aging of America is the cost for medical benefits, particularly Medicare and Medicaid. The current health care "crisis" you read about pales in comparison to the costs of providing medical benefits for retired Americans. To solve this problem will again require more taxes, fewer benefits, or both. Again, we see increasing burdens on your income—higher and higher taxes in the future.

The third stressor is the financial and personal responsibility of providing for your aging parents. Even the most optimistic economists and surveys state that only 1 percent of all retirees are wealthy and an additional 4 percent financially independent.[2] The majority, 95 percent, depend on the government, company pensions (many of which are horribly underfunded), friends, relatives, and charity for their income. These facts do not consider inflation, which will raise prices and put a tighter squeeze on family members.

Never before has one generation been forced to support both its parents and its grown children, many of whom remain in the nest long after adulthood or return home because they are unable to support themselves on their own. More than 20 percent of this year's graduating college class has yet to find employment. Of the 80 percent who have, more than half do not earn enough to live independently.

# 8 Health Care Costs

If your employer provides health care costs you may not feel the strain of paying a greater and greater percentage of your paycheck for health care insurance. Today's problems of AIDS and its cost of $150,000 to $200,000 per patient is just beginning to have the impact we will face in a few years. In real terms, the cost of medical care has tripled in the last generation and a half. We currently have the best medical care available in the world, but the price for the benefit is the highest of any nation on earth. If you think things are bad now, wait until it's "free" from Uncle Sam.

# 9 Information/Technology Explosion

Today we experience another double whammy—declining test scores for the world's most expensive public educational system and an explosion of information and technology. The world's knowledge base and technology are the only things growing faster than our debt. As many as 50 percent of the jobs that will be available in ten years have not been invented today. Career counselors tell me that the average worker entering the work force today at age twenty-one will have to be retrained seven to ten times during his or her working years. Retraining is both time consuming and expensive. All this causes more demands on our calendars that are already overloaded and our incomes that are stretched to the limit. The only good news here is that the opportunities have never been broader or deeper.

# 10 Infinite Options and Detractors

What is the result of trying to balance a finite income with an almost infinite array of choices and options? For most, including many Christians, the result is discontentment, distraction from God's priorities, and a loss of the fruit of the Spirit, especially joy. Everything in our world system is exploding with more choices, requiring more and more of our money. The more we see, the more we want; the more we get, the more we think we need. It's the vicious addictive materialistic cycle which, whether or not we realize it, has affected all of us to some degree. If you believe you aren't infected or you are immune, reserve judgment until you have completed the book, then I'll ask you again whether or not you are a patient with the disease of materialism.

## FEELING BETTER?

These ten factors are the end of the bad news. From here on in we will focus on the good news. Each of these ten factors can be the source of pressure, stress, or pain in your life, or they can be agents used by God to draw you closer to Him and the wisdom of living contained between the covers of the Bible. It all depends on what information you accept as truth and on your attitude. In the pages ahead you will learn how to "respond" rather than "react" to life. The goal is to help you examine and adapt new, more effective information and attitudes. In the Bible far more emphasis is given to attitude than action. For example, the emphasis of Jesus' Sermon on the Mount, Matthew chapters 5 to 7, was on attitude. We shall attempt to focus on both attitude and actions, but attitude is paramount.

## NOTES

1. Larry Burkett, nationally known Christian speaker and author, raises the issue of the cost of government rules and regulations in his best-selling books, *The Coming Economic Earthquake* and *Whatever Happened to the American Dream*. If you want more detailed information or want to become involved, read both books.
2. Social Security survey, 1990.

# CHAPTER 1
# ATTITUDE IS PARAMOUNT

"Godliness actually is a means of great gain, when
accompanied by contentment." 1 Timothy 6:6

Kay Arthur, Bible teacher and founder of Precept Ministries, says,
"Nothing will ever touch your life that has not filtered through the
hands of an all wise, all powerful, all loving God." When my
younger son John was six he fell, cut his head, and required
stitches on the laceration. John has a very low tolerance of pain,
but he loves and trusts me. To many six-year-olds, a parent appears all wise, all powerful, and omnipresent. In trying to calm
John, who was panicked by the flow of blood from his scalp
wound, I asked three questions: "John, do you believe I love you
very, very much? John, do you really trust me to do what is best to
heal your boo-boo? John, do you believe Jesus when He said I will
never leave you or forsake you no matter what?" John gave a yes to
all three questions, and by focusing on the truth and his faith in
his father and his Lord, he came through the pain of disinfecting
his wound and having it stitched up.

If you were on a battlefield during a war and artillery shells
were bursting all around, you wouldn't be human if you didn't
experience fear, stress, despair, hopelessness, or any of a dozen
other similar emotions. So if you face financial challenges today,
the stress you feel is a normal reaction. Your situation may be
more or less severe depending on how these forces have affected
you; the closer you are to the incoming shells the greater the
chance you have of being wounded or shell shocked.

I wonder how often our Lord longs to draw us to Himself to
reassure our fears and panics, clean our wounds, sew up our
gashes so we may heal, and relieve us of the worry and pain

caused by the battles of life. As my son will tell you today, life's a lot different for those who focus on their heavenly Father than it is for those who focus on the explosions, problems, and pain of the moment. When you want to scream *Why?* try asking *What? What, Lord, are You trying to teach me? What, Lord, are You saying to me through these events? What, Lord, can I do so that You may be glorified and honored by this?*

"If then you have been raised up with Christ, keep seeking the things above, where Christ is, seated at the right hand of God. Set your mind on the things above, not on the things that are on earth." (Colossians 3:1–2)

## ETERNAL TRUTHS

The Bible contains both laws and principles. Laws are clear-cut rules we are expected to obey, such as: You shall not murder, You shall not lie, You shall not covet, You shall not commit adultery. Biblical laws, just like traffic signs, *STOP,* are to be obeyed. Failure to obey results in unpleasant consequences. Biblical principles are guidelines like: Be wise and save part of your income, Beware the dangers of debt, Don't start building something if you don't have enough money to finish it. Just like the roadside signs *Slippery when wet,* or, *Drive cautiously,* they are guidelines of good and wise behavior. Let's focus first on four eternal truths or laws. For some, this will be a review and reminder. For others, this may be your first exposure to these truths.

### God's Ownership

*Truth #1: God is the Creator and owner of everything.* In the first book of the Bible, Genesis, we encounter the words, "In the beginning God created the heavens and the earth" (Genesis 1:1). The Hebrew word translated God is the word "Elohim." It means Creator. God is the Creator and thus the owner of everything that exists. Several passages of Scripture confirm the fact of His ownership of the earth: "The earth is the Lord's, and all it contains, the world, and those who dwell in it" (Psalm 24:1). "'The silver is Mine, and the gold is Mine,' declares the Lord of hosts" (Haggai 2:8).

Our constitution provides "rights" for each of us as American citizens. Our citizenship gives us the right to life, liberty, and the pursuit of happiness. Our legal system gives rights to property owners. The property owner may delegate part or all of his rights to another in a legal contract, but if he doesn't sell or transfer his "rights" of ownership they remain his forever. Early in life I learned to label things as "mine." Anything I create I tend to think of as my property—a painting, a book, or a sandwich I make. Too often I forget that all the ingredients with which I create are God's rather than mine. The Bible clearly spells out the law that everything on earth is God's, not mine, when it asks, "What do you have that you did not receive [from Me]?" (1 Corinthians 4:7).

Problems begin when I label as "mine" what really belongs to another, God. Each of us is conditioned to think of "my" house, "my" car, "my" clothes, "my" spouse, "my" children, or even "my" income. We earn our incomes, but the talents, abilities, and time which we trade for a paycheck are gifts from God Himself. "But you shall remember the Lord your God, for it is He who is giving you power to make wealth, that He may confirm His covenant which He swore to your fathers, as it is this day" (Deuteronomy 8:18). We should believe, remember, and act as though it is God's house, God's car, God's clothes, God's child, and God's income, for two very important reasons. I am responsible and accountable for the manner in which I handle the property of another, and *God wants His property managed for His glory, by His rules, and according to His priorities.* God as the owner of everything has rights. We as managers or stewards have responsibilities, and we are accountable to Him for our actions. When you learn to think and act as a manager rather than an owner, your actions and your attitudes will be totally different.

### Corollary 1: We Are Accountable

One of the most awesome concepts in Scripture is that one day every person will be accountable and judged according to his or her acts, words, and even thoughts. The Bible teaches two judgments. First is the Great White Throne Judgment which separates believers from nonbelievers. The Bible calls believers sheep and nonbelievers goats. Believers go to heaven and nonbelievers go to hell. The second judgment is the Bema seat judgment, but it is for believers only. Here the verdict is not punishment, but gain or loss of rewards.[1]

With the exception of self-employed individuals or business owners, most of us work for an individual or company to whom we are both responsible and accountable. The concept of thinking and acting as a manager, rather than an owner, of money and possessions will truly transform your life. Can you imagine one day standing before the risen Christ in all His glory and having to give an account for every action you have ever taken? Every word you have ever spoken? Every thought you have ever had?

The day I first learned the truth that I'm God's manager, not the owner of everything, my life changed and I was freed from part of the bondage of materialism and incorrect thinking. That evening I got down on my knees and made a verbal contract with Elohim. I confessed my ignorance, asked His forgiveness, and dedicated everything I thought I owned to the lawful owner—God! I recognized them as God's checking account, savings account, stocks, bonds, IRAs, home, cars, furniture, personal property, and royalties. Every financial decision now has a spiritual dimension.

If I audited your spending, would you be able to account for 100 percent of what you earned last year? The majority of Christians have no idea where 10 to 15 percent of their take-home pay goes. If you handled your employer or company funds like that, how long do you think you would remain employed? How can you become a better steward? By dedicating everything back to the true owner, acting as a responsible and accountable manager, and seeking God's OK in prayer for every financial decision you consider with His funds.

### Corollary 2: The Implications of Stewardship

Since God is the owner and I'm His manager, several other facts need to be repeated to eliminate confused thinking. Perhaps you can accept that every financial decision has a spiritual dimension and consequences. When you are on a roll and everything is going well, it is pretty easy to praise God for His blessings because just like the Hebrews of Bible times we equate God's blessing with financial success. Conversely, when the bottom falls out, our job is terminated, our pay is cut, or expenses explode, we tend to equate that with God's judgment. Others may look for the evidence of sin in our lives, as they did with Job, to pinpoint the reason for judgment. If it's really God's money, which it is, isn't it His right to give or take His property? How can you be emotionally affected when you lose or give back what was really only a loan?

If you were a guest in "my" home for a week perhaps we could enjoy watching the Phoenix Suns take another shot at the number one spot in the NBA. You would pick your spot in our family room to watch the games on TV. Would you be upset or bothered if I rearranged the furniture in my family room and moved the chair you were used to using into the living room where my wife, Jeanie, was holding her Bible study? Probably not, because you would realize that you were a guest in "my" house. You treat it as my furniture and realize my right to use it as I please. You are not emotionally involved because you haven't nested long enough to begin treating my property as yours. When God allows His property to be removed from your life, remember it is His and He has the right to do with it as He pleases. Financial reversals, losses, and pressure are not God's punishment; neither are financial windfalls, gains, peace, and freedom always evidence of God's blessings. Satan is temporarily the god of this world, and he uses whatever is available in his assault on God's children to lead us to think wrongly of our Lord.

### Corollary 3: The Evidence

Another corollary to the truth that God owns it all is that you can't fake good stewardship. The evidence of your management of His assets is black and white; it is recorded in your checkbook, your credit card statements, and your daily calendar. Let me ask you several revealing questions. If a complete stranger found your checkbook, which recorded all your expenses for the past twelve months, would he know you are a Christian by the way you spend money? Is the first check you write each month your tithe and offering to your local church? If Jesus were to appear for an audit of your spending decisions, what would you shudder to have Him see? What do you think He would say about your decisions and your investments of His assets?

What about your daily calendar? If I examined it would I see evidence of your commitment to Christ first? Your spouse second? Your children third? Or would work and self fill your calendar leaving what's left for God and God's priorities?

Let me ask you another mirror-of-your-heart-attitude question. What is your career or mission? I didn't say your job—but your career. For example, my job is tax, investment, and estate counseling. My career is teaching God's people, ministers, and shepherds God's principles of managing God's assets by God's principles for God's glory and their good.

A philosopher was walking through a construction site, and, being a curious individual, he stopped to visit with a worker. "What are you making?" he asked. "Fourteen dollars and sixty-five cents per hour," replied the worker. The philosopher strolled on to a second worker toiling at his craft. "What are you making?" he asked. "A wall," replied the mason, who returned to trowel the mortar. The philosopher continued down the wall to a third worker engaged in the same task as the first two. "What are you making?" he asked. "A great cathedral for the glory of God," the worker replied. The three men were engaged in the same task but each viewed the same task differently: Two were working at their jobs but one was pursuing his career. Which worker best reflects your attitude to your work?

The way we chose to invest our treasure, time, and talent is a clear testimony, good or bad, of the condition of our heart or attitude. A recent survey I conducted of committed Christians revealed some rather sad statistics. Prior to completing the survey all the participants had to meet two qualifications. First, they said the most important decision of their lives was accepting Jesus Christ as their personal Lord and Savior. Second, they had to have attended church at least three out of every four Sundays for the last six months. Here's their testimony. Only 20 percent gave a tithe (10 percent) or more to the church, 28 percent gave nothing at all, and as a whole, the group paid seven times in personal interest (excluding mortgages) what they gave to God's work. Only 18 percent had a scheduled daily time of prayer, Bible study, or meditation; 26 percent had not opened their Bibles outside of church; and only 20 percent had a planned special time with either their spouse or their children. Fewer than 10 percent had ever thought about or written a career or mission statement for their lives. Most pastors will verify that 80 percent or more of their church resources and programs are funded by less than 20 percent of the membership. Truly a sad testimony for Christ to a lost world looking for a difference in our lives.

It's often unpleasant to be asked the difficult questions, but my charge is to ask you. One: How much of your income last year went to God's work? As you will be reminded, or instructed, in chapter 3, the minimum ever mentioned in the Bible for giving is a tithe (10 percent) of your income. If this were a pass/fail exam, how would you score? If you would like to give more but can't, I guarantee this book will help you find the problems which currently prevent you from giving. More important, you will learn how to eliminate the roadblocks to giving. Question two: Do you have an appointment each day with the Master to pray, worship, meditate, reflect, read, and/or study His Word? If not, I know your life lacks peace, joy, fulfillment, and power. To change what you are and where you are you need to saturate yourself with the presence, Word, and Spirit of the Lord. Last question: What is your career or mission in life? A simple but dynamic answer to the question of what is the purpose of life can be found in a century-old catechism of faith, which says the purpose of life is to glorify God and enjoy Him forever. If you've never tried, stop now and put in writing your life's career, mission, or purpose. The direction, focus, and power a mission statement can have on your life is unbelievable.

## God's Provision

*Truth #2: Jehovah-Jireh means "God Provides."* You know the verse, "God shall supply all your needs according to His riches in glory in Christ Jesus" (Philippians 4:19). This has been one of the most misused verses in the entire Bible because it is too often taken out of context. As a result, believers are filled with disillusionment and doubt rather than confidence and faith.

To see the danger of taking a verse out of context learn from Random Walk. Random was sincerely seeking God's will for his life after being fired from his fourth job in three years. He prayed for God's will, then opened his Bible for direction and guidance as to what he should do. His finger fell on "he [Judas] went away and hanged himself" (Matthew 27:5). A little shocked, he opened the Bible again, and his finger fell on "hurry and do likewise" (Judges 9:48). More than a little shook up, he again let the Bible fall open and placed his finger on "what you do, do quickly" (John 13:27). Scripture must be studied in context to get the complete and accurate meaning of a verse. Taken out of context, you can use Scripture to say almost anything, as you have just seen.

If you read all four chapters of the book of Philippians, you will find that the apostle Paul had several purposes in writing his letter to the church at Philippi. One of his purposes was to thank the Philippians for their recent gifts. Philippi was not a wealthy area; it was what we today would label a third-world country. In verses 15 and 16 of the fourth chapter Paul mentions the fact that on at least two prior occasions the Philippians had sent him a gift. Now read verse 18, and notice how he describes their gift: "But I have received everything in full, and have an abundance; I am amply supplied, having received from Epaphroditus what you have sent, a fragrant aroma, an acceptable sacrifice, well-pleasing to God" (Philippians 4:18). Because the Philippians had sacrificially honored God by their gift to Paul, Paul goes on to promise them, "And my God shall supply all your needs according to His riches in glory in Christ Jesus" (Philippians 4:19).

Whenever I speak with those whose needs are not met, I ask them if they are honoring the Lord with their riches. Unfortunately, fewer than 20 percent are giving at least a tithe to their local church, and a tithe is the minimum standard (or beginning point) in giving ever mentioned in Scripture. If you aren't fulfilling your part of the bargain, is God obligated to meet your needs? I think not. Throughout the Bible obedience is blessed and disobedience is disciplined. Deuteronomy 28 contains fourteen verses of blessings for obedience, followed by fifty-four verses of curses for disobedience. The New Testament confirms the principle of blessing for obedience. The very words of Jesus in the Sermon on the Mount expand the concept of blessing for obedience to include our attitudes as well as our actions. The word "blessed" occurs nine times in Matthew 5:3–11. *If your needs are not being met, is it because of your failure to honor the Lord first with your time, talent, and treasure?*

*Have you mishandled what God has provided?* That is a difficult question to answer because it is so hard to see ourselves objectively. A pastor friend of mine left the ministry due to financial, physical, and personal stresses. He wanted to replace financial insecurity for his family with financial security, because his church subscribed to the philosophy of "You keep him humble, Lord, and we will keep him poor." The year he left the ministry his income tripled from $30,000 to more than $100,000. I met him his fourth year in business when his income plunged from $100,000 back to $30,000. He was unable to meet his needs, had delinquent bills, his cars were being repossessed, and he was three months behind on his mortgage. He was riddled with doubt and disillusioned with God. He asked me why had God not kept His part of the bargain and met his needs? The problem was not lack of giving, because he had honored the Lord by giving more than 10 percent of his earnings over the past three years. His problem was that he mishandled the $210,000 blessing God had allowed to pass through his hands during his three $100,000 years. If he had handled the blessing wisely, he could have been free of consumer debt, had paid-for cars, and have completely paid for the $94,000 mortgage on his home. If you are in a bind today from unemployment, pay cuts, or other factors, ask yourself whether you have mishandled what God has already provided. In my counseling experience I have seen that good stewards are rewarded and poor stewards are chastised.

*Have you improperly defined needs, wants, and desires?* Philippians 4:19 says *"needs"* not *"greeds,"* desires, or wants. What exactly are *needs?* They are whatever it takes to fulfill God's plans for your life. Needs include providing for your family, doing your work, and completing your ministry. Wants refer to quality of goods or services. My four-year-old Honda Civic meets my need for transportation, but it would be nice to have a new Accord with the improved quality and "image." Desires are for surplus funds after all basic obligations are met. If I had the surplus funds, would I love a beautiful new red Porsche convertible to zip around during our great Arizona fall and spring climates? It's easy to confuse needs with wants and desires. I agree that everyone needs transportation, but our city has a fairly good bus system. Does that meet my need for transportation? A beautiful home in the right area meets my need for shelter but so does a single-wide mobile home. The fact is that almost everyone in America operates on wants and desires rather than needs. When you confuse needs with wants and desires, Satan succeeds in his attack—you doubt God's character, goodness, power, and plan for your life.

Satan's strategy is unchanged from the temptation of Eve in the Garden. His first goal is to cause you to *doubt* God's word. "Indeed, has God said, 'You shall not eat from any tree of the garden?'" (Genesis 3:1). Did God say He will meet your needs? How come there is an unmet need in your life? Before you recover from that question you, like Eve, wrongly add to Scripture and *distort* God's Word by replacing the word "needs" with wants or desires. Strategy number two is in full force. All Eve did was add three words to God's command—"or touch it"—and distortion was present. Now comes the knockout punch—*denial:* "You surely shall not die" (Genesis 3:4). In money matters Satan might say God lied and has not met your needs because: He is mad at you, He is not all powerful, He really doesn't care for you, He isn't concerned with money . . . or a host of other lies. Satan's threefold strategy of doubt, distortion, and denial hasn't changed since the Garden because it still works. We are easily led into doubting God or being disillusioned with His plan for our lives. If there are unmet needs in your life now or later, ask yourself three questions: Am I giving firstfruits to God? Have I mishandled His provision? Am I confusing needs with wants and desires? Choose to believe that God provides, and remember the Hebrew name for God, Jehovah-Jireh, meaning God provides. Ponder these truths that will transform your outlook on life: God owns, God controls, God provides, and Christ is my life.

## God's Control

*Truth #3: God is in total control of all the details of life.* Corollary: there is not such a thing as fate, luck, or chance. A third Hebrew word for God, El Elyon, means God is sovereign. Regardless of what may appear to be the case, God is always in total control. He never takes a vacation or a cosmic nap, and absolutely nothing catches Him by surprise. It is easy to say that God is sovereign, but it is even easier to forget that fact in the peaks and valleys of life.

When everything is going our way we take credit for the victories and completely forget about the Lord. Who really needs the

Lord when you're on a roll? Your income keeps rising, blessings and bonuses hit at exactly the right time, and even the traffic lights seem to turn green at precisely the right moment. It is then, lifted up by pride and a false sense of self-security and self-sufficiency, that we are most vulnerable to a fall. Once we forget that our only real security is in Christ and that God desires our dependence on Him, we stumble and crash to the valley.

Remember the great prophet Elijah. After having defeated 400 high priests of Baal in a contest to allow God to demonstrate His power, Elijah fell prey to fear and depression, and in a panic he fled from Queen Jezebel. King David experienced the same fall from the pillar of his success. At the peak of Israel's empire, one evening the monarch took his eyes off the Lord and focused on a scene from an R-rated movie as he surveyed his kingdom from his balcony. That change of focus cost David the rest of his adult life.

Even Jesus, at the start of His public ministry, after He was baptized by John the Baptist, was immediately led by the Spirit into the wilderness for testing and temptation—and He emerged victorious. When you hit your next peak in life be alert, be on guard, for then you are most vulnerable to temptation or a fall. Focus on what you have with contentment and thanksgiving, and remember that it's absolutely calm in the eye of the hurricane, but only half the blow is over.

For every one hundred people who can handle failure, only one can handle success. Maybe that's why we read, "Two things I asked of Thee, do not refuse me before I die: Keep deception and lies far from me, give me neither poverty nor riches; feed me with the food that is my portion, lest I be full and deny Thee and say, 'Who is the Lord?' or lest I be in want and steal, and profane the name of my God" (Proverbs 30:7–9).

For most of us, our focus turns to the Lord when the bottom falls out of our lives. Death, divorce, loss of a job, pay cuts, large and unexpected bills—or maybe a sure deal backfires and multiplies our nest egg by one-third instead of three. Then and only then do we cry out in desperation to God. Our inner nature wants to regain control and correct the things that are wrong with "our" plans for our lives. Being dependent on anyone or anything grates on our prideful nature. If we aren't very careful, we try to step into God's role and tell Him how He should rewrite the current scene. My pastor says all of us, no exception, make lousy gods. When you are flat on your back or the artillery round severs a major artery, look beyond the storm to the Lord.

One of the greatest examples I have ever witnessed of focusing on God rather than circumstances was my father-in-law Edwin Rex Barker. Twenty years ago Rex had a massive heart attack that destroyed half of his heart muscle. Time after time over the next several years Rex was in the emergency room and no one really expected him to survive through the night, but each time he praised God for pulling him through. With half a normal heart and other health problems, Rex required a small pharmacy just to keep going, but grumbling and complaining weren't in his vocabulary. Ask him how he was doing and you would hear all the many blessings God had given him and was continuing to give him. In the valley Rex kept his focus on God.

One night Jeanie, my wife, got another call saying that her dad was again on the way to the emergency room with another round of heart problems. After fifteen years of watching him go in and come out, none of the family really expected Rex to die. On the way to the hospital I reminded Jeanie of all the other times God had pulled her dad through, and remembering all the victories, she perked up for a time.

Sure enough, the next morning Rex had improved and was in stable condition. His second and third days he continued to improve and was allowed a few visitors from his church and Sunday school class. Day four, the trend reversed and he began to lose ground physically, but not emotionally. Day five, the heart specialist again told the family he had done everything possible but Rex was slipping and would be dead before the weekend was over. The doctor told us that he could keep Rex comfortable with medication, but he presented no hope of recovery.

That fifth night in the intensive care unit of Phoenix Baptist Hospital I watched the doctor administer morphine for pain numerous times, but never did I hear Rex Barker complain, blame God, or ask "Why me?" or "Why now?" Instead he recited how great and wonderful God was and recounted again and again, item by item, all the many blessings God had given him and his family. That night, despite intravenous injections of morphine Rex's attitude was the strongest testimony to the power of God I have ever witnessed. The nurse on the ward who had watched many terminal patients meet their Maker said, "You can tell something about what a person believes by how they live, but a lot more by watching how they die." That night Rex met his Master face-to-face. His last words were words of praise and thanksgiving and recollections of God's goodness and blessings on his life. Edwin Rex Barker never forgot that God is El Elyon.

If you are down in the pits, remember our God is the God of all comfort. Believe and accept the sovereignty of God. Let God be God and as best you can, depend and lean on Him. Your God is all-powerful, all-wise, all-present, and all-loving. Ask for His help, His guidance, His strength. In the belly of a fish, a strong-willed man named Jonah gave thanks to the Lord. Regardless of your circumstances, try Jonah's response. Give thanks and choose to believe that God is in control. Notice I did not say "feel" thankful, I said speak words of thankfulness. Saying thank you to God is obedience, and obedience will be blessed. Later your feelings will follow. You may have heard or read "in everything give thanks; for this is God's will for you in Christ Jesus" (1 Thessalonians 5:18). When you are obedient to the clear commands of Scripture, regardless of how you feel or what you think, circumstances will have less and less ability to steal the joy from your life. React scripturally and your life will truly be different. The problems may not evaporate as you would wish, when you wish, or how you wish, but you will find a new real peace and joy in and around your life.

## Our Identity

*Truth #4: Your identity is in Christ.* If I were to ask you the simple question, "Who are you?" how would you answer? For a Christian the answer should involve an eternal, not a temporal, focus. If my identity is based on my job, where am I if I am fired, retired, or demoted? If my identity is in my denomination, then I am putting it above my relationship to Christ. Far too often educational accomplishments and degrees have become our goals, rather than conforming our character to Christ-likeness. As my mentor and teacher at Western Seminary, Dr. Earl Radmacher, warned me when I enrolled, "Knowledge makes arrogant, but love edifies" (1 Corinthians 8:1). The Christian life, said C. S. Lewis, is a balance of love and sound doctrine. If I am weak in doctrine but heavy on the love side of the equation, it is easy to drift or be led into heresy. If I am strong in doctrine but weak in love, compassion, and mercy, then I can join the ranks of the Pharisees and legalists.

If your identity in life is based on your income, your assets, your possessions, who you know, or your positions, your identity is misplaced. The majority of men today have their primary identity, meaning, and purpose in their jobs, while women identify with the home and the family. Neil Anderson points out that in Paul's letter to the Ephesians the phrase "in Christ" or "with Christ" is used more than eighty times.[2] Our identity first and foremost should be in Christ. If I misplace my identity, I encounter a substantial and needless identity crisis when my income reduces, my job ends, my assets wear out, get old, or go away. Paul wrote to his disciple Timothy, "For we have brought nothing into the world, so we cannot take anything out of it either" (1 Timothy 6:7).

We in America have been so brainwashed by our system that teenagers kill each other to get a pair of designer shoes. Where else but here can a garment manufacturer sew on a designer label (for free advertising), then quadruple the price and have people stand in line to buy? Madison Avenue and years of exposure to advertising have trained our society to identify with the symbols of success. To feel better about yourself you need to drive the "right" car, live in the "right" neighborhood, have the "right" degree from the "right" university, have the "right" job, socialize with the "right" people, keep your kids in the "right" schools, wear the "right" jewelry, shop at the "right" stores, and wear the latest and "right" fashions. When you fail to acquire the symbols of success our society says you are a failure, a loser, and a nerd.

Psychologist and author Larry Crabb says that all of us have two deep, powerful needs: the need for security and the need for significance. The needs themselves are not wrong; the problem comes when we attempt to meet real needs for security by looking for love in the wrong places. Only "in Christ" will our deepest needs for security be met. Other solutions are at best temporary, shallow fulfillment, or they are sin (meeting a real need in an inappropriate way). The need for significance is not found in performance, accomplishments, positions, or possessions. The richest, wisest man the world has ever seen put it this way, "He who loves money will not be satisfied with money, nor he who loves abundance with its income. This too is vanity" (Ecclesiastes 5:10).

Wealth and possessions are just like salt water for a sailor adrift on the sea in a lifeboat. Initially the salt water satisfies his thirst, but the salt stimulates his thirst, requiring more salt water, and thus begins the vicious addictive cycle that leads to death.

For those who have lost jobs, homes, assets, or income the following truths from Scripture would be helpful to meditate on or memorize. They will help you remember that true significance, security, and acceptance are only found in Christ.

To learn your true significance ("in Christ") memorize:

| | |
|---|---|
| Matthew 5:13–14 | 2 Corinthians 6:1 |
| John 15:1, 5 | Ephesians 2:6 |
| John 15:16 | Ephesians 2:10 |
| Acts 1:8 | Ephesians 3:12 |
| 1 Corinthians 3:16 | Philippians 4:13 |
| 2 Corinthians 5:17 | |

When you feel insecure try these prescriptions which reflect true security ("in Christ"):

| | |
|---|---|
| Romans 8:28 | Philippians 3:20 |
| Romans 8:31 | Colossians 3:3 |
| Romans 8:35 | 2 Timothy 1:7 |
| 2 Corinthians 1:21–22 | Hebrews 4:16 |
| Philippians 1:6 | |

When you need to feel loved and accepted trust the only truth ("in Christ"):

| | |
|---|---|
| John 1:12 | Ephesians 1:3 |
| John 15:15 | Ephesians 1:5 |
| Romans 5:1 | Ephesians 2:18 |
| 1 Corinthians 6:17 | Colossians 1:14 |
| 1 Corinthians 6:19–20 | Colossians 2:10 |
| 1 Corinthians 12:27 | |

The correct answers to the question "Who are you?" are contained in the above passages. If your identity rests on the foundation of Christ, that structure will never crack or crumble when circumstances (financial, personal, or physical) quake, fracture, or disintegrate. If your identity is proper, whatever happens will not destroy your joy, peace, or value as a person. If your identity rests in your job, education, friends, or possessions, you have built your home on a sand foundation located directly on the San Andreas fault.

## ATTITUDE IS A CHOICE

Time after time Scripture tells us to examine our actions and motives. "Let a man *examine* himself" (1 Corinthians 11:28). "*Test yourselves* to see if you are in the faith, examine yourselves" (2 Corinthians 13:5). "*Examine* everything carefully; hold fast to that which is good" (1 Thessalonians 5:21). The problem is that when we examine our own attitudes we automatically see ourselves in our best light. Since we are all infected with a sin nature, immersed in a sin-filled world, and targeted by the master of sin, our perception of ourselves and our attitudes is distorted. The Bible clearly teaches that we have a sin nature (read Romans 3:10–18 slowly), we live in a world contaminated with sin (Romans 8:19–28; 1 John 2:15–16), and our adversary the devil is the father of sin and our enemy (1 Peter 5:8; 1 John 3:8). Since those are facts, how do I really ever examine my attitude? King David has the clearest answer: "Search me, O God, and know my heart; try me and know my anxious thoughts; and see if there be any hurtful way in me, and lead me in the everlasting way" (Psalm 139:23–24). If you will only ask the Spirit of God to reveal your sinful or incorrect attitude, He will respond. When the Spirit of God turns on the light of truth, the results of examining yourself may horrify you. A spiritual exam is a truly humbling ordeal.

Many years ago our family dog ran under our house, and good old Dad volunteered to retrieve the whimpering animal who was trapped underneath. Our house had about thirty inches of crawl space between our floor and the ground, so I crawled in and started moving toward the sound of the frightened animal. I was able to find and free him because he was only twenty feet from the opening. Just then my friend David turned on the desk lamp he had stretched into the opening through which I had entered. The bright lamp revealed a mass of spider webs, spiders, and other creeping, crawling creatures all around. I could not believe what lived just inches below our floor. The pup and I made a record time retreat and never again have I been under our house. You will experience the same feeling and horror when the Word of God or the Spirit of God responds to your request to reveal to you your own heart. One of the most painful exercises I experienced in seminary was what can be learned by spending fifteen minutes per day, six days per week, for one semester asking God to search my life and to help me to see my attitude, words, and works as He saw them. I obtained enough material to spend several lifetimes trying to correct. If you have never done this, I challenge you to devote your quiet time to asking the Lord to search your attitude, problems, and life from His point of view. Ask Him to let you see yourself as He sees you.

Once you complete your spiritual self-exam you will emerge with a laundry list of bad attitudes, bad choices, poor responses, and wrong decisions. What now? The spiritual cure is simple, but it is seldom taught and very rarely applied. The cure for spiritual problems is what I term the 3 A's: "Acquisition," "Assimilation," and "Application of truth." First, we must learn to *acquire* spiritual truth. I am continually amazed at the ignorance of many Christians who have no clue what the Bible teaches regarding money, possessions, and life. Everything we need to know for right living is contained between the leather covers of our Bibles, but for the few who have actually read what the Word says, even fewer have taken to heart passage after passage which tells us to memorize and meditate, to *assimilate* these truths. "This book of the law shall not depart from your mouth, but you shall meditate on it day and night, so that you may be careful to do according to all that is written in it; for then you will make your way prosperous, and then you will have success" (Joshua 1:8). "Thy word I have treasured in my heart, that I may not sin against Thee" (Psalm 119:11). The final step to recovery is to *apply* what you know, have memorized and meditated upon. The balance of this book will teach, or remind you of, 99 percent of everything you need to know about money and possessions.

If you will commit to a program of memorization and meditation on Scripture, I guarantee that you will replace the pressure and stress in your life with peace and joy. Your problems may not go away, but what used to seem to be merely problems will become opportunities to develop your faith and trust in our all-wise, all-powerful, all-loving Creator and provider—Elohim, Jehovah-Jireh, El Elyon. The Bible never promised us relief from problems, pain, and suffering. But we are promised His presence, His power, and His strength to see us through whatever we experience. When I feel hopeless, I recall "for it is God who is at work in you, both to will and to work for His good pleasure" (Philippians 2:13). When I feel so lost I don't know what to pray for, I recite, "And in the same way ... the Spirit Himself intercedes for us with groanings too deep for words" (Romans 8:26). When I feel weak and helpless, I know I am exactly where God would have me be, so I reflect on "He has said to me, 'My grace is sufficient for you; for power is perfected in weakness.' Most gladly, therefore, I will rather boast about my weaknesses, that the power of Christ may dwell in me" (2 Corinthians 12:9). The painful part is self-examination. Be persistent with a program of self-examination, meditation, and memory. It pays tremendous dividends, and you will find the easy part is application. Once you are saturated with His truth your worldview will be totally different than it is today.

## Choose to Be Content and Thankful

Ask a Christian what's wrong with the Christian community and you will get a yellow pad full of problems. Ask what's right with Christians or churches and more often than not you will get a blank stare. If I asked you now: *What are you discontent with in your life? What needs to be changed? What's wrong with your life?* what would you say? Stop reading and record your answers. It's a good diagnostic of your attitude. Let me tell you simply, unless you are recording ways that your actions and attitudes fail to measure up to God's standards of holiness, your answers are in direct disobedience to God's commands, ownership, provision, and sovereignty. God is the One who has placed you in your circumstances, and it is His will for you to be content there until He moves you somewhere else.

I had the privilege of studying the Old Testament with Dr. Kem Oberholtzer as my professor. Kem is unique because he is both a living testimony of contentment and thankfulness and a master teacher. Have you ever studied the book of Numbers? One assignment we had was to use Numbers 11 to 21 as an example for the command, "Do all things without grumbling or disputing" (Philippians 2:14). If you have never read these eleven chapters, read them to learn the consequences of grumbling and complaining. Eight times the nation of Israel grumbled and complained and the anger of the Lord was kindled against their sin. When we are discontent with our life, our circumstances, our possessions, and our provisions, we sin by grumbling and complaining. The result of Israel's sixth grumbling about Moses' and Aaron's leadership was a plague which killed 14,700 + Israelites (Numbers 16:47–49). I was shocked to realize that discontentment, lack of gratitude, grumbling, and complaining were considered serious sins in God's eyes. God expects obedience, contentment, and thankfulness.

I live in a body contaminated with sin, the world's system is anti-God, and our adversary is familiar with what weaknesses he can exploit in me. Discontentment is a natural response from our old nature, it is hyper-stimulated by our materialistic society, and our adversary delights when he leads us astray and causes us to disobey God. Paul said that *contentment is learned:* "I have learned to be content in whatever circumstances I am" (Philippians 4:11). What if I don't feel content? Am I to ignore my feelings or lie about them? Of course not, but I am to use these feelings as feedback of my incorrect thinking. As the Bible and modern psychology both tell us, feelings follow thinking and thinking follows feelings. When I feel discontent, my thoughts naturally follow and I focus on what's wrong with my life (wrong thinking). What I must do is *choose* to think properly and let my feelings follow. Paul put it this way, "Rejoice always; pray without ceasing; in everything give thanks; for this is God's will for you in Christ Jesus" (1 Thessalonians 5:16–18). Those verses are commands to be obeyed, not suggestions for our evaluation.

Do I mean to say you are to rejoice when your investments crater and you're left with a thirty-year mortgage on your home? Yes. Are you to give thanks when your pay is cut 40 percent or your spouse's job is terminated? Yes. Are you to be content when your spouse dies or leaves you with small children to raise alone as a single parent? Yes. You may not feel like rejoicing, praising God, or giving thanks, but you are commanded to obey out of love. If this sounds impossible, remember your source of power to obey is Christ Himself: "I can do all things through Him who strengthens me" (Philippians 4:13). All you have to do is choose to obey and God will do the rest. Praise, rejoicing, and giving thanks are sources of power seldom plugged into the typical Christian life.

## Choose Perfect Vision

Another real killer of joy is nearsightedness. Nearsightedness is focusing on the temporal, momentary here and now rather than on the permanent eternity we will have after this life is over. Nearsightedness is answering the question who am I by talking about my job, my friends, and my possessions. Perfect vision is choosing to accept my value, security, and significance in Christ. Perfect vision will focus on character, attitude, and contentment, not performance. It isn't your grades, job, education, position, or possessions that matter to God. It isn't who you know, but your relationship with Christ and others that will accompany you to heaven. Keep your focus on Christ and you will quickly sense your feelings falling in line with your correct thinking.

As we move into the topical areas of money—earnings, savings, homes, cars, debt, insurance, planning, and giving—we do not leave the subject of attitude. Behavioral psychology tells us that our attitudes and feelings cause 85 to 95 percent of our behavior and choices. Examine almost any advertisement you see or hear, and you will find it is aimed at your heart not your head. In the few hours that it takes you to complete this book you will be exposed to every significant principle you need to eliminate financial problems. To translate the information to your thinking and then your feelings, however, will require a sustained, consistent, persistent choice. Applying it will take effort over your lifetime to combat our temporary enemy—the world, the flesh, and the devil. If you get only one idea from this chapter, I pray you will take to heart the following and choose to be content in your thoughts. Your feelings will follow.

"Let your character be free from the love of money, being content with what you have; for He Himself has said, 'I will never desert you, nor will I ever forsake you.'" Hebrews 13:5

## ACTION ITEMS

1. Do you believe that God is the owner (Elohim) and we are His stewards? Do you accept your accountability for the way you handle His assets/income? Do you accept that every financial decision has a spiritual dimension? Will the evidence convict you or vindicate you as His steward?

2. Do you believe that God provides (Jehovah-Jireh)? Are you honoring God first with your income and assets? Have you mishandled what He has provided? Have you confused needs with wants and desires?

3. Do you believe that God is sovereign (El Elyon)? Can anything touch you that has not filtered through His hands? Are you focusing on the problems or on the sovereignty of God? Will you memorize 1 Thessalonians 5:18 and respond biblically, or will you react emotionally?

4. Is your identity in Christ? Is your significance in Christ or positions, possessions, and power? Is your security in Christ or in your marriage, education, income, or assets? Is your need for love and acceptance perfectly and completely met in Him?

5. Do you believe that attitude is a choice? Will you examine yourself and your attitude? Will you commit to using the 3 A's to transform yourself?

6. Will you choose to be thankful and content or to grumble and complain?

## NOTES

1. If you want to know more about rewards for the believer, two good sources are: Charles Swindoll's "What It Takes to Win" cassette tapes and study guide (Insight for Living, 1993) and *Going for the Gold: Reward & Loss at the Judgment of Believers* by Joe L. Wall (Chicago: Moody, 1991).

2. Neil Anderson, "Spiritual Disciplines" seminar.

# CHAPTER 2
# YOUR INCOME

"Whatever you do, do your work heartily, as for the Lord
rather than for men; knowing that from the Lord you will
receive the reward of the inheritance. It is the Lord Christ
whom you serve." Colossians 3:23–24

How do you define your work? Is it a necessary evil to be endured? Is it a means to an end? Is it a hassle to be tolerated as a
result of the Fall? If you answered yes to any of these questions,
you need to realize how the Bible describes work. Work is:

- our role
- a good gift from the Lord
- a command to be obeyed
- our testimony
- a calling and
- the method of providing for our families.

## WHY WORK?

As Christians we have dual citizenship: both on earth and in heav-
en. Our work should be a reflection of our eternal citizenship.
Let's begin looking at work by reviewing the basics in the foundation of our faith, the book of Genesis.

### Work Is Our Role

Work is our role in God's economy. "Then the Lord God took
the man and put him into the garden of Eden to cultivate it and
keep it" (Genesis 2:15). The words "cultivate it" and "keep it" are as
valid for us today as they were for Adam. Our charge is to perform

whatever job we have today by His rules for His glory. Work is not a necessary evil to be endured so we can have freedom to indulge our goals and desires. Work is not a curse as a result of the Fall; the Fall did not happen until the third chapter of Genesis. Work is not a means to an end; it is our divine job description. In the first chapter we learned three names for our God: Elohim, El Elyon, and Jehovah-Jireh. God creates, controls, and provides for us by giving us our work whereby we may fulfill His plan for our lives and provide for ourselves and our families.

## Work Is a Gift

The author of Ecclesiastes refers to work as a gift to us from God: "I know that there is nothing better for them than to rejoice and to do good in one's lifetime; moreover, that every man who eats and drinks sees good in all his labor—it is *the gift of God*" (Ecclesiastes 3:12–13). Do you see your work as a gift from God? Do you look for the good in your work? Our old nature and our society do not view work as a noble role. The trend in our society has been toward shorter and shorter workdays to provide more leisure time where we can seek happiness, pleasure, and self-indulgence apart from God.

King Solomon, the wisest and richest man of all time, recounts his search for meaning and purpose in life in the book of Ecclesiastes. Solomon tried wisdom and knowledge; he tried the pleasures (wine, wives, and song); and he pursued the accumulation of wealth. Read his conclusions about work in Ecclesiastes 3:12–13. The proper view of work, according to Solomon, is seeing it as a gift from God. We are to look for the good in our work rather than sin by grumbling and complaining about everything that appears to be wrong. If you have never read this great book of wisdom, begin with Solomon's four conclusions (Ecclesiastes 2:24–26; 3:22; 5:18–20; 12:9–14). The bottom line was the same we found in looking at our attitudes: Choose to be content, enjoy, give thanks for your blessings, and "fear God and keep His commandments . . ." (Ecclesiastes 12:13). I strongly encourage you to begin a study of the book of Ecclesiastes. A lifetime of wisdom for living is found within its twelve short chapters.

## Work Is a Command

Let's begin with the Ten Commandments and see, "Six days you shall labor and do all your work" (Exodus 20:9). Are you surprised to find work addressed in the Ten Commandments? I was.

I was really surprised to find the principle of work put so harshly as Paul stated it when I read,

> Now we *command* you, brethren, in the name of our Lord Jesus Christ, that you keep aloof from every brother who leads an unruly life and not according to the tradition which you received from us. For you yourselves know how you ought to *follow our example,* because we did not act in an undisciplined manner among you, nor did we eat anyone's bread without paying for it, but *with labor and hardship we kept working night and day* so that we might not be a burden to any of you; not because we do not have the right to this, but in order to *offer ourselves as a model for you, that you might follow our example.* For even when we were with you, we used to *give you this order:* if anyone will not work, neither let him eat. For we hear that some among you are leading an undisciplined life, doing no work at all, but acting like busybodies. Now such persons *we command and exhort in the Lord Jesus Christ to work in quiet fashion* and eat their own bread. (2 Thessalonians 3:6–12, italics added)

Work is clearly a command.

## Work Is Our Testimony

In Matthew 5, following the Beatitudes, Jesus calls us to be salt and light to a lost and dying world. He goes on to say, "Let your light shine before men in such a way that they may see your *good works,* and glorify your Father who is in heaven" (v. 16). Pastor after pastor has told me in one-on-one sessions that many Christians' work, the way they handle His money and their careers, and how they choose to invest their discretionary time is a very sad testimony to our Lord and Savior. With our work, our "free time," and our treasures, our mandate is to store up treasures in heaven, not on earth. I urge you to examine your work and your attitude toward it to see what kind of a testimony your work and life are for Christ.

## Work Is a Calling

A most revolutionary concept from Scripture for me was the fact that my work is a calling from the Lord and that He expects me to bloom where He in His wisdom, power, and sovereignty has planted me. "But as God has distributed to every man, as the Lord has called every one, so let him walk. . . . Let every man abide in the same calling wherein he was called" (1 Corinthians 7:17, 20 KJV).

41

Too many times we look across the road at the greener grass God has provided for another rather than giving thanks for where we are, seeking His direction, and planning for where we are right now. I continually wanted to seek work that was more "meaningful" to God than my profession of tax investment and estate counseling. I had friends who were pastors, Christian counselors, and missionaries, and I knew others involved in ministry day to day, rather than my plan of working four days and giving two days per week to Christian service. I enrolled in seminary to find God's will and plan for my life, but to my surprise His plan was to use me right where I was already working. Instead of asking God to lead me to where He wanted me, I should have given thanks for where I was (and am), enjoyed the fruits of my labor, and asked what I should be doing where He had placed me. Our Lord is not impressed with our job but our character, availability, and attitude toward what He has already provided.

## Work Provides for Our Families

One of the reasons God provides work is to enable us to provide for our families. Although 1 Timothy 5 is about our duties toward widows and elders, the text which says that "if anyone does not *provide for his own*, and especially for those of his household, he has denied the faith, and is worse than an unbeliever" (v. 8) can be applied to our work. The Greek word *pronoeo*, which is translated "to provide for" means to "take thought for," "have regard for," "have respect for." The meaning is much broader than mere financial provision for the members of our household.

Providing physical, emotional, financial, and spiritual resources is the responsibility of those in charge of a home. But no matter what our standard of living, there are always those who have more, both greater quantity and greater quality of resources, so the question becomes, "How much is enough?" Do all Christian parents have to provide the cost of a private Christian education for their children? Do parents need to provide a separate bedroom for each child? Do we need a luxury home in the right neighborhood? Must we earn an income high enough to insulate our family from all of life's pressures and disasters? If you feel unlimited pressure on your income, you have probably confused needs with wants and desires.

We also err when we define providing for our loved ones incompletely by seeing it only in financial terms and omitting the more important physical, emotional, and spiritual needs. If all we provide our families are financial resources, we leave a bankrupt legacy. The converse of this truth is that if we fail to provide financial resources we are worse than the heathen (1 Timothy 5:8). It is a difficult balance to achieve, but balance (not excess) and a biblical perspective should be our goal.

## BALANCING WORK AND LEISURE

The biblical plan for living is the playing field for the low-stress, high-joy, Spirit-filled Christian life. In every sport end zones and sidelines mark the boundaries of the playing field. The end zones for your job are called "workaholism" and "sloth." To reduce stress in your life, you need to become aware of the limits and boundaries of your playing field. The Bible commands work and clearly tells us to work hard. "He also who is slack in his work is brother to him who destroys" (Proverbs 18:9).

Scripture addresses the first end zone of workaholism: "It is vain for you to rise up early, to retire late, to eat the bread of painful labors; for He gives to His beloved even in his sleep" (Psalm 127:2). The opposite end zone is sloth, which is repeatedly condemned in the Bible, especially in the book of Proverbs: "The soul of the sluggard craves and gets nothing, but the soul of the diligent is made fat" (13:4).

Failing to stay within proper boundaries too often results in burnout and discouragement. Can you imagine any sport with no time outs, no intervals between plays, and a work-till-you-drop mentality? Jesus Himself in the midst of His Father's business recognized the need for a break from work when He said to His disciples, "Come away by yourselves to a lonely place and rest a while." The text tells us parenthetically, "For there were many people coming and going, and they did not even have time to eat" (Mark 6:31).

Too many players have been injured and overworked by ignoring the sideline of "rest." After eighty hours of nonstop work many people delude themselves that they are indestructible, nonstop working machines. Yet others, after a hard forty-hour week, feel entitled to much more "rest" than is either prudent or effective. The wisdom literature puts it this way: "'A little sleep, a little slumber, a little folding of the hands to rest,' then your poverty will come as a robber, and your want like an armed man" (Proverbs 24:33–34). Balance is the principle, and rest is a real boundary.

## CHARACTERISTICS OF GODLY WORKERS

If you were asked to describe how a Christian could be recognized in the workplace, what would you say? Having asked that question of hundreds of people over the last ten years, I am surprised at the response of both Christian and non-Christian audiences. Our poor testimony in the marketplace is the main reason many nonbelievers cite as their reason never to consider the church as able to do anything positive for their lives.

From God's point of view, we should hear ourselves described first as content. When some Roman soldiers came to John the Baptist to be baptized, they asked John what they should do. John replied, "Do not take money from anyone by force, or accuse anyone falsely, and *be content* with your wages" (Luke 3:14). Again we find the command to be content present in Scripture but noticeably absent in the marketplace. If you are not content with your wages, then one of two things is true. Either everything said about God's sovereignty, provision, power, and goodness is wrong, or you are disobedient to the command to be content. Which is it?

I asked that question of a woman working to support two small children, and she produced a newspaper article which established that women work the same jobs as men for 10 to 40 percent less pay. She said those verses I quoted ignored the fact that women are discriminated against and underpaid for equal work. "Why should I be content?" she asked.

I agree that in the work world, women and many minorities are often not fairly treated. The employers (called masters in the next verse) will answer for their actions as well as the employees (called slaves). "For he who does wrong will receive the consequences of the wrong which he has done, and that without partiality. Masters, grant to your slaves justice and *fairness*, knowing that you too have a Master in heaven" (Colossians 3:25–4:1). For employers the command is justice and fairness; for employees, the command is *be content with your pay*. This woman, who chose to be obedient, began working on giving thanks and learning to be content. She was hired by a competitor ninety days later at 50 percent greater pay. Not always will obedience be so directly blessed here on earth, but what isn't will be rewarded in the eternity that follows.

Do the words *diligence, excellence*, and *quality* describe your work or its results? If so, I congratulate you for being the salt and light we were all called to be; if not, read and ponder the following verses carefully.

"The hand of the diligent will rule, but the slack hand will be put to forced labor." Proverbs 12:24

"Whatever you do, do your work heartily, as for the Lord rather than for men." Colossians 3:23

"Do you see a man skilled in his work? He will stand before kings; he will not stand before obscure men." Proverbs 22:29

Diligence, excellence, and quality are adjectives that should be used when describing the work of a Christian in the marketplace. "Why should I put forth the effort? All I'll ever earn is union scale," replied a journeyman electrician when I asked him if his employer would characterize his work with these words.

"That depends on whom you serve," I told him. Our real employer is the Lord Christ, and our first duty is to serve Him to the best of our ability so God may be glorified. Unfortunately the electrician still serves the same employer today. Nothing has changed except his wages, which have been reduced like many others dependent on the oil industry. Today he is angry, bitter, and still doing just enough to stay on the payroll. I wonder what would have happened if he had pursued contentment, diligence, and excellence?

## MASTER OR SERVANT?

Year after year, management books come out with a new cover on the old biblical theme of servanthood. Jesus Himself came to earth to model servanthood, "For even the Son of Man did not come to be served, but to serve, and to give His life a ransom for many" (Mark 10:45). Time after time Christ's disciples heard the truth "whoever wishes to become great among you shall be your servant, and whoever wishes to be first among you shall be your slave" (Matthew 20:26–27). Passage after passage exhorts us to be unselfish, humble, and other-centered: "Do nothing from selfishness or empty conceit, but with humility of mind let each of you regard one another as more important than himself; do not merely look out for your own personal interests, but also for the interests of others" (Philippians 2:3–4). Yet, as well as we know that even Christ came to earth and lived as a servant, our pride makes the life of a "master" more desirable. Maybe you need to review what the Bible says about masters and servants. We as believers should take these commands to heart and do our best to live by them because of all the marvelous riches we have received in Christ.

The founder of U-Haul, Leonard S. Shoen, attributed U-Haul's success to its corporate goal: "Better and Better Service, to More and More People at a Lower and Lower Price." Part of the reason America has lost much of its leadership is the fact that as a nation we have abandoned biblical principles of success. Instead of the U-Haul slogan, we have learned to ask how little service we can give, to how few people, and how much we can manipulate them to pay.

Before we turn to some specific applications, let me suggest that it's an acceptable philosophy to work for rewards. If the Lord had not wanted us to work for rewards, why are there so many examples throughout the Bible vividly describing the rewards for good behavior and the consequences of bad behavior? I know one nonbeliever who studied the Bible cover to cover when he was young to determine the basic laws of good business. Although he never attended college, he would tell you today that every basic of business needed to build his $500 million business came from a single journey through the Bible in search of a formula for business success. Unfortunately he missed the overall purpose of the Bible, but he realized enough to know that God's Word understands everyday life better than any book written by man. For those of you who are believers, the principles that pay are all biblical, and we work for two rewards. Reward number one is our current income, paid here and now. Reward number two we will receive for our faithfulness when we stand at the judgment seat of Christ.

## SINGLE INDIVIDUALS

If you are single, divorced, or widowed the financial pressures can be tough. May 7, 1993's USA Today statistics showed the average household income was $41,237 for families, the majority of which are two-earner households, while the household income for single people was $18,856. Is it possible to have a $41,237 lifestyle on an income of $18,856? Arithmetically the answer is no, but practically the answer can be yes if you are willing to sacrifice independence. More and more singles are renting or buying apartments and homes together to provide the economics of scale. In Phoenix, a one-bedroom unfurnished apartment rents from $300 to $500 per month, but a two-bedroom unfurnished apartment rents from $350 to $575/month. If I were single, earning an average wage, and I chose to live alone at $400 per month, I'd be paying 25 percent of my income for rent. If I rented a two-bedroom apartment for $462.50 with a roommate, my cost would be $231.25/month, 15 percent of my income. The difference between hassles and encumbrances or joy and peace depends on how you handle the two largest categories of expenditure—your housing and your car. If you refuse to share space with another, you are choosing to overload all the other categories of spending by placing independence above peace.

Besides the economic advantage of sharing housing, other benefits are also very efficient. Counselors tell me that loneliness is a major factor in the lives of singles today. But a roommate can provide companionship and the ability to fairly divide chores instead of having to do everything yourself. Maybe one of you shops and one cleans, one cooks while the other does the dishes, one does laundry while the other irons, or one can help out when the other is loaded down with other tasks. Having a roommate can encourage you to eat at home (it is no fun to make and eat dinner alone), and this can substantially reduce your food costs. Consider this option if you are single; it will de-stress both your life and your income. Seek a spiritually compatible roommate, and consider a written division of duties to prevent and eliminate future conflict.

I know two single engineers who graduated in 1987. Both got hired by a local aerospace company and started work at $18,000 per year. One leased a "cool" furnished apartment for $550/month and a new Acura and began to enjoy the good life. The other rented a room from a Christian family, rebuilt his 1980 vehicle, enrolled in an advanced engineering class, and saved $400/month from his paycheck. The first engineer still lives in the same apartment, now $650/month, drives a new leased Celica, and works at the same job which today pays $22,500. The second engineer has received three promotions at work, earns $38,500/year, and is buying his first home with a $55,000 cash down payment. Live comfortably within your income, and let life's demands take a long vacation. *Set a low, reasonable standard of housing to lower stress.*

## SINGLE PARENTS

The single parent, whether divorced, widowed, or never married, faces the most difficult of all challenges. If you are a single parent, in addition to the burdens of being single you are faced with the physical, emotional, and financial burden of raising children, often with little or no support from your past spouse. *To survive as a single parent you must set conservative, realistic expectations.* Unless you earn substantially more than the $18,856 average wage, have independent income, or receive generous child support, the truth is that you cannot afford independent housing if your children are small and require daily care. After taxes and child care it is not possible to maintain an independent house and meet all the basic desires most people have. Finding a roommate, with or without children, might be an option, especially if you could share child care. Another good option, if you can swallow your pride, is to move in with family, relatives, or another couple who are able and willing to help both with the energy required to parent and the expense of living independently.

I have given this advice to several hundred single parents, and most respond as though I had told them their child was the ugliest kid I had ever seen. Some get angry, some cry, some shout, and others stare off into space in shock. Most ignore the advice the first time and set out to prove me wrong and to demonstrate their self-reliance. They rent the apartment, contract for child care, and rip into the race of life with the pace of a hundred-yard dash. A year or two later they return with broken spirits, a pile of overdue credit cards, and the battle scars of life etched into their faces, minds, and hearts. If you are a single parent, don't be like the salmon who swims so hard upstream to nest that she literally dies from the effort. Even if you earn $25,000/year or more and are able to survive, I don't believe it is always God's plan for you to raise your children alone. Read what Solomon had to say, "Two are better than one because they have a good return for their labor. For if either of them falls, the one will lift up his companion. But woe to the one who falls when there is not another to lift him up. . . . If one can overpower him who is alone, two can resist him. A cord of three strands is not quickly torn apart" (Ecclesiastes 4:9–10, 12).

Mary was a twenty-two-year-old divorcée with three children under six. Mary chose to be realistic about life and moved in with a couple from her church. The couple worked full-time and had two children of their own, ages seven and nine. Mary agreed to provide child care, cook, and clean in return for room, board, and $100/week. Since Mary had quit high school in her junior year, she decided to complete her GED and graduated in less than a year. She knew she needed a skill to be able to earn more than minimum wage, so for the next five years she attended a community college to learn to be a court reporter. More important, she enrolled in a five-year program called Bible Study Fellowship. It was Mary who taught me an ancient Hebrew saying: If you don't teach your son (or daughter) a trade you make him (or her) a thief or a beggar. Today Mary is thirty-two, earns an average family wage, teaches with Bible Study Fellowship, and has a single parent living with her and her three teenagers. *The key to success is to develop godliness and set a long-range goal of learning a trade, craft, or profession (not just getting a degree).* I encourage you to carefully and prayerfully evaluate the independent life.

## YOUNG COUPLES

Steve and Brenda, both in their early twenties, came to see me to deal with financial problems which were putting stress on their marriage. Steve wanted to purchase a nicer home than the one they were renting, upgrade their home furnishings, have Brenda continue to work, and put off starting a family until after he had completed his MBA. Brenda was content with their existing home, thought they couldn't afford to spend $15,000 on new furniture, and wanted a baby now rather than postponing matters until Steve got his MBA. Steve earned $31,000/year in marketing and Brenda earned $22,000 as a legal secretary. They had $200 in savings, owed $9,000 in school loans, and owed $18,000 on two cars that were two years old when we met.

Their case involved three typical decisions faced by young married couples. First, were they going to be a *single- or dual-income* family? Second, did they have a *realistic time frame* for accomplishing goals? Third, what was the *proper sequence* for acquiring possessions, improving income by education, and starting a family? The first question, of whether to build a two-income or one-income family, should be addressed up front by all married couples (before marriage, preferably) and not allowed to just happen. For the great majority of young couples without children both work. They quickly learn to live on both incomes, and when a baby comes there is the double stress of adjusting to parenthood and either cutting living expenses dramatically or living with the expense and pressure of putting a child in day care while both parents continue to work full time.

To address the question of working moms from a financial perspective, let's look at the bottom line for Steve and Brenda. Their combined income is $53,000, and their taxes are $4,055 FICA, $6,570 federal, and $1,445 state. Out of Brenda's $22,000 salary comes $6,400 taxes, leaving $15,600/year. Out of Brenda's wages also come: giving—$1,800/year, transportation to and from work— $1,500/year, work clothing—$1,200/year, and meals out and at work $1,200/year, leaving the family about $9,900/year spendable income from her salary. If she spent $4,000/year for child care, Brenda would have netted $5,900/year, which is only $3.00/hour. Brenda wanted to be a stay-at-home mom, and she agreed to do her part in cutting costs to reduce expenses $6,000/year until their child was school age. Then she could return to work part-time, thirty hours per week.

The second decision concerns realistic time limits for acquiring a home and other things you want and desire. Steve felt that they should have a three-bedroom, two-bath home, furnished nicely so they could entertain business and church friends. His time goal was now. Steve said, "I earn just as much as my father. I feel paying rent on an apartment is a waste of money. Interest rates are starting to rise along with inflation, so waiting to buy costs us money." He knew their cost for housing would go up $350/month, but they would be owners not renters. Steve planned to borrow the down payment of $15,000 from his 401K plan at work, and he had talked to a home builder about buying the furniture from a model home for a $16,000 additional loan secured by a second mortgage. If you haven't figured it out, Steve was the spender and Brenda was the saver. I believe God puts opposites together to balance and complete each other rather than to indulge either extreme. The question for Steve was, How realistic is it to set a goal to own (in his case finance) his furnished home at age twenty-five, having been married less than two years? Comparing himself to his parents was unrealistic, in my opinion, because his parents had twenty-five more years of experience and earnings.

Steve and Brenda had only $200 in savings, and as you will see when we get to buying homes, it is not wise to borrow the down payment, much less to finance $16,000 in furniture over five years at 18 percent interest. One mark of both financial and spiritual maturity is the ability and patience to delay gratification of desires. Steve was skipping some very basic steps in his planning. They had inadequate savings. A conservative guideline would be $15,000–20,000 (we will study savings in depth in a later chapter).

They were financing their two cars rather than saving to pay cash, which would save them $10,000 in non-deductible interest every five years (chapter 6 is all about minimizing your expenses on cars). If this couple chose to follow Steve's wants and desires, they would have committed themselves to at least fifteen years of bondage, if indeed they survived financially or as a couple. There was nothing wrong with Steve's goals, but to balance life and reduce challenges the time line should be lengthened from the first few years of marriage to five or ten years. Much of today's burden results from hasty, impatient decisions focusing on the external signs of success rather than concentrating on character, godliness, and contentment.

The third decision, prioritizing goals, is a common decision facing all individuals and families regardless of ages or dependents. I asked Steve what his goals and plans for the future were, and he said, "I want my MBA—that degree will ratchet my earnings 50 percent. That income will allow Brenda to stay home, and we can start our family. I also feel now is the time to buy our home and furniture. Not only will a nice home to entertain in help my career, but the home will be $5,000 to $10,000 cheaper now than it will be if I wait two years to buy." Where is God in all this? Is Steve's goal godliness with contentment, or is it an MBA and a nicer home? Where is the priority and commitment to their marriage? Does Steve think their marriage will blossom with no time and effort invested? Which is a greater priority: an MBA and a new home, or investing time, talent, and treasure into their marriage and their offspring? Most important, what biblical guidelines speak to these issues? It is easy and painless to focus our resources on the urgent at the expense of the important, to do the job right but ignore the right jobs. To stand our ground, fight our inborn natures, and not compromise with society's expectations and roles take time, planning, effort, and prayer.

## MIDLIFE

In midlife you encounter many of the same problems we examined for other groups of people, but midlife is the point where you face a major decision that will determine your financial destiny. To some extent, the last half of life is determined by earlier decisions, but how you answer the question "now or later?" at midlife is critical. For those who never ask themselves that question, past habits of spending can lead to failure and a miserable life to come. Those who answer the question "now" and spend will have little left later on, and the results are bleak "golden years." The sad facts are that 95 percent of Americans, after forty to fifty years of work, face retirement with insufficient assets to provide for themselves. Only 5 percent, of this the richest nation on earth, are financially independent at age sixty-five. AARP surveys say that the average retiree has less than $10,000 in assets and still owes more than eighteen years of payments on his home. Everyone knows he should save some of his income to provide for the future, but fewer than one out of twenty people actually act on that knowledge. Successful people apply and live what they know. The results are new, more effective, less stressful lives—a witness that cannot be contested.

The choice of spending now means you will have less later on. The formula for financial success has five parts:

(1) Remember it is all God's—honor Him first.
(2) Spend less than you earn.
(3) Do something intelligent with the surplus.
(4) Avoid or eliminate debt.
(5) Set realistic goals based on "needs."

| | $1.00 Principal | | | | $1.00 per Year | | |
|---|---|---|---|---|---|---|---|
| YRS | 4% | 8% | 12% | YRS | 4% | 8% | 12% |
| 10 | 1.48 | 2.15 | 3.10 | 10 | 12.48 | 15.64 | 19.65 |
| 20 | 2.19 | 4.66 | 9.64 | 20 | 30.96 | 49.42 | 80.69 |
| 30 | 3.24 | 10.06 | 29.95 | 30 | 58.32 | 122.34 | 270.29 |
| 40 | 4.80 | 21.72 | 93.05 | 40 | 98.82 | 279.78 | 859.14 |
| 50 | 7.10 | 46.90 | 289.00 | 50 | 158.77 | 619.67 | 2688.02 |

The charts above clearly show the awesome power of compound interest. The chart on the left shows what just one dollar will grow to at three different interest rates over five different time periods. The chart on the right shows the value of one dollar per year deposited at the same three interest rates over the same time periods. If you are forty years old today, you will probably live another forty years to age eighty or beyond. Every dollar you don't spend today is worth $4.80 (at 4 percent), $21.72 (at 8 percent), or $93.05 (at 12 percent) later. If you choose not to spend $83/month ($1,000/year) you could have $95,000 (at 4 percent) or $259,000 (at 8 percent). Put the power of compound interest to work for you by choosing not to spend now but to save for the future. If you are in midlife, this decision will determine your standard of living into retirement.

Jack and Jill were teachers living in Arizona; neither ever earned more than $12,000 a year. By age forty-five, they had put their only son through dental school. They chose to reduce their standard of living and to live on Jack's salary and invest Jill's to provide for their future. From 1962 to 1982 they invested about $10,000 per year into several good mutual funds recommended by a fellow teacher. Their savings grew over time and was worth $1,024,436 in 1982. Ignoring Social Security and their pension from teaching, their 1994 investment income exceeded $100,000/year. If they had both taught full-time in 1992, their wages would have been less than a third of that amount. They are living proof that spending less than you earn and doing something intelligent with the surplus leads to financial freedom. How will you answer the question: Spend—now? or later?

## PAY CUTS AND UNEMPLOYMENT

In the introduction we examined a number of factors that can and do cut income or lead to unemployment. How do you respond when your income drops 20, 30, or 50 percent? What do you do if your job is eliminated and your income stops? We will look at these questions more thoroughly in chapter 5. If you have been working the last decade or two, you either know a victim or have been in that situation yourself. For men at any age, these circumstances are tough, because men tend to have their identity in their jobs and possessions rather than in Christ. If your significance comes from your position, income, and possessions, your world appears to end when income declines or stops. Proper identity is learning and remembering who we are in Christ. It is not what we do, what we earn, or what we possess that counts.

For women, the problem is usually loss of security rather than of identity when income declines or ceases, but the difficulties can be just as real and severe if we let security rest in our incomes or our assets rather than in Christ. The only true and permanent source of security is in Christ who said, "I give eternal life to them, and they shall never perish; and no one shall snatch them out of My hand. My Father, who has given them to Me, is greater than all; and no one is able to snatch them out of the Father's hand" (John 10:28–29). Christ alone is our real and true security.

When disaster strikes it's time to re-examine needs, cut expenses, and learn to give thanks for what you have left. An engineer from our church was recently given the choice to continue working at his present company at 30 percent less pay or to seek employment elsewhere. Being age fifty-three, he decided his best opportunity for continued employment in the defense industry was to retain his existing job, at least until he was fully vested in his employer's pension plan. He knew cutting 30 percent from his spending would be hard, since the only money he was able to save at full pay was the 6 percent of his salary he put into his pension. He was spending his income, but his only debt was his home mortgage, which was less than ten years from being paid off. The engineer and his wife spent most of a month examining, praying, and laboring to accurately define their needs and not be distracted by wants and desires. Although their new plan required some adjustments and time, they reduced their living expenses 38 percent. They were both amazed at the amount of their income they had spent without separating needs from wants and desires.

Prior to learning about his pay cut, they had committed to spend two weeks of ministry in a small town in Mexico 150 miles south of Arizona. Although they were reluctant, they honored their commitment and left as scheduled on the trip. This was the first time either of them had lived outside the U.S. They stayed with a family rather than in a hotel or resort, and they saw first-hand the real difference between needs and wants and desires. They learned that things we take for granted as rights, such as paved streets, cable TV, central air-conditioning, heating, carpet, indoor plumbing, and a room for every family member are wants and desires, not needs. The couple in whose home they stayed were wealthy by local standards, but they would have been considered below the poverty level in the United States.

Those two weeks opened their eyes to all the riches and blessings they still enjoyed with 70 percent of his income. For the first time, he felt blessed and responded in praise and gratitude to the Lord. The experience of realizing that *almost all Americans are rich, but unaware of their riches, and materially blessed, but discontent and ungrateful,* really struck home. Today, four years later, the engineer has the same wages, but, as he would tell you, he is a new man. "I never knew how brainwashed I was or how infected I had become with the disease of materialism until God got my attention with a two-by-four (pay cut), then opened my eyes so I could see my many blessings. I thank God for refocusing my life on proper values, attitudes, and goals," he told our Sunday school class. Again, the principle is *not what happens but how you choose to respond to it determines your attitude, peace, joy, and contentment.*

## RETIREMENT, WIDOWS, AND WIDOWERS

Ask most people nearing or into retirement what their goals are, and nine out of ten say their goal is to indulge themselves. They don't use the word "self-indulgence"; they use innocent phrases like "play golf," "go fishing," "play bridge," "travel," "visit our children," and "enjoy ourselves." They feel entitled to their rewards after forty to fifty years of hard work, paying taxes, and raising kids. Where is God in all this? What does the Bible say about retirement? Is there anything wrong with "self-indulgence"?

Only one verse in the Bible uses the word "retire." Numbers 8:25 says, "At the age of fifty years they [the Levites] shall retire from service in the work [temple services] and not work any more [at this job]." Today's society encourages us to think first about ourselves—our wants, needs, and desires—rather than to consider serving God or others. For Christians, our duty is to serve God and others, not to cater to selfish desires. For the past sixteen years, I have worked as a tax, investment, and estate counselor in a retirement community west of Phoenix, Arizona. Although most members of the community will tell you they are Christians, you can't tell that by looking at their tax returns or their daily calendars. More than 90 percent of my clients give less than 1 percent of their income to charity in any form, and even fewer serve the community or others in any way. What they do with "their money" and "their time" contradicts what they say they are—Christians.

I do not believe that God meant retirement to be stopping work to indulge yourself. Maybe you cannot physically work the hours at seventy-five that you did at fifty-five, but that does not void the biblical principle of work we discussed at the beginning of this chapter. Maybe we can't perform the same duties we used to do, but that does not mean we should not work at all. I am not suggesting you ignore the need to plan for a "nest egg" that can provide or supplement your pension, but to devote all your time, talent, and treasure to build an estate to indulge yourself is incorrect and unbiblical thinking. Ask yourself: Why do I want to retire? How would I use the resource of discretionary time? What would the Lord say if He heard my answers? Best yet—what would He have me do when I am free, partially or totally, of the 8 to 5 work day?

The two basic errors people make in retirement planning are failure to do any planning at all or planning without any consideration of biblical laws, principles, or priorities. If we rely solely on our employers or the government to provide for our retirement, we err in assuming that these funds will fully support us. Today many companies have pension plans that are grossly underfunded, others are reducing or eliminating pension plans due to economic conditions and increased rules and regulations, and others are defaulting on their plans. If you rely on the government and Social Security for retirement, remember 76 million baby boomers will begin to retire in 2010 and Congress can reduce or eliminate current benefits with the stroke of a pen. Most people who try to retire today without personal assets are shocked to find they can't retire anywhere near their current lifestyle. Given the ten factors we studied in the introduction the problems will get worse over time.

The other extreme in retirement planning is to concentrate total energy and time on accumulating money without ever asking yourself: *How much is enough?* Jesus said, "Beware, and be on your guard against every form of greed; for not even when one has an abundance does his life consist of his possessions" (Luke 12:15). In my work I see many people who continue to store treasures on earth and ignore investing any of "their treasure" into the treasury in heaven. Increasing assets and income is a potential addiction which can be broken by answering the question: How much is enough? When you reach the goal of providing for your needs, you are free to serve the Lord and others with part or all of the increase and free time. The Bible advises balance, not extremes. If we make no provision for the future, Proverbs tells us we are fools. "There is precious treasure and oil in the dwelling of the wise, but a foolish man swallows it up" (Proverbs 21:20). If all we do is provide for ourselves, Jesus Himself calls us fools.

> And He told them a parable, saying, "The land of a certain rich man was very productive. And he began reasoning to himself, saying, 'What shall I do, since I have no place to store my crops?' And he said, 'This is what I will do: I will tear down my barns and build larger ones, and there I will store all my grain and my goods. And I will say to my soul, "Soul, you have many goods laid up for many years to come; take your ease, eat, drink and be merry."' But God said to him, 'You fool! This very night your soul is required of you; and now who will own what you have prepared?' So is the man who lays up treasure for himself, and is not rich toward God." (Luke 12:16–21)

Between these two extremes lie peace, joy, contentment, and the balanced Christian life. The principle of saving for the future occupies the entire chapter after next, and it should be used with balance in all stages of your life.

For those of you who find yourselves alone in your later years due to death, divorce, or singleness, think of what you have to give and share with others, not what you lack or have lost. The Bible has verse after verse telling us that wisdom comes with time and experience and that wisdom (not knowledge) is a precious resource. Your most expensive and most painful wisdom probably came in the school of hard knocks. If you are alone, why not invest that wisdom in your family and others? How many young women could be better wives, mothers, and women if only they could learn godly wisdom from mature Christian women? How many men could be better husbands, fathers, and men if only they could receive godly wisdom from mature Christian men? How many ministries, missions, and worthwhile projects go undone because others do not choose to sacrifice their time? If you are alone, you have a precious, irreplaceable resource of discretionary time. I pray you will choose to invest it wisely and give thanks for what you have rather than dwell on what you've lost or what you lack.

## YOUR TAXES

Before we examine some very practical guidelines for managing your income, let's look at the unpleasant topic of taxes. Taxes today consume about 42 percent of the income of all Americans. Social Security and Medicare tax consume 7.65 to 15.3 percent of your gross income. Federal income taxes take another 15 to 39.6 percent. State taxes consume up to 8 percent. When you spend money, sales tax costs another six to eleven cents out of every dollar. In addition, there may be city tax, unemployment tax, property tax, real estate tax, school tax, gas tax, luxury tax, sin tax, use tax, and more. If you are fortunate enough to die with anything left, guess what? Estate, gift, and inheritance taxes may consume part of what you leave behind.

What should be your attitude toward taxes that leave you with an average of fifty-eight cents for every dollar you earn? Paul answered the question this way, "Let every person be in subjection to the governing authorities. For there is no authority except from God, and those which exist are established by God. . . . Wherefore it is necessary to be in subjection, not only because of wrath, but also for conscience' sake. For because of this you also pay taxes, for rulers are servants of God, devoting themselves to this very thing. Render to all what is due them: tax to whom tax is due; custom to whom custom; fear to whom fear; honor to whom honor" (Romans 13:1, 5–7). When Paul penned these words, taxes went to Nero, who persecuted and tortured Christians. I know that many of the policies of today's government are anti-Christian and anti-God, but our command remains clear—be honest and pay what you owe. Then give thanks and be content with the fifty-eight cents you keep out of every earned dollar.

Some of the worst decisions I have seen people make were tax-motivated rather than economic. The era of limited partnerships was tax-motivated, and the results were largely disastrous. Don't let deductibility determine your financial decisions. A look at your major deduction, your home mortgage, in a later chapter might help explain why.

## Six Basic Tax-Planning Techniques

Hundreds of people have reduced their taxes by learning to think like a coach rather than a player or referee. In other words, they've learned to look long-term, at the whole season rather than just one game or one paycheck; and they've learned to look at the whole playing field, all the variables that affect the game plan, rather than just their own position. Here are six basic ideas that you can use to reduce your taxes 10 to 15 percent, within both the letter and spirit of the law. There are no great secrets where tax planning and tax cutting are concerned. The principles around which all tax-cutting strategies revolve can be reduced to these six basics:

1. *INCOME SPLITTING:* Taxes are reduced for the total family unit by shifting income among several family members as legal entities in order to get more of the income taxed at lower rates.

2. *SHIFTING INCOME:* Certain kinds of income (bonuses, dividends, and year-end payments, for example) can be shifted from one year to another in order to have the income fall where it will be taxed at lower rates.

3. *SHIFTING DEDUCTIONS:* As with income, certain deductible expenses can be paid in one year or the next in order to place them where the tax benefit will be greater.

4. *DEFERRING TAX:* Putting money into certain investments or making contributions to a qualified retirement plan (IRA, Keogh, or others) allows you to defer the tax on income until some future year.

5. *TAX-DEDUCTIBLE EXPENDITURES:* Certain expenses can be tax deductible if you meet specific requirements in the tax code. Structuring your affairs to obtain a tax deduction for things you enjoy (within stringent IRS guidelines) is an example of this technique.

6. *TAX-EXEMPT INVESTMENTS:* You can select investments that produce income that is exempt from either federal or state income tax, or both. Become aware of how tax law changes affect you, and make adjustments necessary to lessen the impact of them on your earnings.

All tax planning is based on these six ideas. If you can afford the cost, spend the time and money with a qualified adviser to understand the strategies and then apply them to your life. If you can't afford the price, invest your time to learn the concepts yourself and then use these six ideas to reduce your taxes. I visited a bookstore in a nearby mall and found forty-three books, any one of which was packed with dozens of ideas that can reduce taxes. Most of us ignore tax planning and delegate score keeping to an accountant or a CPA. If you take the time to plan, you will play the game differently. You will be amazed at the difference in your tax liability after you do your homework and adopt some basic tax-planning concepts like these.

## Doublecheck Tax Returns

I just met with an engineer and his wife to help with some financial decisions they were considering. As a matter of planning, I ask everyone to bring in their last three years of tax returns because I know from experience that 20 percent of tax returns are incorrect. The engineer was very bright, but he had always delegated preparing his return to the accountant he had relied on the past fifteen years. I did what my counselee should have done: I examined every bit of data and compared it line by line to his federal and state tax returns. The result was three errors in reporting income, which, when corrected, lowered his federal tax bill $900. The entire process took less than an hour and could have been done by anyone who took the time to learn the tax law and check the accuracy of his own tax return. The more you know, the more valuable your input will be, if you continue to use professional tax preparation. Most taxpayers need no knowledge beyond basic arithmetic to learn to do their own taxes (depending on the complexity of the forms and the amount you earn), and today dozens of programs are available for personal computers that enable you to do your own taxes. Do your homework and learn the basics. Your tax bill will decline as you take advantage of the hundreds of ideas you can use to legally lower your taxes.

## LIVE WISELY ON LESS THAN YOU NET

The fundamental idea to reduce financial trouble is to learn to live wisely on less than your take-home pay. Most Americans these days spend more than they make, and the result is a mountain of consumer debt, installment loans, inadequate savings, pathetic giving, and waves of financial pressure. Overcommitment and over extension have become a way of life not only financially but physically, mentally, and emotionally. Your first prescription to eliminate pressure is to *plan expenses so that you spend less than you earn.*

How many times have you told yourself that despite your good intentions there is always more month left than money? You know your giving should be greater than it is. You know you should be saving part of your income. You also know that living at 100 percent of your income is a formula for disaster; but there seems to be something that prevents you from doing what you know is right. If only you could increase your income 10 to 20 percent, most of your problems would disappear. That's what most of us believe, but that is not the answer. Rather than increasing your income, you must plan a wise lifestyle, then live within that plan, if you want to eliminate financial problems, challenges, and tensions.

Almost all the people I have counseled financially believe the myth that increasing their income would eliminate their financial problems, but it doesn't. It only increases the size of the problems you deal with. If you could observe sessions where I counsel people, you would be shocked to see that people earning double, triple, or even ten times your income face the same problems you do. The only difference is that those with higher incomes have larger problems. It is as easy to overcommit yourself on a $500,000/year income as it is on a $25,000/year income. Increasing your income will not solve your problems, but learning to live wisely with thanksgiving and contentment will eliminate most of your problems.

Wise living is:

- honoring God with the first of your income,
- saving some of what you earn off the top of your income, and
- living with a margin of what's left with thankfulness and contentment.

We will have an entire chapter devoted to giving and to saving, so let's concentrate on the wisdom of living with a margin or surplus in your planned spending. When you first hear the concept of building a financial plan that leaves you with a percentage of your after-giving, after-saving, after-tax income, you probably react, "No way—I can't live on what I earn now, much less increase or start giving, increase or start saving, and then live on a fraction of what is left." Therein lies the problem. If you are now pressured, either change nothing and live with stress the rest of your life, or start now to take steps that will eliminate the problem.

Maybe an example will help. If today you were planning your summer vacation to visit relatives across the country you would gather information on airfares, room rates, and a rental car, and you would estimate the costs of meals, travel, and expenses. Let's say your total expenditure comes out to be $1,500, and that's exactly what you have in your vacation fund. If you leave on your trip with exactly $1,500, your plan has problems. What happens when you want to buy something you hadn't planned on buying? What happens when you get stuck with a medical bill when your daughter slams the car door on your son's finger? What happens when a family member tells you her problems and asks for a small loan until she gets back on her feet? You either overrun your plan, usually on credit, or you lose your good attitude after having to say no the fourth time to an unexpected, unplanned financial demand. That's the problem with living at 100 percent of your income. There is no room for error, problems, and the unforeseen. If you want to eliminate problems, build a plan that allows for Murphy's Law (whatever can go wrong usually does and at the worst possible time).

Living on a plan for 80 to 90 percent of your income is a tall order, but if you approach life in that manner, your life will not be as traumatic when you encounter cost overruns, unforeseen problems, and the unexpected. What if you adjusted your vacation plan and with shopping, a little effort, and some sacrifice of wants and desires, you reduced the costs to $1,200? I advise you not to begin the vacation unless you have an extra $100, $200, or $300 surplus or margin, or you are asking for problems. When you plan wisely (by first allowing for giving, saving, taxes, and a margin for errors), you are planning to reduce or eliminate financial pressure and problems ahead.

So what do you do with a surplus if you don't need to spend it? It depends on your situation, but you might want to leave it in your checking account until it reaches a predetermined amount, then transfer it to savings.

The greater your experience, the lower your margin for error can be, but from years of experience let me recommend at least a 5 to 10 percent margin for error for those of you who are living on a fixed salary. If you are self-employed, in business for yourself, or on a variable or commissioned income, I would raise the margin to a minimum of 10 to 20 percent to eliminate problems and smooth out the peaks and valleys that all of us in business endure. The following example will quantify the principle. It assumes as average an American household earning $40,000/year.

| | |
|---|---|
| Gross earnings | = $40,000 |
| less 10% giving | − 4,000 |
| less 10% saving | − 4,000 |
| less total taxes | − 7,288 |
| less 10% margin | − 4,000 |
| Spendable income | $20,712 or $1,726/month |

The arithmetic is simple, but learning to live with contentment and thankfulness on a realistic bottom line will require effort, prayer, discipline, thrift, and time. To help you be realistic and thankful, you should know that the average global household income is less than $2,000/year, not $20,712/year.

## Have a Plan for the Blessing

For years hundreds of writers have told us that fewer than 5 percent of Americans have written goals for their lives. What is shocking is that many studies over several decades verify that the 5 percent with written goals and plans accomplish more during their lifetimes than the 95 percent combined who have no written goals. The Bible tells us we must have goals, make choices, and be diligent, but beyond that it tells us that only goals made with the Lord's counsel are worth pursuing. "The mind of man plans his way, but the Lord directs his steps" (Proverbs 16:9).

An astounding application of having a goal and a plan for our lives is the simple principle of saving a percentage of our income.

| YRS | CUMULATIVE EARNINGS |
|---|---|
| 10 | $  250,000 |
| 20 | 500,000 |
| 30 | 750,000 |
| 40 | 1,000,000 |
| 50 | 1,250,000 |

The chart on the previous page shows the result of saving a fixed percentage of your income. As you can see, a person who earns $25,000/year has $1,000,000 flow through his hands during forty years of work. If that person had a goal of saving just 10 percent of his income and a plan of having it deducted from his paycheck, he could save $100,000 during his forty years of work.

Our wants and desires consume whatever income we earn and permit them to consume. A simple secret for financial freedom is to have a plan for saving a percentage of your income and pay yourself first. Then, live with contentment and thanksgiving on what is left. To see the tremendous power of compound interest over time, look at what you could accumulate if you earned $25,000/year, saved 10 percent of your earnings, and earned a 10 percent return on your savings. In forty years you would have $1,217,130. Even if you subtract taxes and inflation there is a sizable fortune left. Less than 1 percent of today's retirees have more than $600,000 in assets. All you need to do is *commit to saving a fixed percentage of income and pay yourself first rather than "try" to save what's left.*

| YRS | SAVINGS |
|-----|---------|
| 10  | $   43,828 |
| 20  | 157,506 |
| 30  | 452,356 |
| 40  | 1,217,130 |

To make our picture more realistic let's assume your income rises over time, at the same rate it has the last forty years—4 percent. Look at the chart on the next page, which shows you the result of saving 10 percent of a rising income. By saving only 10 percent of your income, in forty years you could accumulate $196,658, but that is before we compute interest on your savings. If we use a 10 percent return on your savings, compounded over a forty-year working life, you would have accumulated $1,658,046! My goal is not to urge you to accumulate a fortune to retire upon but to show you practically the results that can be achieved by having a goal and plan for your income and to remind you that *your rising income is an asset.* Of course, inflation and taxes will consume some of that money, but the person who is committed to saving some of his income is considerably better off than the person who spends his entire income and then goes in debt.

| YEAR | YEARLY INCOME | ANNUAL SAVINGS | CUMULATIVE SAVINGS | CUMULATIVE SAVINGS at 10% INTEREST |
|---|---|---|---|---|
| 1 | $ 25,000 | $ 2,500 | $ 2,500 | $ 2,750 |
| 10 | 37,006 | 3,701 | 32,019 | 52,460 |
| 20 | 54,778 | 5,478 | 71,691 | 198,856 |
| 30 | 81,085 | 8,109 | 125,007 | 596,224 |
| 40 | 120,026 | 12,003 | 196,658 | 1,658,046 |

See how simple it is to get from financial bondage to financial freedom? All you must do is commit and persist. The sooner you begin, the more dramatic the results. Will you commit to begin today on your journey to freedom?

## Sharpen Your Tools, Talents, and Abilities

The best-seller *Seven Habits of Highly Effective People* by Stephen R. Covey contains a principle called *sharpen the saw*. "Sharpen the saw" means you should spend time, energy, and money to improve yourself and your abilities.

Think of two lumberjacks whose job is to cut down trees with a hand saw. Lumberjack number one puts in his forty-hour week sawing down tree after tree, hour after hour, day after day. Lumberjack number two, at the same job with the same tool, abilities, and strength spends six minutes every two hours sharpening his saw. Who do you think would fell more trees in a week? The same idea can work for you. I encourage you to invest time into sharpening your five saws: financial, family, marriage, physical, and, most important, spiritual. The ten problems we began to examine in the introduction become opportunities if you take the time, effort, and money to acquire or sharpen your tools.

Years ago the actor Ronald Reagan put it this way on a commercial he did for General Electric, "The future belongs to those who prepare for it." Examine the expenses of any of the great companies of our world, and you will find an expenditure labeled "R & D," meaning Research and Development. Depending on the company, expenditures for R & D range from nothing to 5 percent of total income. It is no coincidence that the companies with growing market share, expanding sales, increasing earnings, and rising share prices spend more on R & D than those with shrinking market share, declining sales, declining earnings, and shrinking share prices. The best investment you can make is an investment into making yourself more marketable. In today's marketplace you either improve yourself and your abilities or a few years hence you will be obsolete. It's "grow" or "go," your choice.

Almost ten years ago, I met with a high school senior who had no idea what to do with his life. He had no interest in going to college, he hated his minimum wage job at Burger King, and he met with me merely to get his parents off his back. The only thing he was interested in was drama. He felt he had too little talent to pursue the performing arts as an actor, but he enjoyed drama and volunteered to help build sets for a local community theater. That young man grabbed the idea of sharpening his tools and for the first time really committed himself to being the best he could be as a volunteer set builder. He read, studied, learned, and worked at improving his skills. In less than a year, he was hired by a very large theater in Los Angeles to work full-time building sets. Two years later that young man, age twenty, was earning $30,000/year and studying engineering to further sharpen his tools. Today, six years later, my young friend is a set designer, with an engineering degree, who earns more than $100,000/year doing a job he loves and excels at.

Sharpen your tools in all areas of life. The return on invested time, energy, and capital can be tremendous not only in this life but in the life to come. Take to heart these words written by Paul, "Whatever you do, do your work heartily, as for the Lord rather than for men; knowing that from the Lord you will receive the reward of the inheritance. It is the Lord Christ whom you serve" (Colossians 3:23–24). Incidentally, our young set designer isn't working because he can make $100,000/year, and he didn't get his job by having money as his goal. His goal today is to serve Christ in the ultra-fertile mission field of Hollywood.

## Set Realistic Time Frames and Goals

A sure way to create pressures and problems is by having unrealistic time frames and goals. For those of you just starting your career, try to be realistic in both goals and time lines for accomplishing your material goals. Everyone wants the house of his dreams right now, before prices or mortgage rates climb any higher. Add to that the wish to have the home color keyed, impeccably decorated, and furnished with quality, name-brand furnishings. If those goals are achieved, then we can think about landscaping and adding a swimming pool, saunas, tennis courts, and a gazebo. And we really can't have our old clunkers parked in that three-car garage which has room for a boat, a couple of snowmobiles or maybe a camper, and an ATV or two. The list goes on and on and we accumulate more things until we begin to think we need a larger home and maybe a second home or a time-sharing condo for vacations and retreats. If we listen to our incessant wants and desires, our debt load soon exceeds our income as we try to acquire too much—too fast. The result is discontentment and stress that destroys lives, marriages, and families by unrealistic goals with unrealistic time lines.

For those of you in the middle years when the time and obligations of raising a family hit peak demand, we add to the unrealistic goals and time lines of the younger crowd. We increase the quantity and quality of wants and desires, add impossible goals for retirement in our fifties, and simultaneously seek greater improvements in our lifestyles. Patience as a virtue is drowned out by the instant gratification, buy-now pay-later, I owe it to myself mentality. Contentment is a rare virtue; today we prioritize keeping up with the Joneses, having state-of-the-art everything from computers to cellular phones, and sacrificing whatever's necessary to indulge the desires we have been brainwashed by society to believe we "need" and deserve. The final straw for many lives and marriages is that second, third, or fourth mortgage so we can tell our friends that our children attend Status University.

By the time we approach retirement and figure out that we can't live on Social Security and/or our pension, our peak earning years lie behind us. When we take inventory of our assets we find we have little or no equity, a ton of bills, car payments we strain to meet, and a twenty-five year mortgage on our dream home. What started out as the good life has turned into years of unburdening ourselves from impulsive indulgences. Far too many people face the golden years alienated from their children, enduring the consequences of overtaxing their bodies, tolerating marriages that are empty but an economic necessity, and wishing they could start over again knowing what they know now. No wonder alcoholism, drug abuse, suicide, and divorce are so common at age sixty and beyond.

Every one of these problems could be eliminated or prevented if the people had set some realistic goals and realistic time lines that center around proper spiritual priorities. Here are a few that I suggest you consider, rather than pursuing the acquisition of empty material possessions and status symbols.

(1) a personal relationship with the living Lord,
(2) developing character, godliness, and contentment,

(3) giving something off the top ("first-fruits") of every check to your church,

(4) getting and staying free of consumer (credit card) debt,

(5) saving a percentage of every paycheck you receive,

(6) living on less than your income (with a margin),

(7) saving to buy cars in cash rather than financing or leasing,

(8) paying off your home in ten to fifteen years instead of thirty to forty years,

(9) learning to buy function rather than status, and

(10) learning to make do and do without, with a thankful spirit.

Most financial pressures come from unrealistic objectives, time lines, and attitudes. Reality is never as bad as it appears if we have an eternal perspective, seek meaningful biblical objectives, and remind ourselves that God is our Creator, that He is in total control, and that He has promised to meet our needs. I encourage you to write out your goals and compare them to the ten suggestions above. Are you storing treasures in heaven or on earth? Are you pursuing your goals or God's goals and plans for your life? Are you focused on the problems or the opportunities?

## Problems or Opportunities?

Perhaps your income has been flat while prices continue to rise. Or maybe your income has dropped and it seems impossible to make ends meet. Or perhaps your income is gone and you see years of effort evaporating with each tick of the clock. Any of these circumstances is enough to crush your self-image and self-worth if you forget that your problem is an identity problem rather than a financial problem. Just as riches are not always a sign of God's blessings, problems are not always a sign of God's judgment. Perhaps your problems and feelings are His way of encouraging you to deepen your relationship and commitment to Him and His plans. God is interested in your character, not your position. He wants you to value your relationship with Him above your possessions. He wants you to be content and thankful for all the temporal and eternal riches you have and will have, not depressed and dejected by dwelling on what you have lost.

Each and every day, all of us who call ourselves Christians have a unique opportunity to let others see the difference Christ can make in our lives. Choosing to be content isn't easy, but it can be done. Concentrating on what we have (left) is difficult, but it will make a 100 percent difference in our attitude. Learning to be thankful is not a natural response to adversity or problems, but it is His command, not a suggestion for our consideration.

## ACTION ITEMS

1. Do you believe that work is:
   your role?
   a good gift from God?
   a command to obey?
   your testimony?
   your calling?
   your means of providing for your family?

2. Do you honor the boundaries of work?
   workaholism and sloth
   sufficient rest

3. Is your attitude to your work characterized by: contentment? diligence? excellence? quality?

4. Are you seeking knowledge or wisdom?

5. Is your goal dependence or independence?

6. Are you Spirit-filled and directed or self-filled and directed?

7. Is your goal to be the master or the servant?

8. Which of the six basic tax-planning techniques will you use and apply?

9. Will you choose today to live on *less* than you earn?

10. How will you allocate your blessing?
    _____ % giving
    _____ % saved
    _____ % debt reduction
    _____ % spending

11. Will you commit to save a percentage and pay yourself first starting now?

12. Will you invest time, talent, and energy to sharpening your tools?

13. What are your current long-term or short-term goals?

14. Do you see the problems or the opportunity?

15. Have you memorized Hebrews 13:5 yet?

# CHAPTER 3
# GIVING

"Give, and it will be given to you; good measure, pressed down, shaken together, running over, they will pour into your lap. For by your standard of measure it will be measured to you in return." Luke 6:38

*When you give you are choosing to invest with God.* The world says give it and it's gone, but the Bible says when you give you are investing with God. You reap a tremendous multiple for each seed you sow and each eternal investment you make. Read the parable of the sower in Matthew 13:3–23 and you will find returns of thirtyfold, sixtyfold, or a hundredfold. We have a lemon tree in our backyard that last year produced more than seven hundred lemons. All those lemons came from one tiny seed which year after year bears fruit.

Do you know that the only place in the Bible where God asks people to test Him is in relation to giving? "'Test Me now in this,' says the Lord of hosts, 'if I will not open for you the windows of heaven, and pour out for you a blessing until it overflows. Then I will rebuke the devourer for you, so that it may not destroy the fruits of the ground; nor will your vine in the field cast its grapes,' says the Lord of Hosts" (Malachi 3:10–11).

## YOUR TESTIMONY

It was true in the early church and it is true in life today that the way we view and use our material possessions gives testimony to our relationship with Christ. The entire Bible points toward Christ. Both our attitudes and use of material possessions are methods everyone can use to point others to Him. You encourage others to believe in Christ by your unselfish and generous giving. The results of giving in the early church were identical. People gave generously and unselfishly, their hearts were right, God was praised, the church was blessed, and God added to their number day by day. Your giving encourages others to believe in Christ and to give.

Stop now and get yourself a pen and paper. Don't read on to see what I'm going to say next; find a pen and paper now, then return.

Here's the task. A magic genie appears and says to you, "You can have anything you can write down on your piece of paper in the next three minutes. Get ready to make your list. Ready? Go!" Don't read on, write, the seconds are ticking off.

POOF. By now, you either have a page of wishes, or you are not going to reveal yourself. Look at what you have written and ask yourself whether your wishes represent treasures in earth or treasures in heaven. Having done this hundreds of times with Christian groups, I can tell you that most of our goals relate to building treasure on earth. We all know this shouldn't be our goal, but it is very easy to conform to the world's thinking and to develop bad habits.

Where do you choose to store your treasure? You have only two choices—in heaven or on earth. Your answer to that question determines the direction of your life, and your two possible choices lead in totally different directions. Why can't you do a little of both? Jesus answered that question by saying you cannot serve both God and money. He said that where your treasure is (heaven or earth) there you will find your heart. If you want to know which direction you are headed answer these questions by examining your life. What do you spend more time talking about, heavenly treasure or earthly treasure? Which do you spend more effort creating and building, heavenly treasure or earthly treasure? Where do you invest more money, heavenly treasure or earthly treasure? Be honest and examine your actions, not your intentions. How do you score? Is your purpose to create treasure in heaven or here on earth? Giving is not only a barometer of your true values, it builds up treasure in heaven.

The best way I know to break the bondage of materialism is by giving. We will see later in this chapter that giving has both a corporate aspect (offerings given to the church) and an individual aspect (giving to individuals who need our help). Our lives are blinded by our material culture, and the host of material possessions that surround us makes it difficult to see our need for God and to be a creditable testimony. Jesus confirmed this truth by saying that it is difficult for a rich man to enter into heaven; He knew that materialism blinds people to their need for God. When you give, you recognize and acknowledge that need, open your own eyes, and break the bondage of materialism. You also may open the eyes of others to their need of salvation in Christ. "Blessed are the poor in spirit, for theirs is the kingdom of heaven" (Matthew 5:3). We are not ready for salvation until we recognize our own poverty and need for a Savior.

## Giving Unifies Christ's Church

The results of proper attitudes, use of material assets, and giving produced love and unity in the early church: "All the believers were one in heart and mind" (Acts 4:32 NIV). A church where individual needs are met by church members is characterized by love and unity. Such a church is an undeniable testimony to all non-Christians, and they will want to find out what makes us different. Have you ever realized that giving to the needs of others in your church is a powerful testimony to the world? A way to lead others to Christ?

The Bible tells us that giving alone will not be a testimony, nor will it produce love and unity, unless it is done with the proper attitude. Your giving is acceptable and pleasing to God only when you are in harmony with your fellow believers. Jesus was very clear on this point: "If therefore you are presenting your offering at the altar, and there remember that your brother has something against you, leave your offering there before the altar, and go your way; first, be reconciled to your brother, and then come and present your offering" (Matthew 5:23–24). Giving without an attitude of love and harmony is like planting dead seeds. You must realize that you're giving a dead seed when you are out of fellowship with either God or others. But love and harmony alone cannot produce fruit without your seed or gift. God treasures our relationship with Him and accepts our gifts only when we are in close fellowship with Him and operating on correct biblical attitudes and values.

Jesus said to the Pharisees, "For you tithe mint and dill and cummin, and have neglected the weightier provisions of the law: justice and mercy and faithfulness; but these are the things you should have done [giving] without neglecting the others [loving God and others]" (Matthew 23:23). An improper attitude or fractured relationships, with God or others, nullifies giving. Here as in all areas of life proper attitude must accompany proper action to get proper results.

Do you want to be loved, accepted, and respected by others? For several years that was the desire of my heart, but I found that my church gave only lip service to loving, caring, sharing, and accepting others. I was really beginning to get a negative attitude toward Christianity in general. Where are all the Christians? What makes this group of Christians any different from any other group of people? In fact, I got more love, caring, compassion, encouragement, and strokes from my heathen friends than I did from those professed Christians at church. Do you want to know why I felt that way? I was trying to reap without having sowed. Don't selfishly look for what you can get. Ask yourself, Who in my church needs love, acceptance, encouragement, support, and caring? Then meet those needs. You will find that when you forget about your needs, those needs will be met, because people, believers and nonbelievers alike, love and respond to Christians who are unselfish, generous givers, genuinely concerned with the needs of others. In talking about the recipients of liberal giving and their attitude toward the givers Paul wrote, "Because of the proof given by this ministry [generous gifts], they [the recipients] will glorify God for your obedience to your confession of the gospel of Christ, and for the liberality of your contribution to them and to all, while they also, by prayer on your behalf, yearn for you because of the surpassing grace of God in you" (2 Corinthians 9:13–14). That's the testimony the church needs to present to the world today. If you aren't reaping what you need, try sowing what you need, and your own needs will be met.

Indeed, our jobs, our possessions, our incomes, our degrees, our accomplishments, our material success, and our riches can blind us to the truth that the only true and permanent treasure is the treasure we store up in heaven. Riches and humility blend like water and oil until we add the detergent of giving. We forget that relative to 90 percent of the people alive today, we are rich. Maybe that's why James wrote to people like us in America, "and let the rich man glory in his humiliation, because like flowering grass he will pass away" (James 1:10). Our model for living is Jesus Christ, who described Himself by saying, "...learn from Me, for I am gentle and humble in heart..." (Matthew 11:29). The same concept appears repeatedly throughout Scripture. "Do nothing from selfishness or empty conceit, but with humility of mind let each of you regard one another as more important than himself; do not merely look out for your own personal interests, but also for the interest of others" (Philippians 2:3–4). What a testimony Christ's church could present, if we would focus on heavenly treasure, developing Christ's humble heart, and focusing on giving to meet the needs of others, inside and outside the church. By now I hope you see that giving is much more than money; it's both your attitude and your action.

## Examples, Who and Why

One of the best studies I have completed was the example of the early church in Jerusalem, in Acts 2–6. The church leaders presented a model to emulate, ". . . they were continually devoting themselves to the apostles' teaching and to fellowship, to the breaking of bread and to prayer" (Acts 2:42). That's a rock solid four-part model of how to invest (give) your time, talent, and treasure, isn't it? These leaders were "not self-willed, not quick-tempered, not addicted to wine, not pugnacious, not fond of sordid gain, but hospitable, loving what is good, sensible, just, devout, self-controlled . . ." (Titus 1:7–8). We all need models of leadership, and the best model for your children to observe and replicate is you, mother or father. What you do and your underlying attitude are an indisputable, extremely powerful living testimony.

Each of us is a leader to some extent, and other Christians watch as we give and use our time, talents, and treasure. My favorite example is a man renamed Barnabas by the apostles (which means "Son of Encouragement") "who owned a tract of land, sold it and brought the money and laid it at the apostles' feet" (Acts 4:37). Barnabas's act encouraged others to model correct principles. The results speak for themselves: "For there was not a needy person among them, for all who were owners of land or houses would sell them and bring the proceeds of the sales, and lay them at the apostles' feet; and they would be distributed to each, as any had need" (Acts 4:34–35). You too could be a Barnabas and encourage others by your example. Can you imagine the testimony if we solved today's welfare problem within the church itself? We have a welfare system today because the church has abandoned its responsibility to meet the needs of its members and others. Today, it is the government, not the church, we look to to have our needs met. Be generous and give, and you will encourage others to be more generous by your example.

Every leader, member, and church should be a positive model in the area of giving. If you want to see a model church, read what Paul had to say about the churches of Macedonia: "We wish to make known to you the grace of God which has been given in the churches of Macedonia, that in a great ordeal of affliction their abundance of joy and their deep poverty overflowed in the wealth of their liberality [bountiful giving from deep poverty]. For I testify that according to their ability, and beyond their ability they gave of their own accord, *begging us* with much entreaty *for the favor of participation in the support of the saints*, and this, not as we had expected, but they first gave themselves to the Lord [that's why they did what they did] and to us by the will of God" (2 Corinthians 8:1–5, italics added). A church which committed itself to the Lord, and modeled the Macedonians' attitude and actions, could spark a revival this country desperately needs to see. When our leaders, members, and churches model generous proper giving, that will cause others to praise God. This is the highest and best result of effective giving—"You will be enriched in everything for all liberality, which through us is producing *thanksgiving to God.* For the ministry of this service is not only fully supplying the needs of the saints, but is also overflowing through many *thanks-givings to God.* Because of the proof given by this ministry *they will glorify God* for your obedience ..." (2 Corinthians 9:11–13, italics added). When God gets the praise and glory you know your giving and your attitude are exactly on target.

The early New Testament church was mostly composed of Jews, who usually took their religion very seriously. We can assume that most of them, prior to conversion, practiced the three tithe system as did their ancestors whom God called out of Egypt. The first tithe was 10 percent, hence tenth or tithe, of all produce and of all the cattle and flocks. This tithe was used to support the Levites and priests who ministered to Israel (Leviticus 27:30–33). The second tithe, which was called the "festival tithe" was 10 percent of the 90 percent remaining funds, after the first tithe was given. This tithe was set apart and taken to Jerusalem to pay for the national feasts and offerings. If it was not possible to make the trip to Jerusalem with produce and animals, the possessions could be sold and the money used to take the trip and purchase food or animals for offerings in Jerusalem (Deuteronomy 12:5–7; 14:22–27). The third tithe, called the "charity tithe" was given every third year. It was to be used for widows, orphans, the fatherless, the poor, and strangers (Deuteronomy 14:28–29; 26:12). In addition to these three tithes which averaged 22 percent of annual income, the faithful paid a temple tax, called the two-drachma tax in Matthew 17:24 (NIV), and numerous other gifts and offerings besides the other taxes that were paid both to the Roman government within the empire and in local areas.

The Jewish person was in the habit of giving regularly and systematically because it was a part of his religious training and commitment. Once these converted Jews understood God's grace, contrasted with law, they also gave, and gave generously, the total proceeds from the sale of properties, like Barnabas. "Grace giving" many times exceeded what the law required. The tithe system is not mentioned in the New Testament, but it does serve as a model for regular and systematic giving. Paul wrote to the Corinthians: "On the first day of every week [regularly and systematically] let each one of you [each family member] put aside and save [giving is planned], as he may prosper [giving is proportional], that no collections be made when I come" (1 Corinthians 16:2).

The tithe was required, not voluntary, because Israel was a theocracy, which is a government run by God. The tithes were the revenue or taxes that paid for the theocracy. Over and above the tithes were various "freewill giving" offerings consisting of various gifts and sacrifices. Freewill gifts came from willing, loving hearts and were not a set formula or percentage but a heartfelt expression of gratitude for what God had given the giver. This is the attitude and spirit for giving that God desires us to have. These attitudes and practices of both giving and total money management should be taught by and to our leaders, our members, and our churches. Our declining rate of giving is proof that our attitudes are not God's attitudes about money and possessions. Grateful people give well beyond a tithe instead of today's level of giving of 2 percent of income or less.

An example of people with right attitudes were the Israelites, freed from Egyptian bondage, who chose to build the tabernacle (Exodus 25–28). God told Moses to raise a contribution "from every man whose heart moves him . . ." (Exodus 25:2). What today would cost several hundred million dollars to construct was raised totally by freewill offerings, not required tithes. Eight times in Exodus 35 and 36 the phrases "willing heart," "whose heart stirred," "whose heart moved," or "freewill offering" are used (Exodus 35:5, 21, 22, 26, 29; 36:2). The giving was so bountiful, extravagant, and excessive that Moses had to ask the people to stop bringing contributions. That's what our giving should be like.

## PROPER MOTIVES FOR GIVING

Let's look at proper motives for giving, beginning with a great motivational factor in the way a Christian views and uses his material blessings—*the expectancy of the second coming of Jesus Christ.* The early church expected Christ's return at any moment; this view affected their attitude toward use of their possessions. As time passed, less and less emphasis was placed on Christ's return and more people began to see security and status in their homes, possessions, and assets. This tendency was strong by the end of the first century and continues to this day. When was the last time you heard a sermon on Christ's return or on how you should live today, in light of that fact? What would you say if you were before the judgment seat of Christ and He asked you to account for your use of His riches entrusted to you over the past year? One day— perhaps soon—Jesus will return, and the opportunity of using our riches to meet the needs of others will no longer exist. When you are motivated by His return, your motives are biblical and proper.

A second proper motive for giving is *bringing honor to God, not ourselves*. This motive is contained in several passages quoted earlier, but it bears repeating. Since I have been involved in various fund-raising ventures for Christian organizations over the years, let me tell you from experience, it is much easier to find money for an addition to the college library that is built or dedicated in memory of "Master Materialist," than it is to find funds to re-blacktop the roads and parking lots for a church or Christian college. Both improvements may cost the same, but one caters to the donor's ego and the other to meeting basic needs. Far too many give to bring glory and honor to themselves rather than to bring glory, honor, praise, and thanks to God. Jesus taught that if you give to bring attention to yourself you have your full reward now. The proper motive for giving is to bring honor and praise to God. God rewards and honors honesty, integrity, and sincerity, and He despises dishonesty, lack of integrity, and hypocrisy when it comes to giving.

Remember Barnabas? Contrast his story with God's death sentence for Ananias and Sapphira. God also severely judged the Corinthians because of their flagrant abuse of the Lord's Supper. Paul wrote that many of these believers were "weak and sick," and a number of them actually died (2 Corinthians 11:30). Periodically check your motives to see if they are pure and designed to glorify God rather than yourself. Jesus stressed pure motives when He said, "But when you give alms, do not let your left hand know what your right hand is doing that your alms may be in secret; and your Father who sees in secret will repay you" (Matthew 6:3–4). Some interpret this to prohibit public giving, but Jesus never condemned people who gave publicly. He used the poor widow who put her two pennies into the temple treasury to illustrate the value of sacrificial giving. Jesus was aiming His rebuke at the religious leaders' action of drawing attention to themselves by announcing their gifts with trumpets so as to be "honored by men" (Matthew 6:2) rather than to bring glory to God. Jesus was emphasizing the need to periodically recheck our motives to see if our goal is bringing glory to God or glory to self.

How much time do you spend thinking about money and possessions? worrying about them? being jealous and greedy for more? doing whatever is necessary to acquire whatever you want? keeping and maintaining your material assets and treasures? If your thoughts center around earthly treasure, that's your real treasure. Contrast that to thinking: How can I use my resources to glorify God? meet the needs of others? advance the kingdom of God? invest into eternal treasures? If these thoughts dominate your thinking then you are storing treasure in the heavenly treasury. To check your motives examine your thought life.

*Proper motives for giving stem from a heart of love and concern and are both voluntary and generous.* Peter's rebuke to Ananias is a clear and concise directive on voluntary giving: "While it [the gift] remained unsold, did it not remain your own? And after it was sold, was it not under your control?" (Acts 5:4). Both the heart attitude behind the action and voluntary giving are expressed by "Let each one do just as he has purposed in his heart; not grudgingly or under compulsion; for God loves a cheerful giver" (2 Corinthians 9:7). Does this mean we should not give if we can't give from a thankful spirit? No, or Paul would not have encouraged the Corinthians to give when they had a negative attitude. He hoped that careful planning would redirect their attitudes. Giving has both a planned and a spontaneous dimension. We must be prepared when opportunities arrive, or giving will be accompanied by resentment and resistance when we lack funds. Simultaneously, we must be flexible enough to allow the Holy Spirit to adjust our plans when real needs are suddenly and unexpectedly placed before us. I personally have two giving accounts, both of which are systematically and consistently replenished. A "planned account" is allocated first to my local church and other ministries we support, and a "hilarious giving account" is directed to whatever need the Lord brings to our attention at the moment.

When we truly understand God's love, grace, and mercy, *our giving is motivated by the joy and gratitude we feel toward the greatest act of love, mercy, and grace ever*—the death (and resurrection) of our Lord Jesus Christ. Giving is obedience to the command, and it is motivated by a sincere and grateful heart of love and gratitude for all that Christ has done for us. "I am not speaking this as a command, but as proving through the earnestness of others the sincerity of your love also" (2 Corinthians 8:8). When I consider what Jesus gave for me, the words thankful and grateful don't come close to describing my love for Him. Sometimes when I read, "For you know the grace of our Lord Jesus Christ, that though He was rich, yet for your sake He became poor, that you through His poverty might become rich" (2 Corinthians 8:9), I weep. If your giving doesn't have a dimension of joy, privilege, gratitude, and thanksgiving, you need to learn what your eternal riches in Christ are and study the meanings of the words mercy, grace, and salvation.

May I suggest that to evaluate the validity and reality of your faith you closely *examine your attitude and use of your material assets.* Author Larry Burkett calls giving a spiritual barometer. If real saving faith is present, it will be quantifiably represented in your giving. You don't become more spiritual by giving, but where saving and growing faith lives it is always accompanied by generous giving. James said, "If a brother or sister is without clothing and in need of daily food, and one of you says to them, 'Go in peace, be warmed and be filled,' and yet you do not give them what is necessary for their body, what use is that? Even so faith, if it has no works, is dead, being by itself" (James 2:15–17). The times I have seen people evaluate others' faith for a staff position at church, a teaching position at a Christian school, or acceptance into seminary, I have never seen faith evaluated by the way the candidates view and use their material treasures. Instead questions are proposed about morals, ethics, values, and beliefs. Why not examine their view and use of material treasures as well? It's quantifiable, easy to measure, and impossible to fake. Judge yourself rightly so that you yourself never "come under judgment" (1 Corinthians 11:31 NIV).

The final area under the topic of good motivations is *giving consistently and systematically to remind yourself whose assets you are handling.* When we give the first part of our income each week, we are reminded that God has provided everything we have to enjoy. Giving reminds me that as a faithful steward my charge is to handle all my income as His manager. It is not that 10 percent goes to God and I do what I please with what remains. All of my money is His. Honoring God with the first part of every paycheck is not an option for a committed believer. And the dedicated believer will not show poor stewardship or lack of gratitude for what remains.

## Who to Give to

Begin with your local church; it should be the first priority on your giving list. If you aren't involved in a local church, begin now to search until you find a church where Christ is preeminent, the Bible is taught, and you feel comfortable in mind and spirit. Our pastors, teachers, and leaders themselves should also be on the receiving end of our giving. Paul told us that our pastors, teachers, and leaders deserve support: "Let the one who is taught the word share all good things with him who teaches" (Galatians 6:6). Again from the New Testament, "Let the elders who rule well be considered worthy of double honor, especially those who work hard at preaching and teaching" (1 Timothy 5:17). When we give as we should to our church, pastors, teachers, and leaders it encourages them and enriches their prayer life. The standard is double honor—respect and remuneration. The pay of the Levites and priests was 120 percent of average. Today's standards have plunged to 70–80 percent of the pay of the average member. We should pay our pastors well to free them to serve effectively, not squeeze every last drop possible from the compensation.

Don't forget the evangelist, whose life and ministry is dedicated to fulfilling the Great Commission, when you give. Through Billy Graham's crusades both my wife and my aunt Betty, who led me to Christ, were saved. We continue to support Dr. Graham and other effective evangelists.

When Jesus said, "Go therefore and make disciples of all the nations . . . teaching them to observe all that I commanded you" (Matthew 28:19–20), He was commanding both evangelism and discipleship. Our Christian schools, colleges, universities, seminaries, and many fine parachurch organizations make discipleship their focus. We must also remember them in our giving. We are only one generation away from losing the truth if we fail at discipleship. Evangelism without discipleship is like a car without gas. We will go nowhere unless we have both elements, so our family supports ministries that disciple such as the Navigators, Moody Bible Institute, Christian schools, and seminaries.

Individuals also can be worthy recipients of our giving. An appropriate but often overlooked place to give is to our own family's needs. Certainly our religion must work at home, or we have no right to export it. Many nonbelieving individuals also need our support. When we give to meet their needs we put works behind our words. Indeed money talks—it talks about what you value by what you choose to invest in. The opportunities to invest are numerous. You must learn to be discerning in your giving, to discriminate needs from greeds.

All of us get mail, calls, and requests for support from individuals, organizations, ministries, and even other churches. Before you commit, find out how your dollars are going to be used. Is the request for support meeting a need, want, or desire? What is the lifestyle of the leadership? Does this individual or organization preach Christ and honor God, or is it a monument to a current or former founder? What is their reputation in the Christian community? Do they have a cooperative spirit with other Christian groups, or do they have an isolationist-exclusive air? Is their purpose really to serve others? If so, how? Is the appeal a one-time real emergency or a series of crises created by professional letter writers who know exactly what message will separate you from your money? Beware, there are quite a few wolves in sheep's clothing who prey on gullible Christians and fleece the flock. As we will repeat in the chapter on investing—investigate before you invest. That's good investment counsel, and there is no better investment than giving to God's work.

## Meeting Needs of Individuals

The Bible has more verses devoted to giving than any other area of finances, and, as you would expect, more than half these verses on giving begin with or stress attitude. If the heart is right, and the funds are available, where should your resources be allocated? After you have done your regular giving through your church, the first priority is for money to meet the *material needs within the body of Christ.* Acts 4:34–35 tells us the local early church did not have a needy person among them since generous givers met the needs of all. We have the ability today to meet all the needs (not necessarily all the wants and desires) in the church, but the concept of sacrificial giving is practically non-existent. Meditate on the words of the apostle John who wrote, "For whoever has the world's goods, and beholds his brother in need and closes his heart against him, how does the love of God abide in him? Little children, let us not love with word or with tongue, but in deed and truth" (1 John 3:17–18). When was the last time you made a sacrificial gift to meet the need of a brother or sister in Christ?

Don't limit your giving to those who love and care for you; give to those who resent you or wish you harm. When you return a blessing for a curse, instead of a curse for a curse, you will see people looking closely at your life to try to understand why. When you sow properly, you will be shocked to see how your gift may even be the seed that eventually leads another to Christ. "Give to the one who asks you, and do not turn away from the one who wants to borrow from you" (Matthew 5:42 NIV). When believers are unselfish and benevolent, that is undeniable proof to unbelievers and believers that Jesus Christ is indeed the Son of God. For an excellent example of the testimony of giving read the story of Dorcas in Acts 9:32–43.

*Sometimes needs are temporary, and sometimes they require consistent giving* due to circumstances. Paul devoted half of the fifth chapter in 1 Timothy to instruction on how to care for widows. If a widow was qualified, she was supported by the local church. No Social Security, welfare, aid to dependent children, or other government programs met her needs. The local church meeting the needs of its members and building the love, unity, and testimony is what today's church so desperately needs. Today we have millions of poor single parents, widows, orphans, and elderly being forced to do without, compromise their standards and values, or depend on "big brother" rather than Christ's church. Just imagine again what could be if our hearts were right and we followed the advice of Scripture about giving.

The Bible also says that *children who are able should meet the needs of their parents.* When the Pharisees asked Jesus why His disciples did not honor the traditions of the elders, Jesus answered by saying, "Why do you yourselves transgress the commandment of God for the sake of your tradition? For God said, 'Honor your father and mother' and, 'He who speaks evil of father or mother, let him be put to death.' But you say, 'Whoever shall say to his father or mother, "Anything of mine you might have been helped by has been given to God," he is not to honor his father or his mother.' And thus you invalidated the word of God for the sake of your tradition" (Matthew 15:3–6). The word translated "honor" carries a dual meaning: respect and remuneration. When our parents need help physically, financially, and/or emotionally, God tells us to meet those needs to the best of our abilities. Working in a retirement community the last sixteen years, I have seen the blessing, encouragement, and support some children provide for their parents. Unfortunately, most children meet their parents' physical needs by referring them to a nursing home, their financial needs by suggesting they contact "Uncle Sam," and their emotional needs by voice mail or referral to a shrink. Money and physical needs are important, but even more important is taking the time to listen, to call, to write, and to be available. I hope we as Christians will do a better job in the future accepting responsibility for meeting our parents' basic needs. When you give your parents their double honor you will brighten their lives, provide an excellent testimony to others, be blessed for your obedience to God's commandments, and even lengthen and bless your own life.

*People who have physical needs have a special place in God's heart,* as do those who help meet their needs. James reminds us that how we respond to meeting the needs of children without parents or women without husbands is basic: "This is pure and undefiled religion in the sight of our God and Father, to visit orphans and widows in their distress, and to keep oneself unstained by the world" (James 1:27). Meeting the needs of widows, orphans, and the poor was the purpose of the "charity tithe" collected every third year in Israel. The early church appointed seven highly qualified men to meet the needs of the Grecian widows (Acts 6:1–7). Luke devotes part of his record to describing Dorcas and her ministry to widows, both believers and nonbelievers (Acts 9:32–43) and the giving of Cornelius, a non-Christian, who "gave generously to those in need" (Acts 10:2). Paul also gave detailed instruction of how the church should care for widows in 1 Timothy 5:3–16. If Luke and Paul were writing today, I think they would include single parents and the elderly in this group of people with special and substantial needs waiting to be met.

A general principle of meeting needs is that those *Christians with an abundance of resources should assist those who have a lack or "needs."* "For if the readiness is present, it is acceptable according to what a man has, not according to what he does not have. For this is not for the ease of others and for your affliction, but by way of equality—at this present time your abundance being a supply for their want, that their abundance also may become a supply for your want, that there may be equality; as it is written, 'He who gathered much did not have too much, and he who gathered little had no lack'" (2 Corinthians 8:12–15). The highest and best purpose of a surplus is to use it to meet the needs of others. You find the same principle throughout the Bible. My favorite verse illustrating this principle comes from Ecclesiastes 4:12: "A cord of three strands is not quickly torn apart." Giving to meet needs is always appropriate.

The final area of giving is for Christians who have been blessed with material resources to *use their homes to offer hospitality* to other believers. Demonstrating hospitality to both believers and nonbelievers by entertaining, holding Bible studies, or hosting small groups is an excellent use of your home. You do not have to have a large or lavish home to participate. It is the attitudes of hospitality, friendliness, planning, and service that make any event held in your home a success. I have been part of groups held in homes from a studio apartment all the way up the scale. Some of the meals have been hot dogs and burgers while a few were professionally catered by gourmet chefs. The spirit of giving, caring, and fellowship made the event a success—not the square footage of the home or its location. Who do you know who would like a night out with you and your family? Single parents? Widows, widowers? An elderly person or couple? "Do not neglect to show hospitality to strangers, for by this some have entertained angels without knowing it" (Hebrews 13:2). "Do not neglect doing good and sharing; for with such sacrifices God is pleased" (Hebrews 13:16).

## Barriers to Giving

*Lack of giving can be caused by selfishness.* It may sound biblical to say that God helps those who help themselves, but that cliché has no root in Scripture. God is the One who helps the helpless, and sometimes we are the means whereby He meets their needs. Selfishness is a deadly and subtle sin that is hard to detect in our own lives. Seeing others as more important than ourselves is neither natural nor automatic. *Another very common excuse for not giving is procrastination.* We know we should give, so we tell ourselves we will: right after our raise, after our promotion, as soon as we pay off a few bills, when our car is paid off, when the kids are educated, when.... Unfortunately, these are empty excuses that never end. The cure for procrastination is do it now. The amount doesn't matter. Survey after survey has shown the wealthy actually give less than the average, so don't procrastinate until your income goes up. Start this Sunday and put more (or something) into the offering plate. Commit a part of your blessings in the future and honor your commitment when the blessing comes.

*Most fail to give because they do not have a plan to give first before they spend.* If you spend first, there will be nothing left to give. You are failing if you do not honor God first and if you don't plan first to give, then live. As you will learn in the chapters ahead *many today can't give because they have overcommitted themselves.* If too much of your income is committed to personal debt, such as credit cards, there is little or nothing left to give. If you have overcommitted yourself in car payments there may not be room in your income to honor God or save for the future. Most common of all, you may have bought more home than you need or can afford, and this will leave you with years of mortgage payments and no ability to honor God with the first part of all your income. If you fail to give first, you will never give what you could or should, and you will never experience blessing flowing from the windows of heaven.

# MAKE GIVING YOUR FIRST AND TOP PRIORITY

If you only apply one idea from the dozens in this book, make it the idea to *give first from every check that you receive*. I challenge you to start now and give something, or, if you are giving, increase your giving for one year; then evaluate the results. For years Christians have been asked in financial seminars if the tithe (10 percent) is a binding command for us New Testament believers. The question has been explored extensively elsewhere, with various conclusions reached by different authors. But people who ask the question frequently ignore a more important one: Is giving (not tithing) a valid command and principle God expects us to obey? The answer is an unqualified yes. Before we examine some biblical guidelines for giving I urge you to recall that God owns it all. Our obligation to Him doesn't end at 10, 15, or 20 percent giving. We are responsible to manage the 100 percent of everything we receive, by His rules, for His glory, and for our own good—that's stewardship.

## Guidelines for Giving

*Giving is personally determined and should be proportional to your income.* "Let each one do just as he has purposed in his heart ..." (2 Corinthians 9:7a). "...According to what a man has, not according to what he does not have" (2 Corinthians 8:12b). In theory the more you earn the more you are able to give; but usually the reverse is practiced. Maybe your starting point is 10 percent; for Zacchaeus it was 50 percent (Luke 19:8). A good rule to follow is to start now where you are able and increase your percentage of giving as you are blessed.

*Giving should be regular, systematic, and a top priority.* "On the first day [regularly] of every week [systematically] let each one of you put aside and save ..." (1 Corinthians 16:2). "Honor the Lord from your wealth, and from the first of all your produce ..." (Proverbs 3:9). Our works, not our words, should be proof of our faith. Regular, systematic giving builds proper habits of money management, and the rewards, attitudes, and habits will spread throughout all areas of your life.

*Giving is a command to be obeyed.* "Give [this is an imperative], and it will be given to you ..." (Luke 6:38a). When questioned whether or not it was lawful to pay taxes, Jesus confirmed both taxes and giving as valid biblical principles when He said, "Render to Caesar the things that are Caesar's, and to God the things that are God's" (Matthew 22:21). God expects us to respond now, to the truth we have.

*Don't embarrass your leaders by your failure to give consistently and generously.* Paul wrote regarding unfulfilled promised giving: "But I have sent the brethren, that our boasting about you may not be made empty in this case, that, as I was saying, you may be prepared; lest any Macedonians come with me and find you unprepared [to fulfill your pledged giving], we, (not to speak of you) should be put to shame by this confidence" (2 Corinthians 9:3–4). Don't fail to fulfill your pledges when it is within your power to do so. It is poor stewardship and it embarrasses your leaders.

*Honor your commitments to giving, remembering that you are accountable.* "So I thought it necessary to urge the brethren that they would go on ahead to you and arrange beforehand your previously promised bountiful gift ..." (v. 5). Paul reminds them another time to honor their promises to give. "But now finish doing it also [make your gift]; that just as there was the readiness to desire it, so there may be also the completion of it by your ability" (2 Corinthians 8:11). Nothing is a poorer testimony than an unfulfilled, unhonored pledge to give. You may escape accountability in your church, but not your eventual accountability to God.

*Give willingly and voluntarily.* "Not grudgingly or under compulsion; for God loves a cheerful giver" (2 Corinthians 9:7). "You will be enriched in everything for all liberality ..." (2 Corinthians 9:11). "... and for the liberality of your contribution to them and to all" (2 Corinthians 9:13). God wants us to give willingly out of hearts of love that show our sincere appreciation for His gift of salvation. When giving is willing and voluntary it creates credits in heaven's treasury.

We must *plan ahead so we can give to our church, fellow Christians, and those in need.* "So then, while we have opportunity, let us do good to all men, and especially to those who are of the household of the faith" (Galatians 6:10). We should plan ahead by dedicating the first part of all income received to giving and have enough margin in our plans so that we are able to respond to real but unexpected needs as they present themselves (1 John 3:17–18).

We are to *excel at the grace of giving.* "But just as you abound in everything, in faith and utterance and knowledge and in all earnestness and in the love we inspired in you, see that you abound in this gracious work also" (2 Corinthians 8:7). The grace and joy of giving is something God wants all believers involved in, just as He desires all of us to first give ourselves to Him. "I urge you therefore, brethren, by the mercies of God, to present your bodies a living and holy sacrifice, acceptable to God, which is your spiritual service of worship" (Romans 12:1).

As we have studied, *giving should be both secret and humble* (Matthew 6:1–4), but *sacrificial giving creates the highest praise from the Lord.* "Truly I say to you, this poor widow put in more than all the contributors to the treasury; for they put in out of their surplus, but she, out of her poverty, put in all she owned, all she had to live on" (Mark 12:43–44). An excellent example of sacrificial giving to honor Christ comes right before the final Passover when "a woman came to [Christ] with an alabaster vial of very costly perfume, and she poured it upon His head as He reclined at the table." The disciples questioned this apparent waste of money and the woman's behavior, and Jesus responded, "Why do you bother the woman? For she has done a good deed to Me. For the poor you have with you always; but you do not always have Me. For when she poured this perfume upon My body, she did it to prepare Me for burial. Truly I say to you, wherever this gospel is preached in the whole world, what this woman has done shall also be spoken of in memory of her" (Matthew 26:7–13). My advice to you in your giving—break a vase—try sacrificial giving.

*All Christians are obligated to support God's work with our resources.* Believers in both Macedonia and Acacia gave willingly and sacrificially to support the poor believers in Jerusalem. "...They are indebted to them. For if [since] the Gentiles have shared in their spiritual things, they are indebted to minister to them also in material things" (Romans 15:27). The highest and best use for any surplus is to use it to honor God by giving to the needs both inside and outside the church. *Giving is not limited to money but should include time, talent, thought, and prayer.* If you need more time, give time. If you need more talent, give your talent. If you need prayer, give prayer. If you "need" more money, give money. When you focus on what you can give rather than on what you "need" to get, God will meet your needs. Give in all five areas, beginning with your local church, and God promises that you will be blessed now and/or in eternity.

## Rewards of Giving

God wants us to acknowledge our dependence on Him to provide our daily needs. That's what Jesus taught in the disciples' prayer when He said, "Give us this day our daily bread" (Matthew 6:11). God also wants us to give, and when we do, we have done our part. Then we can claim the promise, "And my God shall supply all your needs according to His riches in glory in Christ Jesus" (Philippians 4:19).

Our first reward of giving is God's promise to meet all our needs. If we do not do our part in proper giving, we have no right to claim the promise.

The second reward of giving is the truth that *obedience is always blessed.* "And God is able to make *all* grace abound to you, that *always* having *all* sufficiency in *everything* you may have an *abundance* for *every* good deed" (2 Corinthians 9:8, italics added). When we "seek first His kingdom and His righteousness; all these things [food and clothing] shall be added to you" (Matthew 6:33).

The third reward of giving is contained in the verse "Now this I say, he who sows sparingly shall also reap sparingly; and he who sows bountifully shall also reap bountifully" (2 Corinthians 9:6). Generous givers will be generously rewarded so that they can continue, and increase, in their generous giving. The proper motive for giving is not to receive blessing, but the result or reward of generous giving will be generous blessings. Your blessings may or may not come during your time on earth, and they may or may not be monetary, but you can always depend on God to be true to His promises and His Word.

When we give, especially sacrificially, we are storing treasure in heaven, keeping our focus on Christ, and serving God rather than money. In speaking of heaven Jesus told us clearly, "But many who are first will be last; and the last, first" (Matthew 19:30). One day the earth and everything it contains will be destroyed by fire, but our good works will survive, and what we have invested into heavenly treasures will remain. In the parable of the unjust steward Jesus put money into its proper perspective and value when He said, "He who is faithful in a very little thing [such as money] is faithful also in much; and he who is unrighteous in a very little thing is unrighteous also in much. If therefore you have not been faithful in the use of unrighteous mammon [money], who will entrust the true riches to you? And if you have not been faithful in the use of that which is another's, who will give you that which is your own?" (Luke 16:10–12). The way we handle and view our material possessions will be in direct proportion to our heavenly treasures, which alone have eternal significance and eternal value.

It isn't wrong to give in the hopes of gaining current blessings. But the higher point of view in Scripture is the eternal reward. The following passage makes clear that our most significant rewards do not come in this life. "And everyone who has left houses or brothers or sisters or father or mother or children or farms for My name's sake, shall receive many times as much, and shall inherit eternal life" (Matthew 19:29). When we receive our rewards at the judgment seat of Christ some will receive crowns for works built with "gold, silver, precious stones" (1 Corinthians 3:12), whereas others will forfeit rewards or crowns when their works will be "burned up" because they consist of "wood, hay, straw" (v. 12). A major reward for following God's plan for giving will be our eternal rewards.

Giving has many special rewards, blessings, and benefits for the giver. Memorize and rest on the truth of Acts 20:35, "In everything I showed you that by working hard in this manner you must help the weak and remember the words of the Lord Jesus, that He Himself said, 'It is more blessed to give than to receive.'"

## ACTION ITEMS

Look at what you gave last year, and set a plan for increased godly giving in the next twelve months by answering the following questions.

1. The next twelve months I will honor God by giving $ _____ per (week, paycheck, or month) regularly and consistently the first part of every income or profit that I receive.

These funds will be allocated as follows:

$ _____ my local church

$ _____ _____

$ _____ _____

$ _____ _____

$ _____ _____

2. In addition to my money, I will give _____ hours per _____ to serve the Lord by _____.

3. To the best of my ability I will allow the Spirit of God to use my spiritual gifts and talents of _____ to _____.

4. If God sees fit to bless me above what I now receive, I will allocate _____ percent of every part of unexpected income or profit that I receive back to giving to His work.

5. What will be your motives for giving?

6. What "needs" right now are there that you can and should meet?

7. What are the barriers that block you from giving more? What will you do to eliminate these barriers?

# CHAPTER 4
# YOUR RESERVES:
# SAVINGS AND INSURANCE

"The wise man saves for the future, but the foolish man spends whatever he gets." Proverbs 21:20 LB

Merriam-Webster's Collegiate Dictionary defines the word "save": "to rescue or deliver from danger or harm; to preserve or guard from injury, destruction, or loss; to put aside as a store or reserve: accumulate . . . maintain, preserve." If I asked whether you think saving is wise planning you would probably say yes. If I asked whether you are consistently and persistently saving something off the top from each paycheck, you would probably answer no. Most of us know better, but we are living like fools according to Proverbs 21:20. Why is it so difficult for us to save? What should we be saving for? What are the reasons to save and the benefits of saving? This chapter addresses the goals, reasons, and benefits of saving (and of buying enough insurance to protect your savings without overspending on insurance). If you want to eliminate problems, this section will tell you what, when, where, why, and how to save.

We saw in chapter 2 how much money flows through our hands during our lifetime. If you will commit to saving first, off the top, then your long-range financial freedom is assured. The best plan for many people is to have savings automatically deducted from their paychecks, just like taxes, and to live on what is left. This plan works because payroll deduction supplies the discipline and persistence required to produce results. Do you recall how easy it was to adjust to your last raise, bonus, or increase?

Our "needs" and desires expand to consume our incomes whether we earn $10,000 per year or ten million. Save first, before you have a chance to spend it.

## THE PRINCIPLE OF SAVING

The first time in the Bible we encounter the principle of saving a part of our income is Genesis 41 when Joseph interpreted Pharaoh's two dreams prophesying seven good years followed by seven bad years. Joseph's solution of saving 20 percent of the harvest of good years (v. 34) would enable Egypt (or you) to weather the coming bad times. A farmer client of mine put it this way, "Don't eat your seed corn." If you consume all your corn, you have nothing to plant when planting season arrives. The writer of Proverbs calls us fools, for good reason, if we consume all of our incomes. Prudent planning, good stewardship, and common sense confirm the fact that saving part of our income will reduce problems in the future when an expanding income contracts or stops.

Albert Einstein called compound interest the most powerful force in the universe. Baron Rothchild, from the European banking family, called compound interest the eighth wonder of the world. The wisdom writer put it this way, "Dishonest money dwindles away, but he who gathers money little by little makes it grow" (Proverbs 13:11 NIV).

If you saved five dollars per day from your eighteenth birthday until you retired at age sixty-seven in EE Savings Bonds earning only 4 percent per year you could accumulate $278,617. If you doubled the return to 8 percent, which is less than the average rate paid on home mortgages today, what effect would that have? By doubling the rate you almost quadruple the results, to $1,047,131. The awesome power of compound interest works for a saver but against a debtor.

To show you the power of saving let's assume that you earn $25,000, which will rise 4 percent per year over the next forty-five working years. This year you decided to start saving, and you put $500 in the bank ($41.67/month), and you determine to save half of all your future increases. At that rate, you will build to less than $300/month in fifty years, so the sooner you begin the better off you are. Your 4 percent raise only covers increases in the cost of living, so you will have to continue to find better and better ways to cut expenses and save money. Look at the rewards over time at three different rates of earnings on your savings. The better rate you earn, the more you will have. Even if you subtract taxes due and the impact of inflation, the results are excellent.

| YEAR | 4% | 7% | 10% |
|------|------|------|------|
| 5 | 2,925 | 3,098 | 3,282 |
| 10 | 7,117 | 8,115 | 9,279 |
| 15 | 12,988 | 15,968 | 19,803 |
| 20 | 21,068 | 27,976 | 37,803 |
| 30 | 46,780 | 72,814 | 118,383 |
| 40 | 86,557 | 156,308 | 304,403 |
| 50 | 170,834 | 372,506 | 919,035 |

Earlier we looked at planning our financial lives with a margin. If you have no margin (savings) for error in your plans, you are planning to create financial pressures and problems in the future because problems do happen. When you spend less than you earn, you create a reserve (savings) to handle what can and does go wrong.

Unfortunately, most Americans today spend more than they earn, and that is how most consumer/credit card debt is created. No one plans not to save, no one sets out to burden himself with debt and future problems, but people tend to be optimistic and to assume good times roll forever. Of course, that assumption is false, but most people don't become realistic until they lose their jobs, their pay is cut, or major expenses appear out of nowhere at the worst possible time. If they have savings to cushion the blow, they manage to steer through the crisis. If they have no savings, they exit the storms of life with a mound of consumer debt to service. Debt further lowers an individual's standard of living by the cost of interest he has to pay. This lower standard of living further limits his income, and he adds to the mountain of debt until it crushes him or steals the joy from his life.

Perhaps the following diagram of debt, compound interest working against you (debt cycle), and compound interest working for you (savings cycle), will solidify the principle: *Save a part of your income, off the top, from every piece of income you receive.* This is the secret of financial freedom that very few really understand and even fewer apply.

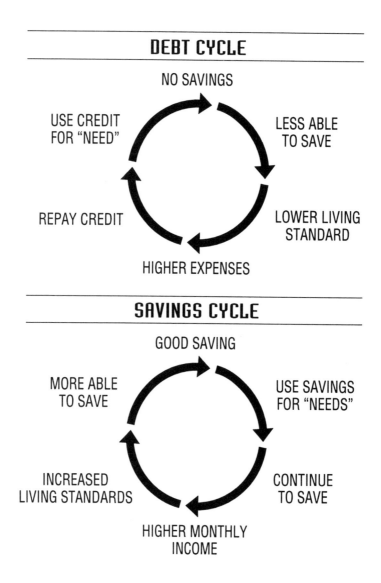

## DEBT CYCLE

NO SAVINGS

USE CREDIT FOR "NEED"

LESS ABLE TO SAVE

REPAY CREDIT

LOWER LIVING STANDARD

HIGHER EXPENSES

## SAVINGS CYCLE

GOOD SAVING

MORE ABLE TO SAVE

USE SAVINGS FOR "NEEDS"

INCREASED LIVING STANDARDS

CONTINUE TO SAVE

HIGHER MONTHLY INCOME

To cement the concept of saving in your life hear Scripture warn against the folly of not saving, "Go to the ant, you sluggard; consider its ways and be wise! It has no commander, no overseer or ruler, yet it stores [saves] its provisions [income] in summer and gathers its food at harvest" (Proverbs 6:6–8 NIV). A friend, who teaches biology in a local Christian school, moved from Minnesota to Arizona a few years back and brought his ant colony, which was part of his doctoral studies, with him. The ant farm contained a queen ant and thousands of tiny workers who gathered food during the summer to feed the colony during the long, harsh Minnesota winter. In Arizona, where we have perpetual summer, the ants continued to work and save for the winter which never came. Saving is instinctive for the ant because the Creator wired in behavior patterns necessary for survival. Saving for us is a choice, and the simple plan *pay yourself first* will help you survive the winters to come if you will choose a painless plan of payroll deduction or any form of consistent savings.

The principle of saving should be followed spiritually, physically, and financially. Why do you think God created the Sabbath as a day of rest? To teach us the concept of reserves—we read the dictionary definition of saving in the first sentence of this chapter. If we fail to keep our eyes on the Creator, we are easily sidetracked by the creation. If we fail to provide a reserve, every material object, including our bodies and our possessions, wears out faster. The same principle works with your income. Saving part will prolong your financial prosperity and peace.

## Faith or Presumption

Sometimes in discussing the principle of saving with Christian groups, the question arises—Isn't saving a lack of faith on our part? Shouldn't I rely on God alone and trust Him to provide for the future? When I save am I not depriving God of the opportunity to meet my needs? Questions like these are very common from those who are employed or who operate "faith ministries." When God fails to provide, is that a divine signal that He is saying no to a decision or direction? To answer that question we must distinguish faith from presumption. The Bible is very clear about our commitment to and faith in God, but that does not eliminate our personal responsibility to make wise judgments and decisions. When the nation of Israel spent forty years wandering in the desert after leaving Egypt, God provided for their needs by supplying manna. The Israelites still had to gather the manna, prepare it, and every sixth day gather enough (save) to consume on the seventh day when manna was not provided. The Lord gave us the Bible and good judgment, both of which He expects us to use wisely and consistently. J. Vernon McGee said it like this: "God indeed feeds the birds of the air but He doesn't do it by causing clouds to rain worms. You gotta do your part too."

Saving is our responsibility with what we have been provided, but we must be aware of the boundaries of the principle of saving. Failure to save anything at all is presumption and foolishness, not faith. But Scripture labels saving to excess as hoarding, which is failure to trust God. Scripture says both: Don't be a fool, save some of your income; and don't store up all your treasures on earth. Since most of the problems I have dealt with in personal financial counseling came from failure to save, we have stressed the necessity of saving. For those of you like me who were raised to over save, learn to ask yourself how much is enough and when you reach the goal stop saving. I know you have heard Charles Dickens's classic tale of Scrooge during the Christmas season. It is as easy to become addicted to saving as it is to spending all your income. The parable of the rich fool (Luke 12:13–21) would be good reading to several "movers and shakers" in this age of entrepreneurs/empire builders who go beyond the boundaries of prudent saving to hoarding.

### Circulation and Balance

I started working full time more than three decades ago. I was raised and trained by my grandmother, who was a child of the depression. My model for income distribution was 10 percent to God, 40 percent for savings, and living on the 50 percent that's left. It never occurred to me that I was erring on the extreme of over saving. I presumed, with no humility, that most people were fools who spent all their income. Then I was exposed to the concept of balance and circulation. Balance is emulating the Sea of Galilee, not the Dead Sea. Both seas are fed by the Jordan River, but the Sea of Galilee contains fish and life and is safe water to drink, whereas the Dead Sea contains no fish and no life and is unsafe and unfit to drink. The Sea of Galilee, fed by the Jordan River, fills its banks, then the overflow empties out into the same Jordan River that provided the water. The Dead Sea takes water from the Jordan but it gives nothing back—it simply hoards its water. Our model for life, financial and spiritual, is the Sea of Galilee. Once you have adequate savings concentrate on giving back—the law of circulation and balance.

## CATEGORIES FOR SAVINGS

Why do I even mention hoarding in a book written to those who have suffered declining or ceasing income? Because I have found that far too many people tend to treat savings and principal as sacred assets since they spent years acquiring the resources. A businessman I will call Don was a vivid example. It took more than a year for us to get his spending less than his income due to some earlier unwise choices. It took another three years for Don to pay off his accumulated debts, and it took six additional years for him to build up adequate savings. Don's major goal was to accumulate two years living expenses in savings to cushion the cyclical income of his business. Just as he reached his goal, the business cycle turned down and required an infusion of savings to dampen the downturn. Don panicked. All he could see was ten years of effort draining away at an alarming pace. Don forgot that the purpose of saving is to cushion a downturn, and, even worse, his security was in his savings rather than in God. As the money dwindled away Don's panic increased until one night he chose to end his life. What a tragedy it is when our security is not in Christ. When your down cycle comes, remember why you saved to begin with and don't treat principal or savings as sacred. Savings are accumulated as a safety net. When you need them, use them.

## (1) Emergency Funds

Everyone should have an emergency fund to provide for the unpredictable problems that occur in every life. What happens when you have a car wreck and you need $500 to cover the deductible? What do you do when your son breaks his arm and you face a $300 bill not covered by insurance? What do you do when you get a call from across the country that summons you to a close family member's funeral? When an earthquake, a mud slide, or a hurricane hits your family, where do you get the funds to cover the emergency costs? You have two choices. Either save beforehand to handle an emergency, or use debt when emergencies strike. If you choose to save beforehand, you have an emergency fund to draw upon. If you assume everyone but you will have problems, then you are simply not being realistic and you will have no choice but to borrow if you fail to save.

Amounts vary from family to family, but a realistic minimum to accumulate for emergencies is $500 to $1,000. If you save only ten dollars a week using payroll deduction or a pay-yourself-first plan, it will not greatly affect your current lifestyle but it will dramatically alter your response to an emergency when one happens. Your credit card is not a suitable alternative for handling emergencies for three reasons. First, the borrowed principal must be repaid and this reduces your spendable income in the future. Second, you have to pay interest on borrowed funds, so now you will have even less spendable income. Third, if you have no savings, an emergency that you could have planned for but chose to ignore traps you in the debt cycle we saw on page 92. You have a simple choice. Save now to eliminate financial pressure and stress when emergencies occur, or live with the foolish belief that emergencies always happen to someone else.

## (2) Repair and Maintenance

Everything on this earth will eventually need repair, maintenance, or replacement. There may be a few people who never get sick, never have an accident, never see a doctor or have any medical problems until the instant they die, but these are very rare individuals. You can choose to believe that you are the exception, or you can be realistic and plan for the probable costs of repair and maintenance of your physical body.

Every car sold carries with it a suggested service schedule for the mechanical parts which will over time need repair, maintenance, or replacement. Either choose to save for these eventual costs for your house, furniture, appliances, and other personal property or ignore the problem and deal with the crisis when it occurs. Very few of us live with a margin that allows us to save for these eventual certainties. Again, we are faced with the choice of living first or saving first. If we save first, we are choosing the path of wisdom and reducing or eliminating financial difficulties ahead.

How much you need to save for repair and maintenance depends on your personal circumstances, but a realistic minimum would be at least enough to cover probable outgo for health, homes, and transportation. If you have medical insurance, it would be wise to save at least twice the deductible on your medical policy. If you have a $250 deductible medical policy, $500 would be a realistic minimum goal to accumulate in savings for medical problems. If you have a car, a conservative guideline would suggest that you save at least your deductible on collision insurance plus probable cost of repairs over your car's mechanical life. My current car has 72,000 miles and I drive about 18,000 miles per year. In the next four years, I can count on replacing tires at least once; replacing my clutch; repairing or replacing the air conditioning compressor; the cost of lube, oil, and filter several times each year; plus three or four major services, suggested every 15,000 miles. I can fool myself and ignore these expenses, or I can choose to save in advance to eliminate the squeeze when these costs must be paid. For me personally a minimum reserve is $1,500 per car. Yours will be more or less depending on your car's age, use, condition, and mileage.

Homes are the major investment most of us make. Over time they too require repair and maintenance, which can be quite expensive. Your needs will vary depending on your home's age and condition, but a conservative guideline for home repair and maintenance would be to accumulate savings equal to 1 to 2 percent of your home's fair market value as a reserve. If you own a $100,000 home, that is $1,000 to $2,000 saved to cover the components that wear out, break down, or require repair, maintenance, and replacement. We just re-roofed our home for $3,000, but the cost was anticipated by planning and saving, so we were able to pay cash rather than borrow the funds. Heating and air conditioning units, refrigerators, washers, dryers, stoves, and other parts of your home will eventually need repair, maintenance, or replacement. Paint, carpet, furniture, computers, plumbing, pools, and saunas will also require dollars to repair and maintain over time. If you ignore these costs, you eventually have to deal with the inevitable problems. When you choose to pay yourself first, you automatically choose a future lifestyle with reduced financial stress and fewer problems.

## (3) Annual Events

Every year the same annual events occur: birthdays, Christmas, anniversaries, school clothes, and vacations. But very few of us look ahead and plan. We procrastinate until the last possible minute so we end up buying now and paying later. The cost of not looking ahead is finance charges, loss of interest we could have earned if we had saved, and the premium we pay for impulse buying. You will see when we discuss making a major purchase that financing costs 47 percent more than saving ahead of time and paying cash. When you discipline yourself to save, you are giving buying impulses time to cool off; more than half of what you think you "need" turns out not to be a true "need."

Take the time to plan for the annual events in your life. Make a list of the people you buy for and the various occasions. In our family, we have sixteen relatives for Christmas and birthdays, two boys to outfit for school, and our wedding anniversary. That's a total of thirty-five events for family each year, not counting another twenty-four people we remember on special occasions. We have chosen to set a dollar figure of $1,500 on these annual events. My wife, Jeanie, makes about thirty of our forty-nine gifts, and that leaves us about $1,300 to spend on nineteen special occasions. Jeanie shops all year with these events in mind. She uses coupons, seeks out sales and bargains, and seldom do we overspend for gifts, birthdays, Christmas, and other special events. To take the pressure off your income, define your needs and decide how much you can afford to spend. In our family we save $30 a week so we can pay cash rather than charge these annual events.

## (4) An Income Cushion

You should have savings for: emergencies, repair and maintenance on physical items, and your largest asset—your income. If I earn $25,000 per year over a forty to fifty year working lifetime, more than one million dollars will flow through my hands. All of us should choose to save part of our incomes to cushion the blow when our income is reduced or interrupted in the unknown future. Maybe you have already experienced a pay reduction or your current status is between jobs/unemployed. If you chose to save part of prior income, today you have savings to cushion the impact. If you have never been informed of the fact that incomes do rise and fall, save now to eliminate problems in the future because over time all of us will probably experience a reduction or interruption of our income.

Those of you who are self-employed, business owners, or on variable or commissioned incomes hold the greatest risk. It is automatic and easy to learn to live on whatever we earn. We experience month after month of increasing or stable wages and we expand our lifestyle on the presumption that things will continue to improve forever into the future. Suddenly circumstances beyond our control strike and our incomes drop 20 percent, 30 percent, 40 percent, or more. What do we do now when our expenses exceed our incomes and we have no reserves to cushion the blow while we attempt to cope with the problems? We suffer the consequences of a prior bad decision of living on 100 percent of our incomes. There is no painless way to soften the blow of earlier bad choices, but we can choose to prevent problems in the future by learning to save and to live on less than we earn in the future. If you are in business for yourself, or on commission, do yourself a favor and choose to live on less than your past three- to five-year average income. All periods of economic expansion and growth eventually are followed by periods of contractions and shrinkage. All bull markets eventually become bear markets, just like all summers eventually turn to fall and winter. If you plan realistically your life in the future will be dramatically different and free of financial affliction.

You must plan and live in the real world with its peaks and valleys. You are creating future problems when you assume your income can never decrease or stop. The ten factors we mentioned in the introduction can cause your income to go down or stop several times over your working years. Financial experts suggest that a good goal to pursue is accumulation in savings of a minimum of ninety days of living expenses, up to a maximum of two years, in savings. If you earn $24,000/year net salary, that's a minimum of $6,000 and a maximum of $48,000 savings required. This and every chapter following will provide you ways to increase savings by decreasing expenses, but if you fail to pay yourself first you will end up with a greater quantity and quality of goods and no savings available when you need them most.

## (5) Education

Those who don't save and invest into improving themselves and their abilities quickly become obsolete in today's global economy. There are numerous areas for education, improvement, and self-development: spiritual, physical, marriage, parenting, personal and social skills, career enhancement, and financial education. The great news is that many resources are available free through your local church or library. Commit your time to making yourself a better person. I have heard that the average adult reads less than one non-fiction book a year after finishing school. No wonder our nation is losing ground in the world market! It is natural to dwell on the urgent and ignore the important. It is human nature to ignore areas of our lives that appear to be OK rather than to invest time and energy into education that can prevent problems or make a good life, marriage, or family better.

I encourage you to plan the time to develop your spiritual life. Your church library probably has volumes of materials you could use to deepen your relationship with the Lord, improve your marriage, better your parenting skills, enhance your character, or widen your knowledge and understanding of the Bible. Your local or college library has thousands of books, magazines, tapes, and videos you could borrow to make yourself more knowledgeable and marketable. Opportunities today are both broader and deeper than they have ever been for those who set out to be the best they can be in their current jobs. Exceptional effort and ability will eventually be rewarded. When you become worth more than you are being paid, very soon you will probably be paid what you are worth. Quality products and services command higher prices than ordinary goods and services, but the proper motive for excellence is not monetary, it is obedience to God's command. By striving for excellence you can bring glory to God.

The most common question in the area of savings for education is how parents should save or invest for their children's education. Let me take some pressure off the back of you parents. Where does the Bible tell a parent that he or she is responsible to provide 100 percent of the cost of education, fees, room, board, and books for his or her children? Where is a child to learn responsibility, reliance on God, industry, and thrift if everything is provided for him? In the Jewish culture a boy becomes a man at his "bar mitzvah." He begins to take adult responsibility and be accountable for future decisions at age thirteen. We Gentiles wrongly assume total responsibility for our children's college and even graduate school and then expect them to exhibit instant responsibility for their lives at graduation. No wonder more than half the children who leave the nest for college turn into homing pigeons at graduation.

If God desires my children to graduate from college is He powerful enough to provide the means? Do you believe as I do that those who work and pay their own way to college put more into the task and as a result emerge better equipped and prepared for the real world? Most parents who provide everything their children "need" produce dependent adults who have learned to rely on their parents rather than their God or themselves. Don't assume 100 percent responsibility; transfer or share that task with your children and help them learn dependence on God, thrift, self-reliance, industry, and the joys of work.

Maybe you can't afford the cost of a private Christian education for your children, but you can model the Christian life, teach Christian principles at home, and have a major influence on your child's character, attitude, and values. My youngest son John never grew more than the year he left a private Christian school and attended a regular public high school. I never spent more time helping John to cope with school than the year he left the private Christian school. Prior to that, I relied upon our church and Christian school to equip John. My investment of time and energy was part of the reason he grew and matured. John learned how to think and how to become more discerning, and he saw Scripture demonstrated and proven in real life. It's one thing to be insulated in a Christian environment where only truth is presented, but John grew a lot more when he had to stand up and defend his faith from real attacks from authority figures such as some of his openly anti-Christian teachers. If it is God's will that your child attend a Christian school, college, or seminary, then it is God's responsibility to provide the means. If you are fortunate enough to have the means to cover the cost, remember you are still responsible for the results of raising your child in the nurture and admonition of the Lord. Don't delegate 100 percent of your job and assume that the church and Christian school will do it all for you. They can't and they won't. Equipping your children is your job; churches and schools are resources that can aid in the process. If you feel guilty because you lack the means to provide private education or a private Christian school, realize that this is false guilt from your adversary, not real guilt from our heavenly Father.

In most states the cost of college is quite inexpensive. In Arizona you can attend a public university and graduate for less than $10,000 including all tuition, books, and fees. That's less than $2,500/year cost if your son or daughter lives at home and you provide room and board. This means that your enterprising offspring can easily work to pay all their own costs for college. By so doing they graduate with pride in their accomplishment, practical work experience, and a transition rather than a leap to self-sufficiency. If minimum wage remains $4.25/hour and a young man or woman worked full-time during the summer (480 hours) and ten hours a week during the school year (400 hours), he or she could earn $3,740 per year. That is enough to honor God with a tithe ($374), put some money in savings ($374), pay the $2,500 school expenses, pay Social Security ($267—automatically deducted from each paycheck), and still have $225 left to spend as he or she chooses. If you teach your children industry; time management; and how to honor God, save money, and be content and thankful for what they have left, those principles will be worth far more over their lifetimes than any sheepskin they acquire in the process. It may not be God's plan that all our children graduate with a four-year degree, but it is God's plan that we help our young men and women learn how to manage His money using His rules and His principles.

## (6) Major Purchases

There are two methods of buying goods and services today, but the vast majority of us buy now and pay later without calculating the cost compared to saving and paying cash. In the next two chapters we will examine the two largest purchases most people make, homes and cars. If you are overcommitted in house and car payments there is no way you can ever balance your life to give, save, and live within your income. The price of balancing your spending may require real sacrifice, learning to be content with needs, and character traits of discipline, persistence, and thrift. Think of your financial life as a marathon, not a series of hundred-yard dashes, and you will deal with much less self-imposed pressure.

The average consumer today finances most of his purchases over time and makes buying decisions on payments rather than price or total cost. Assume that you are looking at an expense of $15,000 for a car, truck, boat, swimming pool, or college education. If you finance $15,000 over six years at 10 percent interest, you make seventy-two payments of $287/month. You have to repay both the $15,000 you borrowed and finance charges of $5,665. But if you choose to save $188.45/month for seventy-two months at 4 percent interest, you can accumulate enough to make the same $15,000 purchase but earn $1,432 in interest instead of paying $5,665 in finance charges. That is $7,097 difference in interest, 47 percent of the price of the item! By saving and buying in cash rather than payments you will stretch your income 47 percent further. Compound interest working for you (saving) rather than against you (financing) has a dynamic effect on both your lifestyle and your buying habits. By the time you have saved $15,000 you may end up repairing what you have, buying used at 10 to 20 percent of the original price, or deciding the item you "need" was really a want or desire you can live without.

## (7) Retirement Planning

Our culture and society put a completely non-biblical emphasis on retirement. The system encourages us to retire early and do what we enjoy: sleep in, relax, travel, play golf, learn new crafts, pursue hobbies, read, join clubs, and socialize. But since according to the Bible the purpose of life is to glorify God, society's goal is in total contrast to God's goal. Our purpose is to glorify God, not to pursue a life of self-indulgence. Ask yourself why you want to retire. Write out your reasons, then review them and ask if your motives are biblically valid, God directed, and God honoring. The Bible encourages us to pursue meaningful, God honoring tasks as long as He gives us life, breath, and energy.

Sometimes God enables men and women to pursue their jobs, excel, and accumulate substantial assets, and then He calls them to full-time Christian service or ministry. Sometimes His plan is to transition from a physically demanding job to one with fewer physical demands. Other times, instead of retiring at sixty-five, people have been led to continue at their same jobs working a reduced number of hours. Another plan I have observed is a change of jobs to a totally new field. The array of possibilities is endless, but He has a unique and perfect plan for each of us designed around our particular circumstances. Study after study has shown that retired people who pursue meaningful goals live longer, healthier, and happier lives. Ask the Lord what goals you should have in your golden years rather than accepting society's answer of retiring early and indulging self.

The familiar name of Moses is an excellent example of a three-career life. The first forty years Moses lived as a prince of Egypt and, if extrabiblical sources are correct, earned a position as a possible heir to the throne. Moses' second forty years were invested as a Midian shepherd whom God prepared for the job of Israel's deliverer from Egyptian slavery and bondage. Moses' third career started at age eighty; he spent forty more years leading the nation of Israel during their days in the desert.

Don't think of retirement as the end of your work; think of retirement as a transition freeing you to be able to serve others, evangelize, disciple, minister, or anything else that unites the body, pursues God ordained goals, or molds you to be the man or woman He would have you become. The major obstacle keeping many people from pursuing these kinds of worthwhile goals is lack of money. How many years are there between now and when you reach age sixty or sixty-five? Assuming Social Security continues in its present form, how much could you expect to receive at age sixty-two? sixty-five? seventy? If you would like to know more about your Social Security benefits, or get an estimate of future benefits, you can call toll-free, 1–800–772–1213 and ask for a Request for Earnings and Benefit Statement or fill out Form SSA 7004 available at your local Social Security office. You will receive a reply including your complete earnings history along with estimates of your benefits for retirement at age sixty-two, full retirement age, or age seventy, plus estimates of disability or survivor benefits that might be payable. If you have a company retirement plan (pension, profit sharing, 401K, 403B, SEPP, or Keogh) what do you project will be available for income at age sixty? sixty-five? seventy? If you don't know find out. The ancient prophet Hosea put it this way, "My people are destroyed for lack of knowledge" (Hosea 4:6).

Let's assume you have thirty-five years to age sixty-seven, your projected Social Security benefits are $1,000/month, and you have no company benefits, but you have saved $2,000/year the last five years into your Individual Retirement Account (IRA), and you currently earn $30,000/year. Further assume you have twenty-five years left to pay on your home mortgage, thirty months left to pay on your car, no credit cards or consumer debt, you are now saving $3,000/year, and you honor the Lord by giving $60 per week to your local church. If you continue your good habits of giving and saving first, and use a few of the principles you will learn in the coming chapters, you are exactly on target for a good retirement plan. Do you realize how much $3,000/year can grow to? In thirty-five years you can accumulate $813,073 at 10 percent, $414,711 at 7 percent, or $220,957 at 4 percent interest. Add to that the value of your current IRA ($12,210 including interest) which becomes $343,131 at 10 percent, $130,361 at 7 percent, or $48,182 at 4 percent. Using the lowest return of 4 percent which is available today in E or EE U.S. Government Savings Bonds, your nest egg is at least $269,139. If you learn a few very simple strategies, your earnings could easily increase from 4 percent to 7 percent. Now you will have $545,072. If you work at it you might earn 10 percent, which is the sixty-eight year average return for common stocks. Now you have accumulated $1,156,204. Granted that is before inflation and taxes, but you have used fewer than a third of the tools you have available in retirement planning.

We assumed that you have twenty-five years left to pay on your house. Let's say you started with a $100,000 mortgage at 8 percent for thirty years, five years ago. Your monthly payments are $740.23/month, not including taxes or insurance. When you check your payment booklet you find your remaining balance is $94,821.30. If you will use one of the many ideas in the next chapter, you can pay off your home in less than twelve and a half years. At that point you would be twenty-two and a half years from retirement. If you then choose to save your house payment for the reminder of the time between your last payment and age sixty-seven, you would have: $1,444,719 at 10 percent, $870,106 at 7 percent, or $533,450 at 4 percent earnings. Even with the worst case of 4 percent you have now doubled your nest egg for retirement, but we are by no means out of tools to use for accumulating for financial freedom.

Saving for retirement is simple if you:

(1) pay yourself first,
(2) set long-range goals and plans, and
(3) manage your increasing income wisely.

All you need to do is be persistent and use ideas like these that work. An illustration of managing your increasing income wisely works like this. First, work at becoming content and thankful for your current lifestyle. Second, commit in advance to save part of every raise, bonus or windfall, or gift that comes your way. Maybe you want to allocate one third to the Lord, one third to savings, and one third for living. Assume your $30,000 per year wages grow at 4 percent per year. This is a fair estimate of inflation over your working years until age sixty-seven since inflation has averaged 3 to 4 percent the past thirty-five years. At the end of year number one you get a 4 percent cost of living raise of $1,200. Give $400 to your church, $400 to savings, and spend the remaining $400 as you choose. Thirty-five years later your salary has grown to be $99,645/year. That is an increase of $69,645 produced by 4 percent per year inflation. If, and this is the key word, you have stuck with your plan, you give $23,215 to your church, save $23,215, and spend the remaining $23,215. Your savings, which came only by saving one third of your increases (this assumes no promotions, no bonus, windfalls, gifts, or inheritances) you continue to accumulate. You would have: $3,704,798 at 10 percent; $1,889,718 at 7 percent; $1,006,783 at 4 percent earnings. Here is our total nest egg from the three simple ideas presented so far.

|  | at 4% | at 7% | at 10% |
|---|---|---|---|
| Age 67 | $1,809,373 | $3,304,896 | $6,305,721 |

Retirement planning is often presented as a very complicated, difficult subject. I have examined some financial plans that took dozens of pages and scores of charts, graphs, and figures which would overwhelm the majority of readers. You do not need advanced math, accounting, or finance. You do not need a computer. All you need is the ability to spend less than you earn over a long period of time and to do something intelligent with the difference. If you are concerned about how you will be able to support yourself in the future, learn and use the three simple rules we have illustrated. Don't waste time looking back over your life asking yourself where you could have been if you had known or used these ideas earlier. Start now and look forward.

Let me illustrate the tremendous power of acting now on the information you possess. The most common plan for saving for retirement is putting $2,000/year into an Individual Retirement Account or IRA. The deadline for putting money into an IRA and being able to deduct it is April 15 of the year following the year for which you are filing your tax return. If you fund your 1995 IRA before April 15, 1996 it is deductible for 1995. The earliest you could fund it is January 1, 1995. What difference does putting money in an IRA 470 days earlier make? The difference is $230,474 more money at retirement, assuming a forty-five year time period (age twenty-one to sixty-seven); $2,000/year contribution, and 10 percent earnings. The moral of the illustration is *do it now!*

## EXCUSES TO PROCRASTINATE

Over the years I have heard the following excuses for failure to save or plan for retirement:

1. I can't make it now—forget the future/savings.
2. Retirement is way down the road. I'll worry about that later.
3. I just don't understand math, finance, and all those technical things.
4. The government will take care of all those things for me.
5. I already have a company retirement plan; why bother?
6. I plan to, just as soon as I . . . (but it never happens).

How would you respond to these excuses with Scripture? The only excuse I have encountered that I had no response to is:

7. My spouse is the only child of parents who are very, very rich, very, very old, in very poor health, and we are their sole beneficiaries!

As the following chart will prove, the longer you procrastinate the harder it gets. This chart provides the percentage of your income you should save assuming you plan to retire at age sixty-seven, earn a 7 percent return on your money, and are able to retire on 70 percent of your pre-retirement income. The earlier you start the smaller the sacrifice. The longer you wait the harder it gets. This same concept applies to every segment of savings we have and will discuss.

| AGE | SAVINGS |
|-----|---------|
| 25 | 10% |
| 30 | 14% |
| 35 | 20% |
| 40 | 28% |
| 45 | 41% |
| 50 | 64% |
| 55 | 114% |

If possible, save with before-tax dollars using a qualified retirement plan like a pension, profit sharing, 401K, 403B, SEPP, Keogh, or IRA. You will have more money working initially, and tax-deferred compounding is dramatic. For example, $10,000 at 10 percent for thirty-five years grows to $281,024, wheareas a 10 percent taxable account (assuming 30 percent for federal, state, and local taxes) grows to only $106,766. Many companies today offer matching deposits for your contribution to a pension plan. For every dollar you contribute they add from fifty cents to a dollar up to some limiting percentage or dollar amount. That is 50 percent to 100 percent immediate *guaranteed return on your deductible investment.* If you work for such a company, by all means take advantage of the opportunity. Nowhere else in the world can you find an investment with a guaranteed immediate return of 50 percent to 100 percent on your contribution.

## WHERE TO SAVE

By definition savings should be safe, accessible without penalty, and pay a fair market return. Banks, credit unions, and mutual funds all offer money market funds which are relatively safe. Most banks and credit unions are 100 percent insured by FDIC or CUNA Mutual for accounts up to $100,000. Mutual funds also offer money market funds that invest into government securities, an array of fixed income securities, and income that can be either taxable or tax-free, depending on your particular needs. Many financial institutions offer interest on checking accounts paid on either your average or lowest monthly account balance. As of the May 15, 1994 *USA Today,* money market mutual funds pay 2.97 percent taxable or 1.92 percent tax-free. When you accumulate more money and are willing to give up immediate access to your funds for a period of time, you can look at one year CDs paying 3.23 percent, one year treasury bills paying 4.89 percent, or a host of other short-term options including EE savings bonds at 4.7 percent. To start with, seek safety and immediate access to your principal without penalty, and don't fret over today's low yields. A young professional recently told me that money market funds are a poor investment if he earns 3 percent, pays 1 percent in taxes, and subtracts 3 percent for inflation. He has a 1 percent loss one year later. He was exactly correct; money market funds are not a good investment. They are savings to provide funds for emergencies, repair and maintenance, annual events, cushioning your income, education, and major purchases.

Some people use savings alone for retirement; I recommend that until you have accumulated $5,000 or more in savings you should stay with money market funds. Do your homework before you "invest," and you will eliminate many unpleasant surprises. (Once you have met the prerequisites for investing—you are out of debt, have adequate money in savings, and are living with a surplus—look at some of the books in the bibliography under the subject "investing.") The young professional I counseled chose to ignore my advice and invest into a sure fire, double his money, new issue stock recommended by a broker rather than let his $3,000 "savings" remain in a 3 percent money market fund. Six months later, he sold his stock for $429. Thereafter, he was a lot wiser and a lot more humble, and he doesn't confuse saving and investing.

If you have surplus funds or savings today, please read the rest of this book before you change anything. We will show you how to calculate real return on investments from: paying down a home mortgage, paying extra car payments, paying off consumer debt, putting money into a qualified retirement plan or pensions, and saving.

Let's apply savings to your income and your individual needs. Fill out the chart below.

PLANNING FOR THE FUTURE

1. Give to God first from all income     _____ %      $ _____

2. Exit the debt cycle—enter the saving cycle. Commit and save for:

    a. Emergencies          $ _____

    b. Repair and Maintenance    $ _____

    c. Annual events         $ _____

    d. Cushioning your income    $ _____

    e. Education            $ _____

    f. Major purchases        $ _____

    g. Retirement           $ _____

3. My next raise, bonus, or windfall will be divided as follows:

    a. _____

    b. _____

    c. _____

Whether you use seven accounts or two is a personal decision that doesn't matter. What matters is that you start today and apply these principles. The next four chapters will help you decrease expenses so you have more discretionary cash flow to save. It is my prayer that you will use part or all that discretionary income to first honor God and second save for the seven items we discussed. To make this plan yours, why not fill in the blanks on the summary on the previous page? What percentage or dollars per pay period will go to the Lord? What percentage or dollar amount per pay period will you commit to savings? How much will you save for emergencies? repair and maintenance? annual events? cushioning your income? education? major purchases? retirement? Most important of all, decide and commit now, before the blessing comes, what percentage of your next raise, bonus, windfall will go to God? to savings? to spending? Once you have made these decisions, you are well on your way to financial freedom.

## SAVING MONEY ON INSURANCE

Insurance can be a major component of your annual spending, so let's look at some ways to determine how much you need and what kinds to buy and then at some strategies to reduce your cost. First, insurance should be bought on a priority basis, based on the probability of a claim. Priority of purchase is: major medical, disability income, property and casualty (home and auto), life insurance, and then other insurance. If you only have enough income to buy part of what you need, start with major medical coverage and go down the list until you run out of funds. What follows is a brief description of all five areas of coverage. If your expense for insurance is substantial, this is an area to explore much deeper. An excellent resource is my booklet *Buying Insurance: Maximum Protection at Minimum Cost.*

*Priority one is adequate major medical coverage,* and good coverage is expensive. Fortunately, most of us are covered by medical insurance at work. If you aren't, you already know that the insurance category of your spending plan exceeds the recommended guideline percentages. First, to reduce your cost look into higher deductibles. The larger the deductible you choose the lower your annual premium. My personal policy has a $10,000 deductible, meaning we are self-insured for any claim under $10,000. The goal of all insurance buying is to purchase maximum coverage at minimal cost. I started out with a $500 deductible and over time increased it to $1,000, then $2,500, then $5,000, and finally my current policy with the $10,000 deductible. Each time I raised my deductible I paid the premiums I saved with a higher deductible into a savings account. In six years we accumulated $10,000 in savings, which allows me to pay premiums that are only 15 percent of what I paid for the $500 deductible policy. I seek protections only from the large loss, rather than pay almost ten times the price so I can recover on every small claim. If all you can afford to purchase is a high deductible policy, buy one, because one single medical problem can wipe out years of effort in a few days.

Avoid all high-cost policy options which cost you more in premiums than you are ever likely to collect. To reduce costs, decline the following options: maternity coverage, dental coverage, prescription drugs, eyeglasses, psychiatric coverage, and accidental death benefits. Stay with basic coverage and as high a deductible as possible.

*Priority two is disability income*, which pays you monthly income if you are disabled and unable to perform your regular job. In 1972, I was disabled for nine months from an auto accident, and if I had not purchased a disability income policy prior to the accident, I would have been financially destroyed. Six basic sources could provide income if you are disabled. They are: Social Security, workman's compensation (if you are disabled at work), company paid or group disability (generally called salary continuation), your spouse and family, your personal assets and savings, and an individual disability income policy. You need to examine your personal situation and provide yourself with a livable income if you are disabled. To reduce your costs: Take long elimination periods (which is the time period between your disability and the beginning of your income), buy only the amount you need, avoid duplicate or overlapping coverage, take a two to three year benefit period rather than five years or longer, and look for policies which are integrated (consider Social Security benefits). Buy only policies that are guaranteed renewable (at your option only, not the company's), provide a partial benefit if you are able to resume work part-time, and have a clear understandable definition of disability.

*Priority three is home and auto insurance*, particularly liability coverage. This is the age of lawsuits, and one accident, whether or not you are at fault, can destroy the results of years of your labor, savings, and effort. We will discuss auto insurance further in the chapter on cars, but let me stress the benefit of shopping and comparing insurance policies. There are no national guidelines or premiums for the same policy, so they can vary in price from 50 to 100 percent. It pays to shop and compare. As a general rule, do not buy your car insurance from your auto dealer, because the price is twice what you can find by shopping around. Never finance your car insurance in your auto loan. You will pay 30 to 40 percent in finance charges over four or five years, and you only buy a one-year policy.

Home insurance is much less expensive than car insurance, but you can still save money by shopping and comparing and being accurate on the value of your home and its contents. If you paid $100,000 for your home, part of the price (15–25 percent) is for land, which doesn't need to be insured. If your lot is worth $20,000, you should insure your home for $80,000, not $100,000, because your insurance premium is based on the home's value. Maybe you paid $40,000 for your furniture and personal property brand new ten years ago, but if you were to hold a garage, estate, or moving sale, you would probably receive $4,000 to $8,000 in cash. Don't pay extra premiums on your home's contents; buy and pay for only what you need, and what is realistic.

*Priority four is life insurance.* To save money, buy term insurance. I explain the reasons in detail in *Buying Insurance*, but in summary: As *insurance* that will pay your beneficiaries in the event of your death, cash value insurance costs much more for the same amount of coverage. And cash value policies have too low a rate of return to be considered good *investments*. Term insurance comes in three types: Annual Renewable Term (ART), Decreasing Term (DT), and Level Term (LT) which has a level premium for a period of time; then it, like ART, goes up in price.

What if you own a policy that is paid up or has substantial cash value? First, ask yourself—do you still need the protection? If you do, buy term insurance, then surrender your policy and use the accumulated surrender value to pay off high interest debt. A paid-up policy is a great deal for the insurance company, because they pay you only 3 to 4 percent and then lend out your cash values at much higher interest rates than they pay you. Insurance companies earn 6 to 12 percent on your money, pay you 3 to 4 percent, and make themselves fantastic profits using your money. You may feel that you are getting free insurance because there are no payments due on a paid-up policy, but they are giving you "free insurance" by paying the cost of insurance out of part of the earnings on your accumulated cash value. Today, there are billions of dollars of cash values inside the 2,000 life insurance companies operating in the U.S., earning the policy holders only 2 to 4 percent interest, while the uninformed policy holder pays 8 to 20 percent on existing consumer and other debt. Now don't rush out and cancel your policy. If you need protection, wait until you have a replacement term policy in your hand.

More and more companies and agents today are pursuing older, retired men and women, to sell them nursing home insurance. The two major financial fears for older people are inflation and ending up destitute in a public or Medicaid nursing home. There are some good policies available, but much of what is marketed by fear is very poor coverage at overpriced premiums. Besides learning the basic components of any good policy so you can intelligently shop and compare, look at the other alternatives available, and learn what is and is not covered before you buy. After the fact is too late to protect yourself, and your premiums are long gone.

Since most insurance is still marketed by commissioned salesmen, realize your salesman has no incentive to reduce your cost. His pay is a percentage of your annual or monthly premium. There are some very good, customer centered salesmen, and there are some very bad, greedy salesmen masquerading as good guys. Do your homework, shop and compare, and you are much less likely to accept either low quality policies or excessive premiums. I almost always advise people to avoid options like waiver of premiums which make premium payments for you (after a six month wait) if you are disabled. If you need disability income buy it direct in a single policy and get the same, or more, coverage for half the price. Accidental death benefit riders or polices may sound like a bargain, but the cost is very high and your chances of collecting are relatively small. If you need life insurance, buy a term policy which pays a death benefit regardless of how you die. Mortgage insurance, which is now marketed by banks, mortgage companies, and insurance agents, is a poor choice. Life insurance or disability insurance included or added to any loan is also extremely overpriced protection, so avoid it. If you need the coverage, buy a single separate policy for either life and disability with benefits equal to your needs. Finally, extended warranties and service contracts are also very expensive options and your chance of collecting benefits equal to or greater than your premium are small. Save your money and resist the sales pitch by reminding yourself that only 15 percent of premiums collected on extended warranties and service agreements go for claims.

I urge you to begin today to learn more about all types of insurance. The more you know the less money you will spend on all types of insurance over your remaining lifespan. If you simply re-read and study these pages, then dig out and analyze all the policies you currently make payments on, you can reduce your costs of insurance 10 to 25 percent. What do you spend each year for: medical, disability, auto, home, life, or other insurance? Does a 10 to 25 percent per year reduction in premiums motivate you to dig deeper into this area?

## ACTION ITEMS

1. Do you understand the awesome power of time and compound interest?

2. Will you commit to paying yourself something out of your next check, regardless of the amount?

3. Will you increase the amount you pay yourself each time you are blessed?

4. Is success in retirement planning a result of excellent investments and a large income or time, discipline, and good habits? How will you begin?

5. Will you memorize Proverbs 21:20? Will you act on its wisdom starting now?

6. What is your cost for:

| | YEARLY | MONTHLY |
|---|---|---|
| Medical Insurance | $ _____ | $ _____ |
| Disability | $ _____ | $ _____ |
| Home Insurance | $ _____ | $ _____ |
| Auto Insurance | $ _____ | $ _____ |

7. What will you do to reduce costs?
   - Shop and compare.
   - Increase deductibles.
   - Buy term insurance.
   - Eliminate unnecessary coverage and expensive options.

# CHAPTER 5
# SPENDING YOUR RESERVES: UNEMPLOYMENT AND UNDEREMPLOYMENT

"Whatever you do in word or deed, do all in the name of the Lord Jesus, giving thanks through Him to God the Father."
Colossians 3:17

What do you do when your income stops or drops? If you haven't had the time to plan before the event, here is the crash course in coping with less or no income. As you might have guessed, the major factor in surviving the situation is developing and maintaining the proper attitude. If your income is down, then concentrate on giving thanks and being content with the income that remains. If your income is gone, remind yourself that God is still in control, He does provide, and it's all His anyway; give thanks and be content with what you do have. What's really important is your identity in Christ, not your income, position, or possessions.

A common but incorrect response to less or no income is to play the blame game; many people blame circumstances for their misfortune and become bitter, negative, and more discontent. When people look for others to blame, they waste time, energy, and thought. If individuals spend their time blaming the economy, their environment, their parents, their mates, or even God, they are only adding fuel to the fire under their negative attitude. Negative attitudes produce negative results, just as positive attitudes produce positive results. Don't invest your time, talent, and energy into destructive activities of blame, guilt, and pessimism.

Instead ask God what you need to learn. Ask Him what you need to do differently. Ask Him to make Himself more real to you. Ask Him to let you experience His love, comfort, and sufficiency. Making these requests will lead to thankfulness and contentment, the spirit we must cultivate and maintain to make it through these trials.

## USE YOUR RESERVES

If you have put aside any money for savings, education, annual events, or even retirement, consider using the funds to bridge the gap until you are re-employed or using these monies to dampen the shock of learning to get by on lower income. Don't be afraid to sell an investment to free up funds you need to live on. While you are taking inventory of your assets, remember that savings come in many forms. One young couple I counseled when the husband's job was suddenly and unexpectedly terminated said they had no reserves or savings at all. When we went through and took inventory of what they did have, guess what we found. The first item was a paid-up insurance policy that had a $825 surrender value. The policy had been a gift from her parents, and the couple had never read the contract or thought that it had any value. Then when we examined his final paycheck I asked about a twelve-dollar deduction into a retirement plan, which was matched by his employer. His vested interest in the retirement plan was worth more than $3,000 after paying taxes in full plus the 10 percent penalty, since they were both under age 59½. In studying their personal property we found two shotguns and a deer rifle that he converted into $950 cash. Finally, they held a garage sale that reduced the clutter in their closets and garage 50 percent and produced another $270 in cash. In almost every case I have examined I have found savings or potential savings from a few hundred dollars to several thousand dollars.

The Scripture passages which have helped me most when problems, reversals, earthquakes, and calamities hit are those written by Peter to a group of Christians experiencing persecution. Peter helped me to see my life as one of personal refinement, not financial reversal, when I reflected on these words, "In this you greatly rejoice, even though now for a little while, if necessary, you have been distressed by various trials, that the proof of your faith, being more precious than gold which is perishable, even though tested by fire, may be found to result in praise and glory and honor at the revelation of Jesus Christ" (1 Peter 1:6–7). James told us to choose an attitude of joy during the trials which refine us: "Consider it all joy, my brethren, when you encounter various trials, knowing that the testing of your faith produces endurance. And let endurance have its perfect result, that you may be perfect and complete, lacking in nothing" (James 1:2–4).

Whether you see events as problems or opportunities is your choice. If you want peace, not pressure, follow Paul's prescription—"Be anxious for nothing, but in everything by prayer and supplication with thanksgiving let your requests be made known to God. And the peace of God, which surpasses all comprehension, shall guard your hearts and your minds in Christ Jesus. Finally, brethren, whatever is true, whatever is honorable, whatever is right, whatever is pure, whatever is lovely, whatever is of good repute, if there is any excellence and if anything worthy of praise, let your mind dwell on these things" (Philippians 4:6–8). Remember our Lord never asks us to do anything that He does not empower us to be able to perform.

## DON'T ADD DEBT, LIGHTEN YOUR LOAD

A logical sounding fix to a short-term cash flow problem of reduced or interrupted income is living off credit cards for a short period of time. Many families have existing lines of credit to draw on, and others turn to friends or family for loans to tide them through until things return to normal. In more than a thousand counseling situations, I have never seen using credit or debt turn out to be a good long-term solution, because eventually all debt must be repaid, both principal and interest. Even if things turn around quickly, the borrowers are left with more outgo than income. Deficit spending is not an option for wise personal planning. I know it is easy and tempting, but resolve to avoid debt as a short-term solution to your current need for income.

Look for financed, depreciating items which you can sell to eliminate debt payments. Almost everything declines in value over time; you can greatly reduce your need for income by eliminating payments and debt on items that you have financed. Could you sell your boat for more than you owe on it? How about your camper, snowmobile, jet skis, stereo, TV, or other personal items? For every dollar of payment you eliminate you reduce the need and pressure to produce more income. If you have debt or installment loans, ask yourself what you could sell to eliminate the loans. Then ask yourself if the item in question fills a "need" or "want/desire."

## Oh No, Not My Home!

I can hear women thinking, *Does this mean he is going to ask me to sell my home?* Only once have I directly recommended the sale of a house. That was years ago, and the couple never came back for the next meeting. Today, when clients ask if they need to sell their home I tell them no, but suggest that they pray about it and ask God if they should sell their house (a home is the family environment created by a family within the structure of the house). Every situation is different, and sometimes the best answer is selling the house to free equity and then renting short-term until the couple learns to respond properly to the changes. Other times trading one house for a smaller house is a better answer. About 20 percent of the time, the best plan is to move in with relatives, friends, or roommates to cut costs. Occasionally people will choose to turn their house into an income generator rather than an income consumer. One widow who faced the challenge of surviving on $600/month Social Security from her deceased husband chose to increase her income by renting out two rooms to four young women who attended a Christian college only four blocks away. The four boarders produced $800/month of additional income, and the five women each shared in groceries, meals, and keeping house. Taking in boarders or becoming one isn't for everyone, but sometimes it is an excellent way to produce income or to cut your personal expenses.

Even if you can't use your home as an income generator you can cut expenses by delaying any improvements, learning how to do your own maintenance, limiting long-distance phone calls, and raising your thermostat in the summer and lowering it in the winter.

## Slash Transportation Costs

Can you eliminate the need for your second and/or third car?

I counseled one family that went from three cars to one for a family of five. Their costs dropped $565/month, but more importantly the event unified their family as they planned and worked together as a team to conquer common problems of living within their reduced income and coping with one car. If you already only own one car, how much could you make or save by trading down to a less expensive transportation car? I know one teacher who traded his thirty-month-old Mustang for $4,500 cash, an eight-year-old transportation car worth $500 with slightly over 100,000 miles, and his car payments of $330/month. Besides the $4,500 cash he netted and elimination of car payments, he reduced his cost of car insurance more than $850/year. Eighteen months later, his situation turned around, and he sold the car for $450, which was his down payment on a nice, lower-mileage, five-year-old transportation car.

Sometimes it may even be necessary to sell your car and ride the bus or pay someone to provide you with transportation to and from wherever you need to go. A draftsman, who had his income cut from $3,000/month to $1,500/month, cushioned the blow by selling his mid-size European sedan for $10,000 and paying a fellow worker $80/month to provide transportation to and from work. He bought a bicycle for trips to the local mall and grocery store, and besides getting some good exercise he reduced his expenses (gas, operation, and car insurance) more than $200/month. By using the equity in his car he survived for seven months at half pay before he found new employment out of state at 40 percent more than he was originally earning. He made other cuts in spending and left Arizona with more than half of the money he received from selling his car.

Regardless of your situation you can reduce the costs of travel by planning your driving to cover maximum necessary stops in minimal time and miles. You can also minimize costs by learning to do your own simple car repairs and maintenance. I have one friend who, after losing his job as an assistant manager, now earns a good living as a mechanic. He takes his mechanical skills to an individual's house or office to save his customers the time and trouble of having to go to an auto repair shop or car dealership. After expenses, he averages more than $22 per hour (double his wage as an assistant manager), and he is hiring a helper to relieve him of the sixty-hour weeks he has been working as his business expands. He learned his trade in less than a year while living rent free with his brother and studying auto mechanics through a local trade program offered in a junior college.

## THE GAME PLAN

Our plan to weather the period of unemployment or pay cuts is the essence of simplicity: Cut your expenses until they equal your income.

There are two ways to approach the solution. First, you can find work at some income and then slash at your expenses until they are less than that income. Second, if you are still employed at some wage you can reduce your expenses to less than your existing income while you seek new work. If you attempt to violate the plan by living on credit or debt, you are simply making your life harder in the future when the debt must be repaid.

When I discuss guidelines with an individual or couple, one of the first areas most choose to begin cutting back is their expense for food.

For more than eight years we have supported a Haitian child through a Christian organization that serves children both physical food and spiritual food. For $30/month our contribution provides our boy, Wilbur, with food that meets all his basic physical needs for a month. When you cut back to the basics you can cut your food bill to $30–$50/month per person. Let me give you a sample of inexpensive foods for breakfast:

grits and other hot cereals (non-instant): 5¢/bowl and up
buttered toast: 1–5¢/slice
boxed cereal: 20¢/bowl and up, including milk
fruit (grapefruit, plums, bananas): 10¢ and up
eggs: 10¢ each
bagels: 10¢ and up
french toast: about 10¢/slice
milk or juice: about 15¢/glass

Note: Sugared cereals and sausage or bacon will multiply both your cost and your cholesterol. Buy only rarely, as a special treat.

For lunch look at inexpensive foods like:

sandwiches: 10¢ (peanut butter) and up
cookies: about 20¢
fruit: about 20¢
soup: about 50¢
homemade tossed salad: about 50¢
leftover fried chicken or frozen pizza: about 20¢/piece

Bag lunches are your least expensive option, but they can easily become boring. Vary the menu some to keep it interesting. You will save money over eating out. View meals out as a special treat; let your children eat in the school cafeteria when it's serving their favorite meal.

For dinner look for good healthy foods at low prices, such as:

casseroles (tuna casserole: tuna, macaroni and cheese, and
    peas): about 75¢/serving
soup: about 50¢/serving
pasta: 10¢/serving and up
vegetables—fresh in season, or frozen: 10¢/serving and up
baked potato with chili and cheese: less than 50¢
tacos: a cheap meal out, or about 50¢ each homemade
lentils cooked with sliced wieners: about 20¢/serving
frozen or homemade pizza: about 50¢/serving and up
grilled cheese sandwiches: 25¢
sardines: about 25¢/serving
homemade nachos (tortilla chips, refried beans, and cheese): 50¢
mini pizzas (English muffins topped with cheese, ketchup,
    and all-spice or ginger): about 25¢/each "pair"

Avoid red meats, except as a special treat, bought on sale. Desserts can be expensive, so if they are traditional in your home, be creative. Inexpensive desserts include Jell-O, watermelon or fruit salad in season, homemade cinnamon rolls or biscuits baked with sliced (raw) apples and cinnamon—and don't forget root beer floats and homemade cookies. Another "cost-cutting" idea: When the grocery store has frozen dinners and pot pies on sale, stock up; having them in your freezer may save you from going out to eat on a day when you just don't feel like having to cook. Remember that rice, potatoes, and beans are cheap, nutritious, and subject to great variation in cooking.

For snacks here are a few inexpensive but nutritious ideas:

granola cereal in sandwich bags
raisins, grapes, plums, and other fruit
homemade nachos
a bowl of cereal, especially at bedtime
homemade cookies and milk
a spoonful of peanut butter
homemade (not microwaved) popcorn
homemade popsicles (try freezing juice, chocolate milk,
    or pop)

The above ideas came from my editor, Cheryl Dunlop. If you want more ideas stop by your library and check out *The Best of the Cheapskate Monthly—Simple Tips for Living Lean in the 90's* by Mary Hunt. Check the bibliography for addresses of newsletters on the same topic.

As for reducing school and child care expenses, try being both frugal and creative. Private schooling is very expensive, and more and more families are turning to home schooling as an alternative. Several excellent curricula are available, and almost every state has an association to share ideas, resources, and events. I know one mother who home schools her three children and three others in return for $300/month plus free child care while she works the second shift. Consider trading child care, and don't forget about family and friends who may welcome the chance to have your little ankle biters around to spice up their lives.

There are dozens of ways to have fun without spending serious money on travel and entertainment. One of my favorite activities is fishing: For only $14 per year for a fishing license I have access to a half dozen lakes within a few minutes of our home. (Remember that we live in the desert.) During the fall and winter Arizona offers an array of hiking and camping trails to explore. If you like outdoor activities, gardening is fun and cheap, and nothing tastes better than home grown fruit, vegetables, and other garden produce. A family of readers will consider it a wonderful treat to spend a half-day at the city library choosing a dozen books each to read at home—and it's free. Finally, there are lots of board games and traditional games such as dominoes, checkers, chess, card games. All these activities build relationships and memories and are very inexpensive ways to entertain yourself and your family.

You can probably eliminate buying clothes for the adults in your family for one to ten years, depending on the current stockpile of your wardrobe closet, but your children just outgrow, rather than wear out, their clothes. In most sections of the country there are a good number of thrift shops and secondhand clothing stores where you can outfit your children for pennies on the dollar. Imagine designer jeans, shirts, skirts, blouses, and shoes for a dollar per item and up. I know one couple from our church who has a teenage son with size 14 shoes who shops at one thrift store where two of the Phoenix Suns basketball team donate their clothing on a seasonal basis. Even better than buying a pair of new Charles Barkley Nikes for $129 is getting a pair of the real Charles Barkley's once-worn shoes for $4. If your home is like ours, 95 percent of the adult clothing we donate isn't worn out or worn; it is simply boring, the wrong size, or less stylish than it was a few years back. Our boys' clothing that they outgrow is slightly worn but very serviceable for several seasons.

## BRINGING HOME THE BACON

By now you have gotten the idea of ways to reduce expenses to your income. Let's focus now on creating or increasing that income. These ideas all come from my counseling experience; there are dozens of other potential sources which you may discover in your own situation. Our most common source of new income is to examine our skills, talents, and abilities and ask ourself what we could market for income that we haven't yet tried. Begin where you are now and determine what you could do for odd jobs or part-time work that would create some cash flow. One young couple who relocated to Arizona was unable to find employment although both had college degrees and good work experience. I visited them in the home they had rented, and the first thing that struck me was the model home look. Everything was neat, clean, and uncluttered. It came out in our conversation that both of them were "neatniks" who thrived on a clean and orderly living environment. When I asked if they had ever considered cleaning homes for others as a way of earning money, they were shocked. Initially the job of cleaning homes sounded demeaning and beneath them (he had an MBA in marketing and she had a master's degree in literary science), but as they hit bottom, pride and image became less and less of an issue. He printed up a one-page advertising circular on their home computer, and they had it copied at a local print shop for five cents per copy. Then they put the fliers on the front doors of a hundred homes in their immediate neighborhood. They acquired four customers within the first week and three more the next, and they earned $120 for less than ten hours of combined labor. Realizing they had found a need which they could fill, they created a data base of homes in their area and outlined a marketing campaign to fill their need for employment of forty hours per week at $12/hour each. In less than ninety days they went from totally unemployed to more than $40,000/year in gross income. Today, six years later, they have two children; the wife is a full-time stay-at-home mom who handles the business, books, and administration; and the husband manages three cleaning crews: a professional window washing group, an industrial janitorial group, and a group of part-time, ambitious young men and women who clean residential homes. Last year their business income approached the six-figure mark, and they have grown tremendously both financially and spiritually through the learning experience of building a service business from scratch.

Don't overlook the possibility of an in-home business to supplement your income or create cash flow if you are between jobs. I have counseled divorcées, single parents, and even couples who turned their homes into income generators by providing day care, secretarial services, computer services, and a host of other in-home businesses without the costly overhead of traditional offices and facilities. One couple in their mid-fifties, who lost their jobs in the defense industry, converted their house and guest house into a "custodial care nursing home" which provided basic care for four elderly individuals. The state pays the couple $1,600/month for each boarder for food and care. Using some of the income the couple hired help to relieve them from 6:00 to 10:00 P.M. daily and all day Saturday and Sunday. After taxes and expenses, they net more income now than they did when both were working in the defense industry.

Another example of using talents and resources to earn money was a forty-year-old single parent who had custody of his two teenage sons, ages thirteen and fifteen. He was terminated as a technical representative of a computer firm, a job which had covered a six-state territory and kept him on the road 80 percent of the time. At first Bill was crushed by the loss of an $80,000 job, and he was both angry and depressed about God's new plan for his life. After several hours with Bill, I discovered that his first love was woodworking and he had natural mechanical ability. Bill's hobby was fixing and making almost anything. He spent most of his free time at home in his garage workshop to shield himself from the deafening sounds of his boys' music. I concluded our first meeting by asking Bill to pray that God would reveal His perfect plan for Bill, and show him what he needed to do differently. Bill also committed to attempt to say thanks for what he had left, and try to learn to be content. He left unconvinced this would help, but he was faithful to his promise.

In less than forty-eight hours Bill called to tell me how God had provided his needs and revealed His perfect plan. Bill realized that his two sons desperately needed an available dad to help them change directions and learn discernment in selecting their friends. This was apparent to everyone but Bill, and the job loss helped him see the problem. Also Bill's neighbor, a custom homebuilder, asked him to build a custom bookcase and desk. In time this single job led Bill to his new career as a handyman and custom cabinet maker. His new job paid him a little less income per year, but it didn't have the drain and expense of traveling over six states.

Another common source of income may be your spouse and your children. A commercial artist and his wife came to our church office for counseling after the husband lost his job when his employer filed for bankruptcy. Before he lost his job he was earning more than $5,000 per month, his wife had been a homemaker for sixteen years, and their two children were both enrolled in a private Christian school that cost about $7,000/year combined. With more than twenty years experience as an artist, the husband had little difficulty in finding work part-time, but his wages were only half of what he had been earning. What could he do to cut family expenses 50 percent or increase family income 100 percent?

First, they tried looking for employment in other areas of the country, but after a few family meetings this option was ruled out. Second, the wife was able to obtain a thirty-hour-per-week job as a girl Friday for their family doctor. This left her home when the children were home from school and reduced their need for income another $1,000/month. Third, both their children volunteered to work after school to help with family expenses and reduce the gap between income and expenses. The younger child went through a class at the local library to become a certified baby-sitter and her first full month she earned more than $200 baby-sitting. The older child was hired by a local retail merchant at $5/hour and was able to work thirty hours per week and hold her B + grade average in school. Then, the family expenses had to be reduced only 14 percent per month and they had a balanced spending plan with each member carrying some of the burden.

## What About Financial Help?

A common question is how Christians should view taking assistance in their time of need. Today many churches have a benevolence fund which is used to help those in need. I wish that all the needs of Christians could be met within the local church, but with more and more of our incomes going to federal, state, and local taxes, and with more of us getting too deeply in debt to give at all, the probability of that happening is becoming lower and lower. If your church offers help, and you need help, don't be proud—accept it. When you are back to normal, you can help those after you who are in need. This is how the early church functioned. Those who had a surplus gave to those in need, and the result was a testimony so strong it spread Christianity around the globe in less than a hundred years from Christ's resurrection.

Funds should be handled during tough times by the same biblical principles explained throughout this book. First, when you earn income remember to honor the Lord with the first part of every check. The amount may not be significant, but start where you can and honor God by first giving something back from every check. Second, regardless of the amount, pay yourself something out of each paycheck. When you develop these two habits in tough times, it will be easier to continue and increase both giving and saving as your income recovers or increases. At less income you may feel that it is not possible to give or save anything, but it is—once you cut expenses enough. Finally, the secret of contentment is to give thanks for what you have and what you earn. That is the best way I know to develop contentment and a better attitude.

## Surviving on Minimum Wage

To show you what can be done, here's a real example of how to handle and think about both income and expenses. A single young woman in her early twenties, whom I will call Shari, lived on the west side of Phoenix and worked at a national drugstore chain near my office in Sun City. For a period of three years she worked at $4.00 per hour gross pay, that is, before taxes. Her pay after taxes and insurance had been deducted was about $6,500 per year or $542/month, take home. Out of that income Shari rented a one-bedroom apartment with her sister, which cost each of them $125/month, for total rent of $250/month. She drove an older car that she had bought for $500 with 113,000 miles on it, and she paid for required liability insurance, gas, and repairs on her car, which together cost about an additional $100/month. The first check off the top of every paycheck was her offering of $50/month written to her local church. Shari's income was low enough that she was turned down for a gasoline credit card she applied for, but she still managed to save enough money that she eventually put herself through college. How did she manage that? By living frugally, with an attitude of thanksgiving and contentment for what she had and what she earned each and every week.

For the three years Shari worked at the drugstore, she managed very well on her income and saved $4,875. That was 25 percent of her income per year saved! Her food budget, including household supplies, was $60/month for both her and her sister. She used every idea we mentioned under cutting food costs, she shopped at low-priced "warehouse" stores, and she took advantage of sales, coupons, and specials. She would tell you that she ate a lot of tuna, macaroni, and canned soup, but the food was healthy and adequate, and she always had milk, fruit, and other basic items on hand. Although she almost never went out to eat, she could have done so if she had chosen to save less for college. She treated her savings account as untouchable except for emergencies, such as car repairs and medical expenses, and those savings started her journey into college in pursuit of a more challenging and rewarding career. She never gave in to the temptation to use credit or debt because she realized that the repayment of any debt would only put more pressure on an already low income. Shari left her drugstore job five years ago, and has since gone on to a professional career and income outside Arizona. As Shari would tell you, if you asked, she was living proof that a person could live well on very little and be thankful, content, honoring God (financially and totally), and saving out of total wages ending at only $4.00/hour.

It may not be easy, and it will require some new habits and different choices, but there are always jobs available at low wages if you want them. If your income has stopped or dropped, start now and do what it takes to cut expenses until they are less than your next job or your temporarily reduced income, even if it is current (1995) minimum wage of $4.25 per hour.

## ACTION ITEMS

1. If you are currently employed, set a goal for reserves to smooth out loss of a job or a pay cut.

2. If necessary, which assets could you sell to reduce or eliminate debt?

3. What can you do to slash your housing costs?

4. What can you do to reduce your cost of transportation?

5. How can you cut your food costs?

6. Do you need professional help?

7. Believe you can succeed and trust God for the ways and means.

# CHAPTER 6
# YOUR HOME

"Finish your outdoor work and get your fields ready; after that, build your house." Proverbs 24:27 NIV

Let's talk about the largest, sometimes only, investment most Americans ever make—their home. Most of us never realize that what we consider a natural right is in reality a privilege most peoples of the world never achieve—owning their own home. If you visit Tokyo, Japan, you will be shocked to find that the average family of five lives in approximately 700 square feet and their real estate prices are more than triple the price of the average American home. Look around Europe and you learn you can buy 60 percent more space than in Tokyo for the average household of 4.3 people, but prices are still higher than in the States. If you check out Africa or South America, you find 6.8 people living in slightly less than 600 square feet. Indoor plumbing, safe drinking water, electricity, sewers, paved roads, a solid roof, central heating and air conditioning, phones, television, fire departments, daily newspapers, mail service, and many other services are indeed luxuries for 80 percent of the world's population. Even those people in the U.S. who live below the official poverty line are rich by worldwide standards.

Realizing these facts may help you separate "needs" from wants and desires with respect to housing. Housing is a need, but a particular square footage, location, furnishings, and exterior landscaping are wants and desires. Your first decision is how much physical space you require. If you use a world standard, the average living space per person is less than 100 square feet. Moving to the industrialized world, space increases to about 160 square feet of living space per person. In the U.S., the average is 375 square feet per person, and the typical household has 3.2 occupants meaning 1,200 square feet of living space. How much space does your family "need"? Do you "need": a bedroom for each child? A living room and a family room? A dining room? Two, three, or four baths? The answer is no, these are not "needs" but wants and desires. Our duty as believers is to learn to be content and thankful with what we have and grateful for the blessing of the largest, least expensive homes in the world. If you have a four person family your "need" space is 400 square feet, your "want" is 640 square feet, and your "desired" space is probably 1,500 square feet or larger.

Location is an extremely large part of the cost of housing. An average home in Beverly Hills, California, sells for more than $450/square foot whereas the same home in Oklahoma City, Oklahoma, would sell for $46/square foot. In Phoenix, Arizona, you can find housing costing from $18/square foot up to $100/square foot or more depending on the area that you select. You might refuse to live in an $18,000/1,000 square foot house in parts of Phoenix, but the majority of people on our planet would see that housing as spacious, luxurious, and something to dream about.

The third variable in housing costs is how we choose to furnish our homes. Your dream could cost $100,000 to furnish if you chose exclusive, expensive, top brand furniture and accessories. Or you could adequately furnish the same home with used furniture purchased at garage or estate sales for $2,000 to $5,000. The first time you encounter the truth about size, location, and furniture it is a shock, because we have all been conditioned with unrealistic desires for space, location, and furniture. The same facts apply to your landscaping. You can hire a landscape architect and spend 25 percent to 50 percent of the price of a home on landscaping, or you can do it yourself with seeds, time, water, and effort for 1 to 5 percent of the price of your home.

## RENT, LEASE, BUY, OR BUILD?

Renting or leasing housing is not a waste of money, and indeed in many areas of the U.S. you can still rent cheaper than you can buy. During the late seventies and early eighties almost everyone in the country made money by owning their own homes. For over a decade we saw prices of homes double, triple, or more. Very quickly we learned the strategy of minimum down payments and maximum mortgages to leverage our net worth. If you put $5,000 down on a $50,000 home in 1970, in 1985 your $45,000, thirty-year mortgage was paid down to $33,000 and you could sell your house for

$100,000, $150,000, or more. With only $5,000 down you had a potential profit of at least $50,000 or $100,000. Just as everyone figured out how to buy more house than they could afford and leverage themselves to wealth, many homes stopped rising in price. Today, in many areas the $100,000 homes we bought in 1985 still sell for $100,000 or less ten years later. Who is better off when prices stay level or fall—the 95 percent who are mortgagees paying payments that are more than they can comfortably handle or the renter with less space and half the payments? Renting can be cheaper than owning, especially for those whose jobs transfer them from one area of the country to another every few years.

The costs of buying a home, including real estate fees, title insurance, etc. are often 8 to 10 percent of the price of the home. Costs of selling a home subtracts another 8 to 10 percent typically non-deductible costs from your sales price. Unfortunately, the loss on selling a personal residence is non-deductible, but the profit on selling a home is taxable (unless you buy a home of equal or greater value or use your one-time $125,000 exemption if you're over fifty-five). So selling one home and buying another can eat up 16 to 20 percent of the price of a home, and since very few pay cash, buying and selling costs can consume up to all your equity. Factor that into your decision making.

Am I forgetting that home owners build equity with each mortgage payment while those who rent or lease have no equity? No, but unless you stay in your home five to ten years the fact is you create very little equity because the early years of a mortgage you pay mostly interest and very little principal. Examine the following chart, which shows the amount of equity you create if you have a $100,000 mortgage at 8 percent interest for a thirty-year term. This is a level payment of $740/month, which is $8,883/year consisting of principal and interest only, not including taxes and insurance costs.

| YEAR | EQUITY | YEAR | EQUITY |
|------|--------|------|--------|
| 1 | $ 883 | 6 | $ 6,476 |
| 2 | 1,836 | 7 | 7,877 |
| 3 | 2,866 | 8 | 9,389 |
| 4 | 3,978 | 9 | 11,023 |
| 5 | 5,179 | 10 | 12,788 |

If you live in a home less than nine years you have built no equity if costs of selling the home total 10 percent of the home's sale price. You might have a profit on your home if home prices rise, or you could have a loss if home prices have fallen. In addition, you will have costs of maintenance, repairs, and taxes as a homeowner that would amount to more money for you than for someone who rents or leases.

If you assume $2,000/year for maintenance, repairs, and taxes, and further assume you could rent suitable living space for $1,000/year less than your mortgage payment, home ownership costs you $3,000/year more than renting. Then there are items like furnishings, landscaping, and decorating that will probably cost you another $1,000/year you would not spend if you rented or leased. Four thousand dollars per year for nine years compounds to $42,331 at 4 percent interest, $47,912 at 7 percent interest, and $54,318 at 10 percent interest. You *might* make as much *if* property values increase but property values don't always go up—sometimes they do down.

If you are uncertain how long you will live in an area, rent because a lease, which is generally less expensive, is a commitment of a year or more that you must honor even if circumstances cause you to move. If you are certain you will live in an area three to five years, then leasing is generally a lower cost. If you feel confident you are going to remain in an area five to ten years, then calculate your own figures based on unique area factors to see which represents lower costs, leasing or owning. For stays over ten years, generally owning has better economics than leasing. Although home ownership has a variety of personal benefits like pride of ownership, sometimes renting or leasing will solve your need for shelter at much less cost. Don't view renting or leasing as a waste of money: You do receive the benefit of housing in return for your monthly obligation.

For a few individuals who have the time, patience, and knowledge, building a home themselves can save some substantial money. You can serve as your own general contractor and hire the subcontractors to pour the foundation, put in the plumbing, do the electrical work, put on the roof, do the carpentry and/or masonry, or any of the components of building a home. By serving as your own contractor you can save money, but you are responsible and liable for your subcontractors. One problem can quickly destroy your savings for the whole house. A friend who paid his plumbing and electrical contractor was shocked to learn the man went bankrupt, spent my friend's money, and failed to pay his workers for their labor. My friend had to pay twice for the same job and ended up spending more than he would have had he not acted as general contractor. Realize there are risks for the rewards and evaluate carefully if the potential savings and rewards of building your own home are worth the potential problems and expenses. If you are skilled and experienced in the trades, by all means use your skills to lower your costs. I know one plumber/carpenter who did his own plumbing, electrical, and carpentry labor and saved $18,000 on the price of his home.

## New or Used

In choosing new or used housing there are both personal and economic components to consider. If you are willing to adapt your wants and desires to what's already built, you can generally buy more house for less money by choosing a resale home. Most existing homes come with upgraded carpet, appliances, drapes, and extras the new home buyer paid for that can be purchased at a discount if you will accept what exists. In Scottsdale, Arizona, for example, many homes come with a swimming pool which cost the new home buyer $10,000 to $12,000 but only add $5,000 to $6,000 to the selling price of a used home. A five-year-old home will come with five-year-old mature landscaping, trees, bushes, and plants that bought new would cost thousands of dollars. Also the new home buyer will have had time to correct all the little bugs you find in any new house. If you can accept what exists rather than design from the ground up, you will spend less money than for comparable new homes by buying a used home.

For those who have time, talent, and motivation, a bargain purchase is the fix-up home. Some home buyers spend no time or money keeping their homes repaired and maintained, and when they sell them those homes can be excellent bargains. The second home I bought was a fix-up special that became available due to a divorce. The home was in an excellent location and was structurally sound, but it had received no maintenance for five years prior to the sale. I estimated the cost to clean up the landscaping, repaint inside and out, recarpet, and replaster the pool at $8,000. Then I offered $15,000 less than a ready-to-sell home in that area would normally be priced. My offer was accepted, I spent less than I projected in repairs (if you don't value by labor), and we sold the home three years later at a substantial profit. Personally I would never do it again, due to the time commitment, but the fix-up special is one way to lower costs in buying homes or to buy more home for less money.

When you move beyond tract homes to semi-custom or custom homes you are well beyond "needs" and into the upper end of wants and desires. Unless you are a home builder or have the ability and the desire to serve as your own general contractor, custom homes are an option to consider only after you have satisfied all your basic needs and wants. A friend of our family recently went through a series of business and personal reversals which necessitated the sale of a large, lovely custom home he had acquired in prior years. Initially the change was devastating, and trading down was a blow to his ego, pride, and self-esteem. Moving out of a 4,500 square foot showplace into a 1,800 square foot tract home destroyed his attitude and temporarily soured his outlook on life until he experienced the fact that neither God nor his real friends valued him for his luxury home. Besides the substantial reduction in house payments, all other expenses associated with his prior high roller lifestyle were now removed from his monthly outgo. Today, he works a four-day week, has real time for his wife and family, and volunteers several hours each week at church serving others. If you offered my friend a choice between his prior and present lifestyle, he would choose today in a heartbeat. If today you are going through a reducing stage, choose to believe that God owns, controls, and provides, and remember that your true identity is in Christ not in your possessions, positions, income, or home.

## Roommates and Family

The largest blows to our egos come when circumstances force us to either take in roommates or move in with friends or family. We value independence and devalue dependence. Pride stresses self, freedom, and individuality, while humility exalts others, accountability, and interdependency. The entire New Testament is filled with example after example of the virtues of humility, accountability, unity, and dependence on God. Read Jesus' prayer for Himself, His disciples, and us today in John 17. If circumstances are forcing you to consider moving in with friends or family, perhaps this is God's method of reminding you that He wants you dependent upon Him. The concept of Christ's church is a unified body, not a collection of individuals on an organization chart. If you feel crushed, angry, and disillusioned by circumstances beyond your control, remember the words of the apostle Paul when he was tormented by circumstances beyond his control—"And He [God] said to me, 'My grace is sufficient for you, for power is perfected in weakness.' Most gladly, therefore, I will rather boast about my weaknesses, that the power of Christ may dwell in me. Therefore I am well content with weakness . . . for when I am weak, then I am strong" (2 Corinthians 12:9–10).

By living with other people you can dramatically lower your

cost of housing by sharing kitchens, living rooms, family rooms, bedrooms, baths, and other components of your home. My grandmother's old saying that two can live as cheaply as one isn't mathematically precise but the principle is true. If two single parents become roommates, their costs may not drop 50 percent each but they will reduce housing costs for each family 40 to 45 percent. Besides filling the void of loneliness, friends or family can share meal preparation, shopping, housework, yard work, carpooling, and a host of other time-consuming, costly necessities. The adjustment is in attitudes, not economics. What we are taught to expect/believe and demand as entitlements today in this country are often unrealistic and founded on selfishness, pride, independence, and autonomy.

The choice of independent housing is the largest single item in an individual's monthly expenditures nationwide. It should be made on economic realities not emotional desires. If you today approached a mortgage company to see how much you could afford to finance (or rent) they would use a maximum of 28 to 32 percent of your gross income. If you have no debt on paper you can obtain a mortgage with maximum payments of 32 percent of your monthly gross income (28 percent if you have debts). There are two dangers in working from these guidelines that people learn the hard way—after the fact. First, it is unwise to commit yourself to the maximum and eliminate any margin from your life. Second, if you look only at payments you are considering only two-thirds the cost of housing and guaranteeing yourself a lifestyle of financial bondage. Later chapters will show percentage guidelines for housing and all other expense categories, but first let's examine the question deeper.

## HOUSING: HOW MUCH CAN YOU AFFORD TO SPEND?

With a $40,000/year household income (charted on page 62), you should first allow for giving (or choose to rob God), saving (or live like fools), and taxes (federal, state, FICA, and Medicare). A family of four is left with real spendable income of $24,712/year, which is $2,060/month. If we use typical lending guidelines for maximum mortgages, we come up with payments of $933 to $1,067 per month ($3,333/month X 28 to 32 percent). If you live to the maximum, you have overcommitted yourself and probably made it impossible to give, save, and live free of pressure because mortgage or rent payments are only part of the cost of housing. The column below gives typical monthly expenses for mortgage payments (principal and interest only), property taxes, home-owners insurance, utilities, telephone, maintenance, and improvements. As you can see, the payment ($933/month) is only two-thirds the total monthly cost of housing ($1,388). If you commit to the maximum house payment, you have committed 67 percent of your $2,060/month spendable income to housing. There is absolutely no way you can stretch what is left, $672/month, to cover all the other expenses: giving, saving, transportation, food, insurance, debts, entertainment, clothing, medical, school and child care, and miscellaneous. Since $672/month cannot adequately cover these expenses, to survive you spend what you could have given and saved just to make ends meet. Even then it is extremely tight and you are living with no margin for error.

| | |
|---|---:|
| PAYMENTS | $ 933 |
| TAXES | 80 |
| INSURANCE | 25 |
| UTILITIES | 200 |
| TELEPHONE | 40 |
| MAINTENANCE | 50 |
| IMPROVEMENTS | 60 |
| TOTAL | $1,388 |

Maybe you can lower your gas, electric, and water bills some by raising and lowering the thermostat and conserving water, but you can't totally eliminate these expenses. If things really get tight, you could choose to disconnect your phone, but most families cut giving or saving first. For a while you can defer home maintenance, repair, and improvements, but over time discipline fades, money must be spent, and you end up charging these items and repaying the costs at 18 percent interest. If you have a mortgage you have no option on property tax and home insurance because these amounts are collected monthly along with your mortgage payment. The largest single reason for financial problems in the American home is that we have overcommitted ourselves on our "need" for housing. To live a stress-free financial life you should *commit no more to total housing costs than 32 to 40 percent of your after-giving, after-saving, after-tax income.* In the example above of $40,000 gross with $24,712 spendable income, that means between $7,980 and $9,885/year for total housing costs!

Having showed this principle to thousands of people over the years I anticipate your response. Some will say that I don't understand the cost of housing in your area. Others say that they cannot live on that little amount of money for housing. A few will rework the numbers as shown below.

| | | | |
|---|---:|---|---|
| SALARY | $40,000 | | |
| GIVING | 800 | | |
| SAVINGS | 100 | | |
| TAXES | 6,604 | | |
| SPENDABLE | $32,496 | = | $2,708/month |
| PAYMENTS | $ 933 | | |
| TAXES | 80 | | |
| INSURANCE | 25 | | |
| UTILITIES | 150 | | |
| TELEPHONE | 25 | | |
| MAINTENANCE | 10 | | |
| IMPROVEMENTS | 0 | | |
| TOTAL | $ 1,223 | | |

First they cut or eliminate giving, slash or eliminate saving, and reduce federal taxes withheld due to deductibility of mortgage interest to leave themselves with more spendable income. They use ten dollars for maintenance and nothing for improvements. This family is creating future tension by violating five basic rules: (1) First honor the Lord, (2) save some of your income off the top, (3) look at *all* the costs of housing: taxes, insurance, utilities, telephone, maintenance and other, not just the payment, (4) don't go to the maximum in financing your home or anything else, and (5) be realistic about the cost of maintenance and improvements.

Maintenance and improvements can be substantial expenses, and the longer you put off spending the money the more you are apt to spend. Look at all the costs and be realistic. No home can run forever without some money spent for repairs and maintenance. If you don't plan for the expense either a problem causes you to do repairs on credit, or your house begins to decline in value as maintenance items build up. Regarding home improvements, either plan for costs, or accept the fact that it will be obvious to everyone that you bought more house than you could afford and have no money left to decorate, furnish, or landscape. A salesman friend of mind, who earns an excellent six-figure income, purchased a luxury home two years ago. He borrowed 32 percent of his gross income, the maximum a lender would lend, hoping that over time his commissions would increase allowing him to furnish the home, give something to the church, and save a part of his income. Today his luxury home has little furniture (two rooms), no landscaping, and no drapes or blinds, since his expected increase didn't materialize. If he had only examined all the costs, been realistic for maintenance and improvement, and bought within his income, rather than finance to the maximum, his financial problems would be gone rather than ongoing.

My salesman friend's wife recently went over a list of what it would take to make her home what she wanted. She had shopped, listed the improvements she wanted inside and out, and estimated a total cost of $45,000. She was angry that her husband could play golf any time he wanted and still had his toys (jet ski, motorcycle, new golf clubs, and a bass boat) while she lived in an unfurnished house. To the salesman, golf and toys were "needs," but his wife saw them as "wants and desires" while her "need" for furniture was a real need. What would you say if you were counseling this couple? My solution was to sell the jet ski for $4,000, sell the bass boat for $8,000, and limit his golf from twice a week to once weekly. His wife was ecstatic. The $12,000 from selling the jet ski and the bass boat would be the down payment to furnish and landscape her home. Then I explained that they had no savings, no giving, and no margin left to make payments on a $33,000 loan. I did agree that the Ethan Allen dining room table, chairs, and hutch were lovely, but I pointed out that by searching for used furniture and shopping at estate and garage sales they could buy the same set used for $1,000 to $1,600 rather than the $8,000 figure she had on her list. Six months later my friends had a completely furnished home with no additional debt and they were completing a do-it-yourself landscaping plan.

If you don't allow for improvements and extras in your home you are kidding yourself and unnecessarily stressing yourself, your marriage, and your family.

## FINANCING A HOME

As we have seen, size, location, furnishing, and landscaping are major variables in the price of your home, but the way you finance your home can cost you even more than your home if you approach the decision carelessly. Let's look at what we have been conditioned to accept: minimum down payments and a thirty-year mortgage. If you price a $100,000 mortgage at 8 percent, assuming $10,000 down already applied on a $110,000 house, your payments are $740/month PI only for 360 months. Since your equity is less than 20 percent you have an extra one-half percent ($35/month) added to your 8 percent mortgage, and that is before you calculate for property taxes and homeowner's insurance, which will be added to your payment [PI $740/month; plus mortgage insurance, $35/month; plus taxes and insurance, $105/month]—TOTAL payment $875/month PITI. Did you ever stop to figure out what the cost of interest is on a thirty-year loan? You make 360 payments of $740/month PI only for a total repayment of $266,400. Subtract the amount you borrowed ($100,000) from your total paid, and you find your interest charge is $166,400. That's 1.63 times the amount you financed! What if you considered a fifteen-year mortgage? Your interest rate would drop from 8½ percent to 7¾ percent, and your new payments would be $959/month for 180 months. That's a total repayment of $172,620 on a $100,000 mortgage leaving you an interest cost of $72,620. By financing your home fifteen years instead of thirty, you raise your payments 24 percent but you save yourself $93,780 in interest. *Finance your mortgage less than thirty years and slash your costs of interest 50 percent!*

Principle: *The more you put down the better off you are.* If in the above example we elected a 20 percent down payment we could obtain 7.8 percent interest for thirty years or 7.55 percent for fifteen years because the more you put down the lower your interest rate. This is pure interest savings of $17,682 to $108,693 over the life of your loan. We do not suggest that you use all your savings for a down payment as you would be vulnerable to problems if they occurred and you had no reserves. Neither do you want to borrow the down payment from parents, family, friends, or anyone. Too many times parents or others try to help children buy a home by lending the down payment interest free. In more than 60 percent of the cases I have counseled, the children bought too much house and the eventual result was foreclosure and loss of all equity. If you, your children, or family members do not have the income, persistence, or discipline to save a reasonable down payment, don't borrow (or lend it to them). The majority of families will tell you that they or others they know wish that they had never made family loans. Family loans are bad business; they destroy relationships and create problems. If you must lend a down payment make it a gift not a loan, and make sure your gift won't be used to help others bury themselves financially into more home (or car) than they can realistically afford.

A common question is whether an individual should acquire a fixed or a variable rate mortgage. The first year variable rate mortgages, also called adjustable rate mortgages or ARMs, offer a cheaper payment than fixed rates, but the cost over the life of the loan is determined by unknown future interest rates. If you are certain interest rates will stay level or decline, purchase an ARM. If you are certain rates will rise, purchase a fixed rate plan. If you own an ARM and are wrong about the direction of interest rates, make certain you can handle the maximum payment, which is usually a 5 to 6 percent higher interest rate than your initial rate. If you select a fixed mortgage and are wrong about the direction of interest rates, you can always refinance at a lower rate if interest rates decline. Interest rates declined from 1980 and reached a twenty-three year low for treasury bonds (a twenty-five year low for mortgages) in October 1993. Since then interest rates have gone up and probably will continue to rise. I generally prefer and recommend fixed rates since I saw far too many people lose their homes when rates rose in 1979–80 and 1986–87.

## PREPAYING YOUR MORTGAGE

One of the best investments you can make is to pre-pay principal on your existing mortgage. We saw earlier how little equity was built in the first ten years of a thirty-year mortgage (page 131). During the life of a thirty-year fixed-rate mortgage of $100,000 at 8½ percent, here is the breakdown of principal and interest for several payments. Each payment remains level at $775/month, but the principal increases over time and the amount that goes to interest decreases over time. If you have an existing mortgage, ask your lender to send you an "amortization schedule" which lists all 360 payments and how each payment is divided between principal and interest. Then consider one of the following four methods to save thousands in interest over time.

| PMT. | PRIN. | INT. |
|------|-------|------|
| 001  | $60   | $715 |
| 002  | 60    | 715  |
| 003  | 60    | 715  |
| 004  | 61    | 714  |
| 012  | 65    | 710  |
| 024  | 71    | 704  |
| 036  | 77    | 698  |
| 048  | 84    | 691  |
| 060  | 91    | 684  |
| 120  | 139   | 636  |
| 180  | 213   | 562  |
| 240  | 327   | 448  |
| 300  | 501   | 274  |

## Method 1: Make Extra Principal Payments Each Month

Make an extra principal payment each month to slash your finance charges. Payment number four of $775 is $61 principal plus $714 interest. If with payment three ($775) you add an extra $61 to be applied to loan principal you eliminate the fourth payment and save yourself $714 in interest. Your return on an investment of $61 is 1,170 percent, or $714. If you adopt this simple strategy you could pay off a thirty-year loan in fifteen years and save yourself $89,500 in interest costs. Can you imagine the financial freedom of not having to make house payments the next fifteen years? If you continued to invest the $775 house payment for the next fifteen years you could accumulate $282,399 if you earned the same 8½ percent you were paying your mortgage company, plus you own a paid-for home.

## Method 2: Make a Constant Extra Principal Payment Each Month

If instead of your regular $775 payment you paid $1,000, $225/month would be used to reduce principal, not counting the principal payment included in your regular payment. You would have a paid-for home in 177 months, which is fourteen years and nine months. Total interest saved $102,152—again more than the price of your house.

## Method 3: Choose Bi-Monthly Payments

In some cases it is possible to finance or refinance a mortgage with bi-monthly payments, meaning a payment is due every two weeks instead of once a month. If you are currently paid every other week you know that twice a year you get three paychecks during a month. Your third monthly check applied to your principal will shorten your mortgage life, since the extra payment is applied to the principal and that eliminates interest. If you paid $338 every two weeks on the same $100,000 mortgage at 8½ percent your home would be completely paid for with 567 payments, which is twenty-one years and ten months. That's eight years and two months early, and your interest savings are $59,156 over the conventional thirty-year loan paid monthly.

## Method 4: Use Raises, Bonuses, Windfalls, and Gifts to Pay Principal

If I added an extra $743 to my first payment on our $100,000, 8½ percent, thirty-year loan, I could eliminate twelve months of interest, saving $8,557 in interest. When a windfall, gift, inheritance, or bonus comes, consider using part or all of it to prepay principal on your mortgage. If one year into a thirty-year mortgage you inherit $20,000 give God a double tithe ($4,000), save $2,000, put $10,000 onto your mortgage, and enjoy/spend the remaining $4,000. By prepaying $10,000 principal you have eliminated 104 payments and saved yourself $70,600 in interest. The best strategy to plan and follow is to allocate every raise, bonus, windfall, gift, or inheritance *before it arrives*. Part should go to your church, part should be saved, part should be applied to your mortgage, and part could be spent. If you allocate one fourth to each of these four areas your giving will exceed most, you are exercising wisdom and saving, your debts are decreasing, and you can live better. This fourth method will save you thousands in interest over your life, and, more importantly, the method produces a balanced lifestyle of giving, saving, debt reduction, and spending. Regardless of the method you select start applying it now. You will never regret the decision.

## WHAT ABOUT TAXES?

When I mention paying off a home mortgage the first objection I get is that this would raise taxes because mortgage interest is tax-deductible. Yes, mortgage interest is deductible for taxpayers who itemize deductions, but only the amount over the standard deduction saves you taxes. During the fourth year of the $100,000, thirty-year, 8½ percent mortgage you make twelve payments of $775, of which $1,046 goes to principal and $8,254 goes to interest. If you are married filing joint, you have a standard deduction of $6,350 for 1994, meaning your deductions, over the standard deduction ($8,254 − $6,350), is $1,904. If your federal and state taxes are 18 percent you save $343 in taxes, and at 33 percent you save $635 in taxes. Is that a good return on your investment? Would you spend $8,254 to get a return of $635? What would your return be if you had a paid-for home, put your house payment interest into savings, and spent $1,046 principal for living? On $9,300 earnings ($8,254 + $1,046) use the same $6,350 standard deduction, and assuming a 33 percent tax rate you would pay taxes of $983 ([9,300 − 6,350] x ⅓). With a mortgage, your bottom line is $1,046 more equity plus $635 taxes saved for $1,681 net. Without a mortgage you spend $1,046, pay $983 in taxes, and have $7,271 net. You are more than four times better off without a mortgage. Reread the example and check the arithmetic. At first it sounds crazy but it is absolutely accurate. Don't let the tail (taxes/deductions) wag the dog (good stewardship of your income).

## REFINANCING PROS AND CONS

Any time you can lower the cost of a loan (not just home mortgages) 1 or 2 percent interest, refinancing makes economic sense if you will keep the loan long enough to recover the cost of refinancing. You have a fixed rate $100,000 mortgage at 9½ percent interest for thirty years, and your payments are $847/month. If you refinanced the loan at 7¾ percent for thirty years, your payments would be $723/month. Your savings are $124/month for 360 payments, or $44,640. If total costs to refinance are $1,500, you make a profit the thirteenth month (13 x $124 = $1,612). Many people refinanced their homes between 1980 and 1993 because interest rates have declined, reaching a twenty-five year low in the fall of 1993. Unfortunately, most people refinanced incorrectly. First, they lowered their monthly payments rather than shortening the life of the mortgage. Second, they extended rather than retained the original length of their mortgage.

Let's look at shortening the term of your mortgage rather than cutting the payments. By refinancing a 9½ percent, $100,000, thirty-year loan at 7¾ percent you cut your payments $124/month. Ninety-eight percent of the time that $124/month gets spent or recommitted to other payments. What would happen if you kept your payments at $847/month with a 7¾ percent rate? You could pay off your home in twenty years and save $101,680 in interest. That is more than double your savings if you lowered the payment (saving $44,640). A mortgage broker friend tells me only one out of fifty people shortens term, forty-nine out of fifty choose to lower payments.

Secondly, even if you don't shorten the term of your loan, retain—don't extend—the term of the loan you refinance. Assume your $100,000, thirty-year, 9½ percent loan is four years old. You have made forty-eight payments of $847 and have another 312 payments to go. If you refinance at 7¾ percent for thirty years (which adds four years to the twenty-six you now owe), your payments drop to $723/month. If you refinance your balance for twenty-six years, your payments would be $731. That's eight dollars per month more payment, but you would have your home paid for four years sooner, saving yourself $35,088 ($731 x 48). Eight dollars a month over twenty-six years is $2,496 invested, for a return of $35,088 or fourteen times your investment. If you refinance remember these two rules: *Cut the time, not the payment, and maintain or shorten the term of your loan.*

## HOME EQUITY LOANS (HELS)

Maybe you need a new car and you learn you can use the equity in your home rather than the car as collateral for a loan. You know that home interest is deductible but interest on car loans is not deductible. Is an HEL a good deal? Maybe you have a $10,000 total balance on six credit cards costing you 18 percent interest. Would it be wise to cut your interest cost 50 percent and make the interest tax-deductible with a HEL? Maybe it is $15,000 for a pool or home furnishings you want. Is an HEL better than a separate, higher rate, non-deductible pool loan? In theory the answer is yes, but in reality the answer is no because people usually end up spending the amount their payment drops. If you refinance or use HELs to lower your payments you are treating the symptom (payments) not the problem (controlling spending and paying cash for purchases). In fifteen years of family counseling never have I seen a family that did not spend the amount the payment dropped by refinancing, or worse yet, by committing the freed payment to more long- or short-term debt.

HELs offer much longer terms, and people look at the payment, not the rate of interest or total interest cost. If I just can't live without that 1995 red Mustang convertible, I end up with a $20,000 HEL at 12 percent interest for ten years and payments of $287/month because I couldn't afford payments of $406/month for sixty months at 8 percent interest from the Ford dealer. Unfortunately an HEL costs $10,080 more interest than the car loan, and my convertible is worn out or traded long before my payments end. In practice I never recommend consolidation loans, HELs, or changing to credit cards with lower rates until the individual has established good habits (giving, saving, and spending with a margin) and demonstrated discipline and self-control by staying with his plan for a period of time.

## TRADING DOWN

Now that you have the majority of tools you will ever need for home buying decisions, let's examine a tough but very real possibility of trading down. For some a paycut necessitates downsizing their homes. Sometimes health or circumstances turn a two-earner household into a single-earner household. Other times people accept the fact that they have overcommitted themselves and rather than live with continued pressure they choose to trade down. If today your total cost for housing (payments, taxes, insurance, utilities, telephone, maintenance, and improvements) exceeds 40 percent of your spendable income (after giving, saving, and taxes), you should consider downsizing houses, taking in a boarder, or moving in with friends or family. It is easy to write these words, but it is difficult to accept if you are the one downsizing or doubling up. For most men, this issue is performance and significance because we men wrongly evaluate ourselves by our performance, possessions, and material provisions for our family. We know we should have our identity in Christ but years of brainwashing and programming by society are difficult to face and overcome. For women the issue is security. If we men were more sensitive to a woman's needs, we could make the transition less painful and less traumatic. If women realized men are wired to value performance, possessions, and providing for our families (because we wrongly derive our significance from accomplishments rather than Christ), they could help their men reduce the pain and trauma of downsizing.

It is no wonder finances are a major cause of divorce. When things get tough or you face the humbling experience of stepping down, consider that a reminder to ask yourself: Is God really first in my life? Is my mate really my second priority? Is my family more important than my home? Trading down can be a great learning and growth experience. It can strengthen your walk with God, strengthen your marriage, unify your family, and help you to remember what priorities are truly important. Facing and working through a problem will either break or bond your marriage. The results will depend on your attitude toward what happens, not what happens. If today you are facing downsizing, realize that after the pain of trading down will come a life of peace, rest, joy, balance, and relief from financial burdens. Once you have downsized you will have the ability to give God a meaningful share, save, and live with thankfulness and contentment for what you have. Keep your focus on the Lord. He is your source of strength, comfort, provision, and wisdom while you endure the temporary pain of transition from an unwise overcommitment to good stewardship of living within your income.

The average family moves every five to eight years. When you first move into a home you believe this will be your home for a long, long time, but in reality, most of us live in a home only five years. Review the equity you build in a home over the years (page 131). The fifth year you have about 5 percent equity and a 95 percent mortgage with twenty-five years to go on your payments. When you purchase your second home, put all your equity down and finance the balance no more than twenty-five years. At the end of the tenth year you will have 12 percent equity (more if you prepay mortgage or refinance to shorten the term of the mortgage) and 88 percent mortgage. In year ten when you move again, again put all your equity down and finance no more than twenty years. At the end of the fifteenth year when you trade again, follow the plan and put all your equity down and finance no more than fifteen years. By following this plan and a plan to prepay principal, you will have a paid-for home in less than fifteen years. At worst case stick with this plan alone and you'll have no payments in thirty years. Remember most retirees age sixty-five still owe twenty-three more years on their home mortgage. Set a goal today for your mortgage burning party—you will probably make it ahead of schedule. A paid-for home is your ticket to major financial freedom. What would you do with the money if you never again had to pay that monthly mortgage payment?

## ACTION ITEMS

Whether you are starting out, starting over, or stepping up, remember the principles we have covered in this chapter on homes.

1. What are your "needs" for space? location? furnishing? and landscaping?

2. Should you rent? lease? or buy?

3. Should you buy new? or used?

4. Is independent housing a "need" or a desire?

5. Look at all the cost. How much can you afford? Fill in the blanks.

| PAYMENTS | $ _____ | GROSS INCOME | $ _____ |
|---|---|---|---|
| TAXES | _____ | GIVING - | _____ |
| INSURANCE | _____ | SAVING - | _____ |
| UTILITIES | _____ | TAXES - | _____ |
| TELEPHONE | _____ | | |
| MAINTENANCE | _____ | SPENDABLE INCOME | $ _____ |
| IMPROVEMENTS | _____ | | |
| OTHER | _____ | | |
| TOTAL COST | $ _____ | (Guideline for total housing costs is 32 to 40 percent of spendable income.) | |

6. Does your total cost exceed 32 to 40 percent of spendable income?

7. If not, congratulations. If so, how will you solve this problem?

8. Will you live to the financial limit or with a margin for error?

9. How long should you finance? 25 Years? 20 Years? 15 Years? Or less?

10. Should you obtain a fixed or variable rate mortgage?

11. Which of the four plans will you use to prepay your mortgage? Starting when?

12. Should you refinance? Will it be to shorten term (save interest), not lower payments?

13. Will you avoid home equity loans? Consolidation loans?

14. Will you choose to believe God is sufficient when (or if) you trade down?

15. Will you commit to staying with your plan?

# CHAPTER 7
# YOUR CAR

"Do not lay up for yourselves treasures upon earth, where moth and rust destroy, and where thieves break in and steal." Matthew 6:19

**N**ext to housing, transportation is your largest expense, and it's another category where overspending can be tempting. When I was sixteen I saw a movie called "Thunder Road" starring Robert Mitchum, who drove a hot 1957 Ford Fairlane. The movie's theme song described the sound of the car's exhaust as thunder. Guess what I bought for my first car? Eighteen months later, as I prepared to enter my first year of college, I had been saturated with Jan and Dean's hits about fast cars and a number of car songs by the Beach Boys, which described what I thought I needed for my new collegian image. I upgraded to a brand new 1964 Impala Super Sport with a 327 cubic inch engine, four-barreled carburetor, 300 horsepower with positraction, and bucket seats! The Impala was great for a year, but the Corvette Stingray was the "in car," so the next year I bought a 365 horsepower convertible "Vet" and for the first and last time in my life, I experienced car payments for the next eighteen months. Since I worked full-time, the car payments were manageable, but after two accidents and eight traffic tickets, my car insurance cost twice my car payment. During the last two years of high school and the first years of college, I owned five cars, and they took all my excess income. During those years, several older and wiser adults tried to tell me that cars were transportation, not status and image, but I was deaf to the truth.

## TRANSPORTATION, NOT STATUS

Today buying a car costs the average household twenty-six weeks of after-tax income. Ten years ago it took twenty-two weeks of income, and twenty years ago it cost seventeen weeks of income. If cars seem to cost you more, that's because they do.

Examine the commercials on television from car manufacturers who sell "image," "status," "power," "prestige," and "luxury." These ads, which cost millions of dollars to create and run, are produced to condition us to believe we become different people if we drive the right car. After dozens of exposures to these ads, we begin to believe the myth that our self-image is determined by the type and model we drive. Pride is a powerful emotion, and everyone wants to look his best in public. The hard question: Is the price we pay for image, success symbols, and luxury worth it?

Compare the six top-selling luxury models—Lexus, Mercedes, BMW, Infinity, Volvo, and Jaguar—with the same size non-luxury vehicles at half the price (or less). What do you get for twice the cost, if you don't count status? Both types depreciate in value over time, both get comparable gas mileage, both are expensive to insure, both take me from Point A to Point B, and both are safe, reliable transportation. If you drive a luxury model vehicle, I don't condemn or judge you to be wasteful or a poor steward, but I hope you aren't driving status by sacrificing giving, saving, and providing for your other basic needs. If you have consulted the Lord about how to spend His money and He doesn't object, then neither do I—enjoy the blessing of your labors.

### Purchase, Don't Lease

A major question for individuals today is, Should I purchase or lease my vehicles? The number of cars leased today is four times what it was only fifteen years ago, and industry experts tell us that 50 percent of all new cars on the road will be leased in another ten years. How come? There are two main reasons that people lease. First, leasing offers lower payments for the same car, or allows me more luxury for the same payment as a purchase. Second, leasing (which is long-term car rental) temporarily solves my permanent need for transportation.

All things being equal, most people examine the payments much more closely than they do the price of a car. We make decisions about tens of thousands of dollars not on the cost, the interest, or the value, but the payment. In the last chapter, we studied housing and saw that the price of interest is generally several times the price of your house. The same principle is true in buying a car. When I financed my first car in 1965 the maximum car loans available were twenty-four months. Today you can finance your car five, six, or even seven years, and by so doing lower your payments to what you can afford. Leasing is a method of financing. A car depreciates over the time of the lease, and since all you pay for is the depreciation, leasing lowers the monthly payments. At the end of your lease you "own" nothing. Leasing is a long-term rental; instead of a daily or weekly rental rate you are committed for a period of twenty-four to forty-eight months. Naturally, leasing is cheaper because you have no ownership or equity. At the end of your lease, you can choose to buy the vehicle, but most people opt for another new car rather than make car payments on a used car. If you want maximum value for transportation, and if you have a permanent need for transportation, purchase rather than leasing; you will conserve money over the long haul.

I have counseled several people who learned the hard way that a lease is a commitment that you cannot just walk away from. You are obligated to fulfill the term of a lease. Since leasing builds no equity, termination of a lease early leaves you with no transportation, plus a cost for getting out of your lease that can amount to several thousand dollars. One couple who returned their leased vehicle when they were unable to make the monthly payment got a $2,500 penalty for excess mileage plus a $5,500 deficiency judgment when the lease company auctioned the car and then sued them for the loss. When you add the legal costs of $2,000, the couple lost a total of $10,000 on a lease and learned to read the contract (beyond the payments) before they committed themselves. Leases are 30 percent more profitable than sales according to *Automotive Age*, since people don't know they can negotiate purchase price, residual value (car value at the end of the lease), or interest rates. When all you see are the payments, you generally overpay for both merchandise and finance charges. The couple with the $10,000 judgment learned after the fact that they had received only a $500 discount on a $23,000 car. What they thought was an 8 percent interest rate really amounted to 17.94 percent.

If you earn enough to splurge and you pray about God's plan and direction before you commit, go ahead and lease "your image." For most of us leasing is a very poor and expensive way of solving our need for permanent transportation.

## New or Used

Many people hate the idea of buying a used car for fear of buying a problem car that consumes income like teenagers consume pizza. Even dealers for used cars label the lot "re-sale" or "pre-owned" to avoid the negative label of "used cars." Years of exposure to auto manufacturer ads have convinced most Americans that when our cars are paid for and four to five years old, it makes good economic sense to trade rather than to pour hundreds of dollars of repairs and maintenance into a used car. The truth is, the cheapest car you can drive is the car you are driving now, once it is paid for.

If an average owner drives 10,000 to 12,000 miles per year, a five-year-old car will have 50,000 to 60,000 miles. If properly maintained and serviced, today's vehicles have a realistic life span of 150,000 to 200,000 miles. A five-year-old car with average mileage has two-thirds of its mechanical life still left, but it can be purchased at one-third to one-half of what it cost brand new. Let's say that five years ago you bought a new Honda Accord for $15,000, and it now has approximately 60,000 miles on it. If you traded today and received $7,500 as a trade-in, your cost to drive the car would have been 12.5 cents per mile ($7,500/60,000 miles). Someone else buys your pre-owned model for $7,500, drives it ten years and 120,000 miles, spending 6.25 cents per mile ($7,500/120,000 miles). You paid double the cost of transportation for the same outlay (assuming you paid cash, which most don't). Here you may want to argue that you will pay more for repairs on the older car, so it's really cheaper after all to buy a new one. But if the car you have bought is a reliable make, costs should not increase that dramatically as the car ages (the more expensive repairs are once- or twice-in-a-car-lifetime repairs, and you've already made some of them), and the used car will probably save enough money on insurance to cover the difference.

All cars depreciate in value over time, and the drop in value is greatest the first year for a new car. If you look at depreciation of all cars sold new, the average loss in value is 28 percent—year one; 20 percent—year two; 16 percent—year three; 8 percent—year four; and 6 percent—year five. If you shop and compare prices and avoid the "status" cars you can buy a two- to three-year-old car for 48 to 64 percent off list price, and your "pre-owned" car still has 75 to 85 percent of its useful life remaining. Separate the need for efficient, functional transportation from the desire for luxury and status.

How much you save depends on the type of used car you buy. A three-year-old Mercedes may cost you $25,000 or more, but a three-year-old Chevy can be bought today for less than $10,000. If you are a Chevy buyer let's calculate what you would save by buying a three-year-old car and driving it for twelve years. Obviously, a car accident, rusted exterior, or other factors may make it impossible to drive a particular car for twelve years, but let's look at the figures to see what your potential savings could add up to. Assume you are age thirty. In the next forty-eight years you will buy five cars, with your final car purchased at age seventy-eight. You die at age ninety, leaving your fifth and final car to your great-grandson who just turned sixteen. During your lifetime you spent $50,000, ignoring inflation, to buy your five cars. Compare that to another person who buys a $20,000 new Chevy every five years. During his sixty years of driving he spends $240,000 for twelve new Chevys, but his five-year-old used cars are worth $90,000 in trade-in value, assuming $7,500 per car. Net outlay for the buy new, trade every five year buyer—$150,000. Your net outlay is $50,000. You have a savings or nest egg of $100,000 plus interest you could have earned had you saved or invested the difference instead of coughing up bucks for the thrill of the expensive drive off the dealer's showroom floor, new car smell feeling! (Some car washes now have air freshener for your car in "New Car Scent"—you can spend five bucks and get that same smell as owning a new car and save $10,000. Both scents last about the same length of time!) If you put the $100,000 ($1,667/year) over time into an investment you would have $550,115 at 4 percent, $3,859,311 at 7 percent, or $22,345,320 at 10 percent interest (another example of the power of compound interest working for you)! Deciding to buy "pre-owned" rather than brand new is literally the second largest good investment decision you can make. The next time you pass a car dealership praise God for the car you are driving and realize the price others are paying for "new" status, image, and prestige. Thank God your identity is in Christ and not depreciating in the driveway or garage.

## Pay Cash, Don't Finance

As I prepared for this chapter, I examined car ads in the three newspapers I read daily, looked at the ads in all the magazines we subscribe to at the office, and observed more than a hundred TV commercials for new vehicles. Of the ads discussing price, more than 90 percent sold the payment not the price. The average new car buyer commits to sixty payments of $365.45 per month, not an $18,100 price less $900 down payment. *Automotive News*, a trade monthly paper for the industry, cited statistics that more than 85 percent of all new car purchases are over time rather than for cash. When you multiply a $365.45 payment by sixty months, you find your total repayment is $22,827, including the down payment, if the interest rate is 10 percent. This is $4,727 interest, which is 27 percent of the price of the car. If you committed to saving $252.92 per month into one year Treasury Bills, currently paying 5 percent, in five years you could accumulate $17,200 and buy your car in cash. By saving you would earn interest of $2,025 rather than paying interest of $4,727. The difference is $6,752, which is 39 percent of the typical $17,200 car purchase. See why it makes sense to save and pay cash?

You can cut your cost of transportation 39 percent if you will commit to driving your current car until it is paid for, then continuing to make car payments to your savings account until you have enough to replace or rebuild the car you are now driving. The price is discipline and persistence, but the rewards are enormous over time. The chart below assumes: You purchase a new car every fifth year, cars rise in price at a 4 percent per year rate, finance charges are 10 percent, earnings on savings are 5 percent, and payments are made for sixty months. Savings is the sum of interest earned by the saver and interest paid by the borrower. Cumulative savings is the sum of savings for the selected time periods. If you are age thirty, look at forty-five years. Your finance charge at age seventy-five would be $27,245 and your cumulative savings by following the save now and pay later plan is $145,187. See what the cumulative benefit would be for you, and commit now to save and pay cash rather than finance.

| YEAR | SAVINGS | CUMULATIVE SAVINGS |
|---|---|---|
| 1 | $ 6,752 | $ 6,752 |
| 5 | 7,677 | 14,429 |
| 10 | 8,804 | 23,233 |
| 15 | 10,173 | 33,406 |
| 20 | 11,839 | 45,245 |
| 25 | 13,866 | 59,111 |
| 30 | 16,333 | 75,444 |
| 35 | 19,334 | 94,778 |
| 40 | 22,984 | 117,762 |
| 45 | 27,425 | 145,187 |
| 50 | 32,830 | 178,017 |

## Repair, Don't Trade

Despite what you have been told, repairing your existing car is probably much cheaper than buying either a new or newer car, if your vehicle's frame and body are sound. A twelve-year-old Chevy Impala Sedan with 175,000 miles which needs a new engine and transmission would bring $300 to $500 for salvage. If you look at a newer, three-year-old Chevy with 36,000 miles, prices range from $6,000 to $8,000 depending on optional equipment, the car's condition, and the area of the country where you live. If you sold your trade for $400 and bought a $7,000 "pre-owned" car you would withdraw $6,600 from savings rather than finance $6,400 for thirty-six payments at 14 percent interest. Right? If you had your 175,000 mile engine completely rebuilt for $2,500, and rebuilt the transmission for $1,000, you would have a brand new mechanical car, in a twelve-year-old body, for an outlay of only $3,500. You save $2,900, if you can be content with a mechanical rather than a cosmetic overhaul. In some areas of the country, winter snows and salt or ocean spray rust a car's body and make this idea impractical, but for many, rebuilding a car will save several thousand dollars. In addition, it is much cheaper to insure and pay license, fees, and taxes on a twelve-year-old car than it is on a three-year-old car. Perhaps in your area of the country, a six- or seven-year-old car can be purchased for the same amount of money as rebuilding the twelve-year-old car. My point is that you need to consider all your options and not assume that the crowd's advice is always the best financially.

If this counsel sounds solid but you want confirmation, ask any company that operates business transportation vehicles such as cars, vans, buses, trucks, cabs, police cars, or even airplanes. They will confirm that it is much less expensive to repair or rebuild than to replace transportation. If you want to relieve financial constraints from transportation expenses: Buy transportation, not status; buy, don't lease; buy used; save and pay cash; repair/rebuild; and drive 'em till they disintegrate.

## Shop and Compare

To save money on cars or trucks decide what you need, then do your homework so you receive maximum value for minimum outlay. For most, buying a newer car is an emotional experience they treat themselves to every fifth year. To minimize outlay, let your head moderate your heart and limit outgo to needs. Within a particular style of vehicle you will find two to four models with labels like basic, deluxe, luxury, and super deluxe. The fancier the label the higher the price. My car, for example, is a Honda Civic. It currently comes in three models: DX, LX, and EX. The difference between the basic Civic DX (deluxe), and the most expensive EX model (extra luxury) is 40 percent of the price of the car. What I get for 20 to 50 percent above the bottom of the line model is status, trim, toys, and image. To minimize expense buy the bottom of the line. If you just can't live without the top of the line super-duper deluxe luxury label, wait one, two, or three years and buy the image at ten to twenty cents on the dollar. To reduce your outlay, set your limits before you visit a showroom or lot.

Most optional equipment loses half to 90 percent of its value in three years, so if you're buying new, the fewer options the better. If you buy used, remember expensive optional equipment and high-tech toys are very expensive to repair or replace. Options like power windows, power seats, stereo CD systems, fancy wheels and tires, sun roofs, plush interior, etc. are luxuries not necessities. Even the "standard" options—automatic transmission, power steering, and air conditioning—may cost more than you are willing to pay if you really consider the price. The less you pile onto the base model, the lower your cost.

Next, either educate yourself or find a friend in your church who is an expert at buying cars. John Grogan and Jennifer Trip are the brightest, best informed consumers I have ever met. John starts car shopping by pulling out the last ten years of *Consumer Reports* to educate me to safety ratings, reliability, dependability, and resale values of any type vehicle I am considering buying. Jennifer provides dealer cost for new models from her credit union or wholesale values from "Kelly Blue Book" or "NADA Used Car Guide" for used vehicles. If you want to know what the dealer paid for the new car consult:

Edmund's New Car Prices ($6)—check your library or bookstore.
Consumer Reports Auto Price Service—(303–745–1700)
   $11 for one car, $20 for two cars, and $27 for three cars.
Compuserve 1–800–848–8199
Delphi Internet 1–800–695–4005

Since most new cars ordered for the display showroom are not equipped for needs but wants and desires, John would help me spec out a basic car and order it through a local broker or dealer if

I wanted to buy a new car. If I needed a "pre-owned" car Jenny would introduce me to dealer auctions, repossessed cars on sale, estate sales, bankruptcy sales, and an array of for-sale-by-owner options. Once I found the right used car and negotiated for minimum price, John reminded me to have the car inspected and evaluated by a professional mechanic to make certain it was mechanically sound.

Doing your homework in advance will save you thousands of dollars. If your church doesn't contain a John or Jennifer, why not become one yourself? A great untapped resource is the tremendous talents, gifts, interests, and abilities of different church members.

The last skill you need to borrow or develop is the ability to negotiate. Although most people hate to negotiate, I love it and have probably helped to buy and sell more cars, homes, and assorted items than most people you will encounter. Negotiating is getting maximum value for minimal outlay of the Lord's cash. (Note, though, that Proverbs 20:14 does not speak well of the person who negotiates dishonestly.) When you buy anything, especially cars, think of yourself as God's purchasing agent whose goal is maximum value for minimum cash. When you sell merchandise your task is to obtain a fair price and deliver fair value. By spending an extra hour or two negotiating you can earn $100 to $500 per hour, and that is after-tax money. Major purchases like home and cars are items you must negotiate to minimize outlay. If you are bashful, proud, or unskilled, look within your church for a horse trader like my uncle Ham. Uncle Ham was a professional musician who trained me how to haggle by buying musical instruments from one pawn shop and selling them to another shop. I was only fourteen years old, but I learned how to negotiate from a pro. Not only did I learn the street value of merchandise, I learned how to dicker without being disagreeable.

## HOW MUCH CAN YOU SPEND?

To avoid or reduce financial difficulties from your life you must be realistic and consider the total cost of transportation, not just the payments. Record your total costs as shown below.

| | |
|---|---|
| Payments | $ _____ |
| Gas & Oil | _____ |
| Insurance | _____ |
| Tax/License | _____ |
| Repairs | _____ |
| Replacement | _____ |
| TOTAL COST | $ _____ |

To reduce strain on your income, reduce your total commitment to transportation to 12 percent to 15 percent of your after-giving, after-saving, after-tax income. If housing and cars take more than 55 percent of your net income you need to adjust now. If you wait until you have maxed out your credit cards and are getting second notices and calls from collection agencies, the problems will be more severe and the time required to unburden yourself from problems gets longer.

Let's look at the amounts for our example family, with an income of $40,000. From gross income they honor God with $4,000 in tithes, save $4,000, and their total taxes deducted for their family of three are $7,597. Their spendable income is $24,403/year, or $2,034/month. Guideline transportation expense (12–15 percent) would be $244 to $305 per month for payments, gas, oil, insurance, tax, license, repairs, and replacement. If car insurance is $50/month, gas and oil $80/month, license and tax $20/month, and they figure from the maximum of $305/month for transportation they have $155/month left for payments, repairs, and replacements.

Do your own calculations, but if you don't allow something for repairs and maintenance, how will you handle the expense when your brakes need re-lining, the alternator needs to be replaced, the timing belt breaks, the tires wear out, or the starter breaks? If you don't have your car regularly serviced, you shorten the life of your vehicle. If you don't save something now for replacement of your vehicle, you are deceiving yourself and choosing a lifetime of bondage to car payments. What is the solution? How do you make it if there is only $155 left for transportation and you "need" two cars since both of you work and your son is turning sixteen and wants use of a family car?

First, get realistic, calculate what you can afford, and learn to be content and give thanks for what you have, rather than concentrating on what you lack. Second, cut expenses to the minimum and stretch your income to the maximum. A pastor and his wife addressed this situation recently and decided they would become a one-car family rather than straining to support two vehicles and their family. By doing their homework, they cut their car insurance $20/month, planned their driving and shaved $25/month off their gas bills, and sold their second car and cut their license expense to $15/month. Moreover, he learned to do his own basic car repairs. Their six-year-old, 60,000 mile car was worth $4,000 and was paid for, but they committed to save $150/month now for future repairs and eventual replacement. They explained the situation to their son and gave him the choice of driving and paying for the increase in insurance or not driving; he chose to spend his income from a part-time job on items other than car insurance. For the first time in twenty years of marriage this family is saving $250 for the future and spending $240/month for transportation (notice that is less than the guideline). In slightly over three years they will have $5,000 saved to purchase a newer "pre-owned" car, and their savings account will contain $10,000. The process of change was difficult, and it required adjustment and effort, but the financial tension has been relieved and both their family life and their ministry have never been more effective.

The road to financial freedom and the release from financial stress and bondage await you. I strongly urge you to examine your current commitment to both housing and cars. If you exceed the maximum expenditure I hope you will honestly face the problem and make whatever changes are necessary to live within the guidelines. If you ignore the truth, your problems will not go away; they will grow and get more severe over time. The solution is not longer hours, a second job, and increasing your income. The solution is learning to live within your current income and giving thanks for what you have by learning to be content.

## SAVE MONEY ON VEHICLES

To save money on vehicles do not buy extended warranties or service agreements. Did you know that less than 15 percent of the dollars collected from all extended warranties and service agreements are spent on repairs? The 85 percent that is left goes to the selling merchant and the issuing insurance company. Extended warranties are very profitable sales items, so raise your sales resistance. Save 15 percent of a policy's cost for eventual repair and maintenance, and do something wise with the money you could have spent on extended warranties. The same principle applies to extended warranties on all items you buy.

Learn to do your own repairs and practice preventative maintenance on cars and all mechanical items you use. Trained mechanics at garages and dealerships charge from $35/hour to $60/hour for labor. I am not suggesting you learn to rebuild your own engine, but a set of tools, a repair manual, and a course or two at a local college can save you hundreds of dollars when you learn to do your own simple repairs. If you aren't mechanical, perhaps you can share a skill you have with someone who is and reduce or trade your services. A single mom who types one hundred words per minute and occasionally baby-sits could trade her skills to a mechanic who does $1,200 in repairs to her car for $175 worth of parts, bought at his mechanic's discount.

Preventative maintenance is simply good business. The better you service and maintain any mechanical device, the longer it will last and the lower your cost of owning the item. All vehicles come with an owner's manual which suggests service for various parts and systems of your car at various time intervals. Unfortunately, very few ever study a car owner's manual and most put off suggested service until they can afford to have the work done. When the lining on your brakes reaches a certain thickness, have the lining replaced for $50. If you wait until the lining is gone and you hear the screech of metal on metal as you brake, you have turned a $50 repair into a $200 repair. Plan, commit, and persist with a proper preventative maintenance program and you can get 175,000 miles or more from your present vehicle.

## Do Extra Car Payments Help?

You don't always save money by making extra car payments, because interest on a car loan is figured differently than on a home mortgage. Many lenders apply early payments to the end of the loan rather than the beginning, where interest is highest, so before you invest, investigate to determine your best return. Find out exactly how much interest you can save by pre-paying and determine if that is the best use for your extra funds.

## FISBOs (For Sale by Owners)

You can generally get money by selling your present car rather than trading it in, and you can usually buy cheaper from an individual than from a car lot or dealership. During my fifteen years in practice in Sun City, a retirement community, I have seen and helped several hundred people sell their cars for several hundred dollars more than they were offered in trade by a dealer. I have also seen hundreds of low mileage, well-maintained, pre-owned cars at hundreds of dollars less than they were advertised on local lots, dealerships, and showrooms. You must be careful in either buying or selling from or to private parties, so if you aren't knowledgeable or experienced, find a friend who can assist you. Any time a client of mine sells his car, a simple one-paragraph contract is provided which eliminates potential liability, and we deliver title only after being paid in cash or cashier's check. Any pre-owned car purchase should also be accompanied by a simple agreement where the seller certifies mileage and good title and affirms that he is not aware of any existing problems with the vehicle. These forms are now standard in buying or selling a home and will be in the future for purchase or sale of both cars and trucks. The last thing you need is a lawsuit from the buyer of your old car, so protect yourself from liability when you sell. If a potential seller won't sign a simple statement on the car you intend to buy, don't gamble; continue to shop for one who will.

You can save thousands of dollars on car insurance if you will take the time to learn the basics of car insurance. Forgive the commercial, but the best four-dollar investment you could make is to purchase my book, *Buying Insurance: Maximum Protection at Minimum Cost* (Moody, 1994). It covers all insurances, including major medical, disability, auto, home, and life.

Here is a summary of ideas to reduce cost on car insurance from *Buying Insurance: Maximum Protection at Minimum Cost:*

1. Shop and compare—rates vary 100 percent or more from company to company.

2. Buy liability equal to your net worth plus potential legal fees.

3. If you have a large net worth, check out "umbrella" liability coverage.

4. Avoid credit life and disability on car loans.

5. Don't buy coverage (unless required by state law) you don't need such as no fault, uninsured motorist, underinsured motorist, medical coverage, emergency road service, car rental expense, and specialty coverage for car stereos.

6. Raise deductibles on collision and comprehensive to cut cost, and, depending on your car's age and value, consider dropping both collision and comprehensive.

7. Never file a claim for under $500 without checking out the increase in premium rates.

8. Find out insurance rates before you buy the car, not after.

9. Find out how much a ticket or accident will raise your premium.

10. Ask for all possible discounts: multi-car, driver training, good driver, anti-theft equipment, safety equipment, long-time customer, senior citizen, non-smoker/drinker, etc.

11. Don't have teenage drivers, especially boys—consider suspended animation from age sixteen to twenty-five or until your children can afford to buy and insure their own cars.

Right now you know 90 percent of what you need to know to escape financial weights as you motor down the highway to heaven. Let's review: Attitude is paramount, but we have all been conditioned to confuse "needs" with wants and desires. Plan now how you will handle your next raise, bonus, or windfall profit and stick with your plan. Honor the Lord with the first part of every bit of income or profit that comes your way. Be wise and save a part of each piece of income or profit. Don't overcommit on housing or cars. Count your blessings, give thanks for what you have, and learn to be content. The majority of believers today exist day-to-day with needless strain because they don't know or use these simple financial principles. Welcome to the winner's circle.

## ACTION ITEMS

There is a lot of information in this chapter. Pray, plan, and commit to a plan to reduce financial stress by adopting one or more of these suggestions to cut your cost of transportation:

1. Separate "needs" from wants and desires, and decide to buy transportation, not status.

2. Buy, rather than lease, if you have a permanent need for transportation.

3. Buy used rather than new to cut costs 50 percent or more.

4. Commit to saving and paying cash, rather than financing your future vehicles.

5. Plan on driving your vehicle 150,000 to 200,000 miles before you replace or rebuild.

6. Decide what you need and do your homework, including price, before you go car shopping.

7. Buy basic models, with minimal optional equipment, to cut expenses.

8. Commit no more than 12 to 15 percent of your net spendable income (after giving, saving, and taxes) to total transportation costs. If you are over the guideline, how will you handle the problem?

9. Save money by declining extended warranties, doing your own repairs, buying and/or selling direct, and cutting the cost of car insurance.

10. Commit and persist with your plan. As you have seen, good decisions regarding transportation will save you several hundred thousand dollars over your driving lifetime.

# CHAPTER 8
# DEBT—THE BLACK HOLE

"The rich rules over the poor, and the borrower becomes the lender's slave." Proverbs 22:7

I have yet to meet any individual or family that set out with a goal of accumulating credit card debt. Credit card balances start small. Initially we pay our bills in full at the end of the month, until one month when the balance is too high, so we opt for minimum payments and vow to pay our remaining balance as soon as possible. Time passes and we don't notice our unpaid balance is growing larger each month since we focus on our minimum monthly payments, not the unpaid balance. No problem, we get solicitations for a new card with no fees and pretty soon both cards have reached their limits. We get our credit limits raised several times, since we are making payments due and on time, and we seldom calculate the total interest being consumed by the black hole of credit card debt. Five to ten years from our beginning, we have eight or ten credit cards, our minimum payments consume 5, 10, or 15 percent of our income, and we are really feeling the pressure of making all those payments on time, so we choose a consolidation loan or a home equity loan to reduce our monthly expenses. We experience instant relief as our credit cards are paid off, our monthly payments drop one to three hundred dollars, and we think we have things under control. Just then another unexpected expense, a pay cut, or loss of our job puts us in a real dilemma. The only solution appears to be to use our credit card and operate on credit until things turn around, the expenses are paid off, or until we get that raise or new job. For 80 percent of us credit cards have become a way of life. Tomorrow, when you buy anything, look and see that most people are paying by plastic rather than

check or cash. Most financial publications and advisers treat credit cards as a fact of modern life and don't consider them wrong,
dangerous, or harmful as long as the monthly payments consume
less than 15 to 20 percent of an individual's income. Above those
levels most advisers say problems begin because it becomes difficult or impossible to make either timely payments or required
minimum payments. Look at credit card debt as proof of Proverbs
22:7: "The rich rules over the poor, and the borrower becomes the
lender's slave."

If today you have outstanding balances on your credit cards
which you do not pay off completely when you receive your statement, you are failing to realize that you are gradually being sucked
into the black hole of bondage—consumer debt. We will examine
exactly what the Bible says about debt later, but debt causes financial failure in four ways. First, debt consumes a large part or all of
what we should be giving to God. Second, debt consumes part or
all of what we should be saving so we end up living like fools rather than wise men and women. Third, debt allows us to plan poor-
ly and incompletely since cost overruns, unexpected expenses, or
problems are temporarily buffered by our line of credit. Fourth,
debt causes financial burdens since we wrongly believe credit is a
form of wealth. When we fail to give, save, and plan, and we
wrongly treat credit as wealth, we are formulating a plan for failure.

My son J. T., who just turned eighteen and graduated from
high school, was impressed when he received several unsolicited
applications for credit cards through the mail. He filled out the
forms, returned them, and in less than three weeks was approved
for a $500 credit card limit. J. T., who earns about $400 per month
from his after-school job, really felt wealthy when his shiny new
credit card arrived in the mail. No more problem cashing checks,
since he had a bank credit card and what he thought was an extra
$500 to spend as he chose. The next day he went to the mall, visit-
ed a pet shop, and returned home with a fifty-gallon aquarium,
stand, filter, heater, gravel, plants, and nine pretty freshwater fish.
The following day at school, someone slashed two tires on his car.
He was angry, but he charged the new tires and a $20 auto detail
on his new plastic wealth. That afternoon he visited his favorite
record shop and treated himself to three new CDs that he had
wanted but had been unable to afford. A few weeks later the $498
bill came from the credit card company, but J. T. did not have
$500 to pay his bill in full. He sent away his check for the mini-
mum payment of $25. A week later he had the unpleasant and

embarrassing experience of having his credit card rejected when he tried to purchase a $110 sound board for his guitar because he was over his credit limit.

Another month passed and a new statement arrived with a $505 balance including interest at 18.96 percent. We reviewed J. T.'s income and expenses and now he is on a two-year plan to pay back three days of indulgence. J. T., like many others, wrongly assumed that a $500 credit card is like $500 cash. It isn't. A credit card is a tool to create long-term future liabilities today. It's fun to spend money, but the thrill of purchases is long gone after a few days, and the payments seem to run forever. I define a credit card as "a means of buying what you feel you 'need,' with money you don't have, at prices you can't afford, to impress people you don't even know." If you ask J. T. if he really had a "need" for a fish tank, he would tell you that he confused needs with wants and desires. Today he has learned that credit is not wealth, but a means of indulging now, followed by months of payments. After buying his $400 new aquarium he learned that a cheaper method is to look in the classified section of the newspaper and buy used. When we looked at a slightly larger aquarium fully equipped including fish that we found advertised in the newspaper for $95, J. T. realized impulse buying cost him $305 plus $100 in finance charges. That is an entire month's earnings for J. T.

## BE A NON-CONFORMIST

The average consumer or family holds eight to ten different credit cards, owes a combined balance of $15,000, and has payments that consume 10 to 15 percent of the paycheck. In counseling and speaking to thousands of individuals and couples over the past fifteen years, I can tell you that we Christians are no different than our non-Christian counterparts. One of the reasons total giving to the Lord's work is less than 2 percent of incomes is that people have overcommitted themselves to installment debt leaving little or nothing with which to honor God. Credit card debt also diminishes or eliminates our ability to save because we forget to pay ourselves first, and after debt service there is nothing left to save. If you compare the U.S. to other major industrial nations of the world, we rank at the bottom in terms of personal savings even though we are at or near the top in per capita income. The voracious appetite of the black hole of finance (your credit card) is the major factor preventing both saving and greater proportional giving. Paul wrote to the Romans—"Do not be conformed to this world . . ." (Romans 12:2). Begin today to reduce or eliminate use of credit cards.

Our government today is an excellent example of how not to manage money wisely. Each year since 1971 the Federal Government has spent more than it earned by using credit. The term "deficit spending" means spending more than your income; governments and people do so by using debt or credit. Unfortunately the trend is getting worse not better. Today interest on the national debt consumes fifteen cents out of every dollar of taxes collected. Interest on our country's debt is the third largest item in our national budget, and if we do not address the problem honestly and realistically now, the solutions will become more painful, more difficult, and more expensive the longer we wait. Don't emulate the government and burden yourself with debt. Conform to Christ's image and set your goal to become debt-free so you are free to serve Him when and how He calls. Choosing to free yourself permanently from the bondage of debt is a difficult choice. Most individuals, our Federal Government, and the vast majority of businesses avoid the road less traveled of choosing to live free of debt.

## WARNINGS ABOUT DEBT

Before we examine ten biblical warnings against debt, I want you to understand the various theological positions individuals assume about debt. One extreme is to assume that the passage "Owe nothing to anyone except to love one another" (Romans 13:8a) is a command to avoid all debt at all times. A few even go so far as to label debt as a sin. The opposite extreme assumes that debt is acceptable, normal, and often God's way of meeting our needs, which He promised to do. My personal view is that debt is not a sin to avoid, but a dangerous tool which must be used with extreme caution due to its potential for enslaving people in financial bondage. I further believe voluntary bankruptcy is not an option for a committed Christian (see Psalm 37:21), and I interpret Scripture as instructing, not commanding, us to avoid cosigning for loans or pledging other assets as surety (collateral) for a loan. The following ten warnings about debt are my rationale for saying debt is extremely dangerous and should be used with extreme caution and after much prayer, if at all.

ONE: Debt presumes on the future and Scripture clearly says, "Do not boast about tomorrow, for you do not know what a day may bring forth" (Proverbs 27:1). The same principle is confirmed in the New Testament: "Yet you do not know what your life will be like tomorrow. You are just a vapor that appears for a little while and then vanishes away . . ." (James 4:14). When you commit yourself to payments over time, you are presuming: no pay reductions, no loss of job, and no unexpected expenses. That is a dangerous and improbable assumption. If you knew you would lose your job, have a pay cut, or incur sudden and large expenses, would you still commit to debt? Do you know that you could still honor your vows despite potential problems? If not, I suggest you pray and reconsider using debt to finance whatever you are considering buying.

TWO: Debt lowers your standard of living in the future. Money that you borrow today must be repaid over time plus the cost of renting the money, which is interest.

If I charge $2,000/per year in living expenses on my credit card, I have spent $2,000 I did not have. The first year my payments, interest only, amount to only $30 per month. If I continue this pattern of overspending $2,000/year for ten years my credit card balance is $20,000, my monthly (interest only) payment is $300/month, and I have paid $19,800 in interest over the ten years. To get debt free, I must quit overspending $2,000/year or $167/month and repay principal and interest over another ten years with monthly payments of $314/month. The second ten years my interest cost totals $17,715. Total interest paid is now almost double the amount I originally spent. I don't care who you are, a $481/month ($167 habitual overspending + $314 repayment) reduction in your spendable income won't be painless. Do you see how debt lowers the amount of money you will have in the future to spend?

THREE: Debt avoids making the decision of whether or not an individual can afford to buy an item by focusing on the low payment rather than on the cost of the item. Ask a young couple if they can afford $3,500 for a new big screen TV, and they will most likely say no. Ask the same couple could they handle $89/month for a new big screen TV, and you will have a much greater chance of getting a yes. Yet $89/month x 60 months = $5,340, of which $1,840 (51 percent of the cost of the TV) is interest charges. The question of whether you can afford it should include all the cost: purchase price, operational expense, and finance charges. Credit is dangerous because it is too easy to say yes to low payments over time and ignore the real decision—can I afford it, and do I need it?

FOUR: When you borrow you have the awesome power of compound interest working against you. One of the major consequences of debt is the huge cost of interest. We looked at home mortgages and car loans earlier, but here is an example for credit card debt. If you borrow $100 on your credit card and make only minimum payments, do you know how long it will take to repay the loan? Would you believe up to thirty years? Would you ever guess your total payments over the life of the loan amount to $500? Also, since what you bought isn't tax deductible and credit card interest also is non-deductible, you must earn $700 to $800 gross pay to have enough after-tax income to repay the debt on a $100 purchase. Items charged on your Master Card can cost you seven to eight times the purchase price!

FIVE: Debt may delay God's plan for your life or cause you to forfeit a blessing God had planned to give. A single parent I counseled recently was grappling with whether or not to replace a completely worn out car by buying a three-year-old $6,000 replacement vehicle. She had saved $1,500, but the thirty payments of $175 per month would really stress her income. Since she was giving a first part of her income to God, saving part, and living a very frugal life, I suggested she make her need for transportation a matter of prayer for a few weeks before committing herself to two and a half years of car payments. She agreed and four days later received as a gift an almost identical two-year-old car from a relative that she had not spoken with in ten years. Before you obligate yourself to payments give God a chance to provide your needs.

SIX: Debt evades the necessary self-evaluation to distinguish wants and desires from real "needs." In our home we have what we call the "I want list." The "I want list" has two rules. First, not more than five items are allowed on the list at one time. Second, we have to wait thirty days after the item is entered on the list before it can be purchased. You would be amazed how much wants and desires fade over the thirty days and the amount of impulse buying that is eliminated. During our thirty-day time out, we ask God's wisdom in discerning "needs" from non-needs and ask Him to provide, guide, and lead our decision making. This simple idea has helped to transform me from an chronic impulse buyer into a much better steward of His assets.

SEVEN: Debt encourages impulse buying and overspending. When the chief financial officer of a national credit card company said that consumers will spend 27 percent more on plastic than they would with cash or check, I was stunned. I thought that may be true of the average person but it could not be true for me. I haven't paid a penny in credit card interest in more than twenty years, since I pay my balance in full whenever I receive the monthly statement. I have taught classes telling students that the first month they can't pay their credit card bill in full, they need to offer up their cards as a burnt offering. If you sense a little pride and conceit in the attitude I had, you read me correctly. Shortly thereafter, I felt a strong conviction to put away my plastic, so as not to be a stumbling block to my Christian brothers. I felt convicted that it would be wrong to say I handle credit wisely so it is OK for me to charge, but you should burn your card rather than rely on your own self-control and discipline as I do. A year later in summarizing my expenditures I found an almost exact 27 percent drop in spending. I was both shocked and humbled to learn I was not immune to impulse buying and overspending when I use a credit card. Any merchant who accepts plastic will verify that consumers will spend 25 to 30 percent more with plastic. That is why businesses pay a fee of 1 to 7 percent of every purchase you make on plastic for the privilege of accepting your credit cards. Try my method—write a check or pay cash and ask for the cash discount that otherwise would go to the credit card company. You will find many merchants agreeable to a 3 to 5 percent cash discount.

EIGHT: Debt and credit cards stifle creativity and resourcefulness. I was raised by a grandmother who was sixty-four the year I was born and her younger sister, Rene. Both of them were raised on a cotton farm in south Texas. They used words like "make do," "do without," and "fix it" that are rare today. If we want something today, we charge it rather than "make do" with what we have. We feel entitled to what we want, when we want it, so we automatically head to the mall, never considering a simpler, less expensive choice: "doing without." It is not fashionable today to re-sole our shoes, repair our cars, or mend whatever wears out; we simply replace them. If we lack the funds to write a check or pay cash, we use our credit cards to consume rather than conserve income by making do, doing without, and repairing.

NINE: Credit cards eliminate margin in our lives, since we use plastic as our margin. Rather than planning what we need and allowing a margin for errors or overruns, we "charge" ahead and spend, thinking that if we must write a check that we don't have sufficient funds to cover, we have overdraft protection with our credit line. Living without a margin for error is asking for problems. Your credit card is not an asset but a potential future liability which becomes a liability when you use it.

TEN: If you want to teach your children bad habits teach them how to use credit cards, obtain car loans, and apply for student loans. You will equip them to begin life with a mountain of debt that creates years of financial bondage. When I began counseling young people (in their early twenties) I was astounded by the size of the debt load many of them had accumulated. Many had graduated from private Christian colleges or seminaries by borrowing the costs and living to the limit of their credit cards. They had never considered paying cash for transportation or anything else.

One young pastor came in with $60,000 worth of student loans, $10,000 charged on six credit cards, and two car loans with payments of $450/month, wondering how he and his wife could get by on the $30,000 per year he was offered as a beginning associate pastor. The young man had godly parents, but they had taught him to rely on credit which he believed was God's way of providing his needs. To service his school loans would require payments of $779/month for ten years. His payments to the credit cards took another $254/month for five years, and the $450/month car payments ran for sixty-three more months. How would you handle $1,483/month payments on a $2,500/month income? I honestly believe if God calls me to a particular task, education, or job, He can and will provide the means without saddling me with debt and asking me to run the marathon of life carrying a one-hundred pound backpack of consumer debt.

The young pastor and his wife agreed to move in with her parents, put off raising a family until they were debt free, and sell their financed car. With both of them working full-time we constructed a plan that would lead to total freedom from debt in less than thirty-six months. After a year their $70,000 debt was reduced to $46,000; at the end of year two only $22,500 of debt remained. In the coming eighteen months their goals were to pay off the remaining debt, save $10,000, and begin their family with the pastor's wife as a stay-at-home mom until the youngest child entered grade school.

Unfortunately, the young pastor was sidelined by sexual sin twenty-five months from our beginning. He left the state and his wife, leaving the debt for his ex-wife and her parents to finish paying two years later.

## THE RISKS OF DEBT

Credit cards and debt are not a sin, but they are potentially as dangerous and addictive as many drugs. We will discuss later a plan to free yourself once and forever from the bondage of debt, but first let's look beyond the symptom of debt to common causes of debt that are really spiritual problems reflecting themselves by the financial symptoms of excess debt.

You can be harmed by ignorance of two simple facts: the power of compound interest working against you, and your current financial condition. We have shown the tremendous effect of compound interest over time so remember that at 15, 18, or 21 percent interest or more, debt expands at an unbelievable rate! Let's look at where you are now and eliminate the second half of the problem of ignorance of your current condition. Remember the advice from Scripture, "Be sure you know the condition of your flocks, give careful attention to your herds; for riches do not endure forever, and a crown is not secure for all generations" (Proverbs 27:23–24 NIV). Good stewards are responsible for knowing where they are financially. You probably don't have flocks and herds, but you do have income, expenses, and bills. It is your job to be aware of your condition and act as a responsible steward. To start, fill out the following chart.

| DEBT | BALANCE DUE | INTEREST RATE | MONTHLY PAYMENT | REMAINING PAYMENTS |
|------|-------------|---------------|-----------------|--------------------|
| 1. _____ | $ _____ | _____ | $ _____ | _____ |
| 2. _____ | _____ | _____ | _____ | _____ |
| 3. _____ | _____ | _____ | _____ | _____ |
| 4. _____ | _____ | _____ | _____ | _____ |
| 5. _____ | _____ | _____ | _____ | _____ |
| 6. _____ | _____ | _____ | _____ | _____ |
| 7. _____ | _____ | _____ | _____ | _____ |
| 8. _____ | _____ | _____ | _____ | _____ |
| 9. _____ | _____ | _____ | _____ | _____ |
| 10. _____ | _____ | _____ | _____ | _____ |
| TOTAL | $ _____ | | $ _____ | |

When you complete the chart, you will know exactly where you stand. That is the first step toward financial freedom and release. Most people are shocked to see how much debt they owe, the rates of interest, and the total of their monthly payments. The good news is that 95 percent of you can be rid of all these debts in eighteen to thirty-six months and never again have to struggle with the bondage of debt and the burden of never-ending payments. Imagine how different your life would be if you owed no bills. What would you do with the extra $200, $300, $500, or more you currently pay out each month for debts? Naturally you would honor God first and save some, but you would have money left, free to use as you choose. If you haven't completed the chart, stop and do so now so you will have conquered the problem of ignorance of your current condition.

Debt is caused by overspending. Unless you have a printing press to print money, you spend more than you earn when you use your credit cards or other types of debt. Why do people overspend? Sometimes it is ignorance of the cost of debt or the facts of their situation, but many times they overspend due to *problems like discontentment, poor or improper priorities, a get-rich-quick mentality, impatience, laziness, self-indulgence, covetousness, greed, and pride.* These are spiritual problems that manifest themselves financially by overspending using debt or credit as the means. To solve the symptom (excess debt/overspending) you must deal with the underlying spiritual problem or cause.

We know the Bible commands us to be content and give thanks for what we have. That is difficult to do if we aren't careful where we go, what we see, what we listen to, what we think, and what we talk about. If you want to lose your contentment, turn on QVC, the shopping cable TV channel, which runs twenty-four hours a day, and you will certainly find a few items at great prices that you really "need." If you don't have cable TV, a trip to the local mall will give you sensory overload and stimulate your lust for more items you also "need." Go into a new car dealership and look at all the beautiful new models, colors, and options, and your old car will never look quite as good as it did before. Last, go look at new model homes, immaculately landscaped, beautifully furnished, with the size and amenities you want. *The formula to develop your discontentment is to compare yourself and what you have with others. The formula to develop contentment is to avoid comparisons and choose to count your blessings and give thanks for all that God has given you.*

After His resurrection, Jesus spoke with the apostle Peter. After asking Peter three times, "Do you love Me?" He commanded Peter to "follow Me." As they were walking along, Peter looked back and noticed that following along behind was the apostle John. Peter asked Jesus, "What about John? What plan do You have for him?" Jesus responded by saying twice, "Don't compare yourself to John; you concentrate on following Me." Jesus knew the danger of comparison and its ability to destroy contentment. Read the message yourself in John 21:15–25; it contains other valuable applications for living as well.

*Poor or improper priorities* in life are another spiritual root cause of problems that surface as overspending and excess debt. Ask a Christian to state his priorities for living, and you will probably hear: God first, family second, and work third. We parrot the correct responses, but if you examine our checkbooks, credit card statements, tax returns, or daily calendars, what you see often reflects totally different priorities, habits, and patterns. We know we are to use things and love people, but it is very easy to learn to love things and use people. We all know the value of daily time alone with God, prayer, Bible study, and worship, but too often the urgent replaces the important and we drift into bad habits. We know our spouses, children, and family are a higher priority than accumulating material treasures, but we con ourselves into believing we are climbing the corporate ladder to provide for our loved ones. I encourage you to look at your life and ask yourself if you are investing your time, talent, and His treasure by His priorities. Are you living by what you know are proper biblical priorities?

Except for Hawaii and Utah, all fifty states today offer gambling, lotteries, and other methods to indulge the desire to *get rich quick*. Both gambling and debt cater to our sin nature to get rich quick or to get something for nothing. Our society tells us we are all entitled to what we want, when we want it. The philosophy of buy-now-pay-later, microwave meals, instant coffee, and *instant gratification* of all wants, needs, and desires is the exact opposite of patience, prayer, dependence on God, and industry that Scripture commands. Spending is exciting and fun, and it appears painless for a time, until the bills start to arrive in the mail. Then the price of self-indulgence surfaces—payments that never end for most Americans. *Self-indulgence* is short-term gain for long-range pain, which is why the Bible warns us of the consequence of living without considering the consequences of today's acts. God doesn't want to kill our joy, and He doesn't call everyone to a monastic, spartan lifestyle. The biblical principles about finances are given to protect us from the pain and difficulties that poor choices today have for tomorrow.

*Pride, greed, and covetousness* are the motives that today's consumer marketing professionals use to distract us from the biblical virtues of humility, moderation, and contentment, and to plunge us into consumer debt. We know intellectually that pride is one of the seven deadly sins, but when it becomes our driving force, we are seldom aware of our true motives. A few years back pride grabbed our sons J. T. and John. J. T. wanted a pair of $150 designer sunglasses, and John was consumed with desire for a $150 pair of pump-up tennis shoes. When I tried to reason with J. T. about the value in a pair of Oakley sunglasses, he told me about the quality optics, the interchangeable side rails (arms), and the fact that all the guys were wearing either Oakley's or Rayban's. John made sure I saw the Air Jordan ads during the slam dunk contest, told me the shoes would last three times longer than normal, and complained that he didn't want to wear a pair of cheap "nerdie" shoes to school. Pride and peer pressure are tremendously powerful motivators. I solved the problem by making both boys responsible for their actions and choices and giving them a clothing allowance that I set. Jeanie bought J. T. a pair of imitation Oakley's at a local flea market for six dollars, and he exchanged the side rails for fifteen dollars in the mall; not even the clerk could spot the counterfeit Oakley's. John bought his pumps, but he learned the hard way the consequences of using one-third of his annual clothing budget on one pair of shoes. Thank God neither had credit cards back then, or they would have been ready for bankruptcy before they could vote!

You may laugh at pre-teens' desires for designer labels, but the same pride, greed, and covetousness sells billions of dollars of luxury cars, estates (a fancy word for large homes), watches, rings, designer clothing, and other adult status symbols and toys. Two years ago I watched a top salesman for a computer firm show off his Rolex Presidente solid gold "certified Swiss chronometer" at a sales meeting. In less than a year, more than half of the sales force sported their own Rolexes, with most of them financed. Can you imagine thirty-six payments of $325/month for a watch? Pardon me, a "certified Swiss chronometer." The world's self-proclaimed most successful car salesman, Joe Girrard, capitalizes on people's desire to keep up with the Joneses by prospecting the ten homes nearest to the home where he sells a new Chevrolet. Would you believe 40 percent of the neighbors of a new car buyer go out and buy a new car for themselves within ninety days? Before you finance anything check your motives; ask yourself is this a "need," want, or desire; and don't forget whose money it is you are spending.

# REFINANCING

As we learned in refinancing homes, the goal is not to reduce the size of your payment but to reduce the time and finance charges on your debt. In every case I have observed, where people refinance debt to lower their monthly payments they end up committing the freed payment to service more debt and bury themselves deeper under a pile of debt. The same principle works with consumer debt like credit cards. The problem is not cash flow (lower payments or greater income); the problem is proper spending and proper biblical attitudes.

A business owner I will call Vic and his wife Joan represent a good case study. Although the numbers were quite large the same principle will work at any income level. Although Vic and Joan's combined income was $97,000 per year, they sought my help on April 13 because they owed $13,200 in self-employment tax and income taxes two days later and had no way to pay. Their total debt, including taxes, was $109,500 spread over twenty-one loans with monthly payments of $5,252. They did not own a home, but they had three vehicles which cost $980/month in lease and purchase payments. This was Vic's second marriage, and he was paying $750/month in child support. They had been married thirteen months, and the relationship seemed doubtful at best. We went through their records and recorded their total income and expenses for the past year to find that their outgo ($111,400) exceeded their income about $1,200/month. Part of their debt came from bad business decisions ($35,000), and part came from a medical problem ($6,300), but the balance ($55,000) came from overspending and prior consolidation loans. To simplify the example I have combined some of the loans, but here is the debt analysis including the current year's unpaid tax bill.

| LENDER | BALANCE DUE | INTEREST RATE | MONTHLY PAYMENT | REMAINING PAYMENTS |
|---|---|---|---|---|
| I.R.S. | $ 13,200 | 12% | ? | ? |
| Business Loan | 35,000 | 14% | $  956 | 48 |
| Medical Loan | 6,300 | 10% | 554 | 12 |
| Credit Cards | 15,000 | 21% | 406 | 60 |
| Consolidation #1 | 30,000 | 24% | 1,586 | 24 |
| Consolidation #2 | 10,000 | 17% | 1,750 | 6 |
|  | $109,500 |  | $5,252 |  |

177

They had $300 in savings, no giving, and, as you can calculate, their loan payment, car payments, and child support totaled $6,982/month, leaving $1,101/month for: taxes, housing, food, insurance, entertainment, clothing, medical, and miscellaneous spending. When Joan saw the figures that day, the first time Vic let her see their total financial condition, she was ready to abandon the marriage. Neither had discussed finances prior to marriage, and with the exception of the medical bills and taxes incurred during the marriage, Joan did not feel responsible for Vic's prior problems. Joan came from a conservative background, and she owed nothing other than a $201/month car payment on her two-year-old car. Vic, who came from a wealthy family, assumed that another consolidation loan, this time from his parents, would solve their financial problems and produce enough money to pay their $13,200 tax bill, leaving them with income equal to outgo. He figured they needed $2,385/month to live like they were living, and a consolidation loan from his dad for $109,500, payable at $3,218/month, with no interest, over thirty-four months. For the third time in his life, Vic felt sure his solution to consolidate debts and lower payments would solve their problem by reducing their payments $2,032/month.

Vic was speechless when his dad refused the consolidation loan and demanded that Vic be self-reliant and accountable and learn financial responsibility. The next day Vic and I visited the IRS office, where we worked out a plan that required payments of $1,000/month for fifteen months. Next we constructed a spending plan that allowed Vic and Joan $1,200/month in living expenses (down from $2,385/month). Vic sold his recreational vehicle, which reduced their car payments from $980/month to $410/month. This left $4,723/month, after the $750/month child support, free to apply to the remaining debt of $96,300, which required $5,252 in monthly payments. We contacted each of the twenty-one creditors, presented them a copy of the monthly spending plan, the

| LENDER | BALANCE DUE | MONTHLY PAYMENT | REMAINING PAYMENTS |
|---|---|---|---|
| Consolidation #2 | $10,000 | $1,698 | 6 |
| Medical Loan | 6,300 | 545 | 12 |
| Consolidation #1 | 30,000 | 1,344 | 24 |
| Business Loan | 35,000 | 838 | 48 |
| Credit Cards | 15,000 | 298 | 60 |
|  | $96,300 | $4,723 |  |

agreement with the IRS, and their tax return, and we proposed the preceding repayment plan. Notice that we reordered the loans by the time remaining until the loans were paid off.

As you can see, each lender would be repaid in full but would have to agree to a reduction of interest rate (we negotiated for 7 percent on each debt) and payments for the plan to work. Praise the Lord, all twenty-one lenders agreed to work with our plan as long as Vic and Joan made their payments on time. Joan agreed to a six-month trial commitment to their marriage, and both entered marriage counseling at their church reinforced by a weekly accountability/mentoring experience with a mature Christian couple to deal with finances and other areas where they were struggling as a couple.

Normally, when I go through debt repayment with an individual or a couple, we divide the freed payments from the first debt between giving, saving, and debt repayment, but Vic insisted that he needed the self-control of getting out of debt before he looked at any other area of finances. Six months from the day we began, we reevaluated their financial condition. They still owed $69,774, and their monthly payments were still $4,723, but the $10,000 consolidation loan (#2) was completely paid off. As they had agreed at the outset, they added the entire $1,698 freed payment to Vic's medical loan payment of $545 which now had a remaining balance of $3,150. Month eight, the medical loan was paid off and they had $1,336 left to apply to the original consolidation loan. At the end of fourteen months, consolidation loan #1 was paid off, only two loans remained, and they had $2,804 left, which was applied to the business loan. With payments of $4,425/month the business loan was completely paid off at the end of the nineteenth month, and they had $137 left over to reduce their remaining credit card loan balance to $10,250. By sticking with the plan of *using each paid-off loan payment to reduce the next remaining loan balances*, their $4,723 payment paid off their last remaining credit card bill in three months, and they had $3,782 left over. In only twenty-two months from the date we began, they were completely out of debt. More importantly, Vic had learned spending control, patience, self-discipline, and good stewardship habits.

## GETTING OUT OF DEBT—PERMANENTLY

Remember the IRS payments of $1,000/month? That debt was paid off the fifteenth month, and Vic and Joan saved the payment so they accumulated $7,000 in savings at the end of the twenty-second month, which they used to pay off both car loans and free up what had been $410 in car payments. They stayed with our original plan, and at the end of their second year, they were debt-free, free of car payments, and had accumulated more than $12,000 in savings. In only two years, Vic and Joan went from personal debt equal to 113 percent of their take-home pay to debt free; from car payments costing 13 percent of their income to no car payments; from 0.3 percent of their income in savings to 14 percent of their income in savings; and from no giving at all to giving 11 percent of their income. You can do the same thing if you use this simple plan to get debt free.

1. Record your bills starting with the bill that has the least remaining payments.

2. Put all your energies into paying off the bill at the top of the list. Decide now how you will divide the freed payment, when all the loans are paid off, between: giving _____ %, saving _____ %, debt reduction _____ %, and spending _____ %.

3. Continue the process until all your bills are paid off. Ninety-five percent of people in debt can be totally debt free in eighteen to thirty-six months.

The process is simple but effective, and as each bill in turn is paid off, you build momentum, victory, and a success attitude that will spread throughout all areas of your life. There are organizations that help people plan their way out of debt. Many times these organizations are able to reduce interest to zero, extend repayment terms where necessary, and provide general financial guidance and information besides debt counseling. Three nonprofit organizations that I have worked with over time are:

CONSUMER CREDIT COUNSELING—2,200 offices nationwide —look in your yellow pages or call 1–800–388–2227 to find the office nearest you.

CHRISTIAN FINANCIAL CONCEPTS—1,000 Christian counselors nationwide with excellent educational materials available. For more information or a counselor in your area call 1–800–722–1976.

FAMILY LIFE CREDIT SERVICES—Christian counterpart of Consumer Credit Counseling. For more information and available counselors in your area call 1–800–747–9307.

Consolidation loans are a poor long-range answer because they do not address the problem of overspending. If you consolidate your bills to lower payments, 99.9 percent of the time, two years later you will be deeper in debt than when you began. Home equity loans are also a poor plan if you are using the loan to lower payments, lower interest rates, or extend the term of a loan beyond what you can obtain at a traditional lender. Consider consolidation loans and home equity loans as powerful and dangerous as nitroglycerin. Handle with care if you must use them. My advice is to avoid them altogether.

What about refinancing existing credit card balances if you can find a credit card with lower interest rates, lower fees, or no fees? The idea is economically sound, but again it is potentially dangerous for two reasons. First, the more credit cards you have, the more chance you have to run multiple cards up to multiple limits, so consider destroying the card(s) you're "replacing." Second, if you refinance a $15,000 credit card balance that is now at 19 percent interest (with payments of $305/month, for eight more years) to a new card at 9 percent interest (with payments of $220/month), what will you do with your savings in payments? Determine to pay your balance off early with the difference, which will free you to begin putting your former debt repayment into savings. Don't be like the vast majority of people who refinance, then continue to charge until their new card has a balance due of $20,819 and payments of $305/month. When interest rates rise a few points, their payments increase to $338/month, and they are worse off than when they began, having greater debt and higher payments. If you must refinance keep payments level and pay off the loan as quickly as possible; don't refinance just to lower your payments. That's looking at the symptom of stretching your income rather than the real problem, which is spending control.

Every other issue *Money* magazine provides a list of credit card companies with no fees, lower rates, or both. RAM Research of Frederick Maryland says today's average rates have fallen from 18 to 15 percent and credit card companies are scrambling to steal business from competitors by offering lower rates. The lowest rate in the May 1994 issue of RAM's Research monthly newsletter was 5.9 percent! A copy of RAM's *Cardtrak*, a 12–16 page monthly newsletter that covers approximately 500 low-rate, no-fee, gold or secured credit cards, can be obtained for $5 by writing: RAM Research Corp., P.O. Box 1700, Frederick, MD 21702. Do not refinance until you are certain that you will use lower rates to reduce the term of the loan and/or the cost of financing. If you refinanced a $15,000, eight year, 19 percent interest credit card requiring $305/month in payments, at 5.9 percent interest, with the same $305/month payments, you would be debt free in fifty-seven months and save yourself $11,895 in interest, assuming your new card doesn't raise the rate before your loan is paid off.

## Cosigning

The Bible is very clear of the dangers of becoming surety for a loan. Surety is pledging yourself and/or your assets to a lender to guarantee or secure a loan. The most common examples are co-signing for someone else's loan or pledging assets other than the asset you are borrowing to buy. Let the Bible speak to the issue of surety:

"My son, if you have become surety for your neighbor, have given a pledge for a stranger, if you have been snared with the words of your mouth, have been caught with the words of your mouth, do this then, my son, and deliver yourself; since you have come into the hand of your neighbor, go, humble yourself, and importune your neighbor. Do not give sleep to your eyes, nor slumber to your eyelids; deliver yourself like a gazelle from the hunter's hand, and like a bird from the hand of the fowler." (Proverbs 6:1–5)

"He who is surety for a stranger will surely suffer for it, but he who hates going surety is safe." (Proverbs 11:15)

"A man lacking in sense pledges, and becomes surety in the presence of his neighbor." (Proverbs 17:18)

If you ask a lender what percentage of cosigned loans end up being paid by the cosigner, the answer you will hear varies from 50 to 85 percent depending on the lender, the risk, and the item financed. Besides the economic risk, you may be helping another person to do what is outside God's desire for his life. Perhaps God wants to bless this person by providing, but when you enable another to trust in credit, you may be hindering, rather than helping, him move toward God's perfect plan for his life. Parents, when you are tempted to cosign for your child's first car or home, ask yourself if what you are doing is in your child's best long-range interest. Rather than training your children to use plastic or debt, perhaps you should teach them God's principles for handling money wisely, including the clear warnings from Scripture about debt. Grandparents, when you give your children a down payment on a new home or a car, are you really helping, or are you encouraging them to commit to five to thirty years of bondage using debt? To me, Scripture is clear and neither surety nor cosigning is an option. If you are sure God would have you help this person, and you have the financial resources, a better way of helping—*after* you are sure the person has wisely figured out how much house he or she can afford and has saved an adequate down payment—would be to reward the person's wisdom by doubling the down payment (as a gift, not a loan), thus lowering his or her monthly payments.

## Bankruptcy

For more than a million Americans this year bankruptcy is the method to legally discharge debts and relieve financial and personal pain and pressures in life. Why bother to suffer the two years of grinding it out like Vic and Joan, when for a few hundred dollars you can legally discharge all your debts and start over fresh by declaring bankruptcy? If you find that you or your partner is pregnant, why bother to bring an unwanted child into the world? If you are bored with your mate, why not shop around for a better or more attractive, exciting sexual partner? Our society views all these as acceptable options. God, on the other hand, views bankruptcy as breaking a vow, labels abortion murder, hates divorce, and refers to sex outside marriage as adultery or fornication. Bankruptcy may be a legal right, but it is not an option for those seeking to live by a biblical standard. The Bible calls one who defaults on his debts wicked: "The wicked borrows and does not pay back, but the righteous is gracious and gives" (Psalm 37:21). When you take out a loan, you sign an agreement to repay both interest and principal in a timely manner. The Bible refers to a promise to do something as a vow, and vows were a very serious matter: "When you make a vow to God, do not be late in paying it, for He takes no delight in fools. Pay what you vow! It is better that you should not vow than that you should vow and not pay" (Ecclesiastes 5:4–5). Breaking a vow, promise, or pledge is a serious matter in God's eyes, and He can and does deal swiftly and harshly with the offenders.

Ananias and Sapphira were members of the early church who promised (vowed) to sell a piece of property and donate the proceeds to the church. After the sale of their property, they probably counted the proceeds several times and agreed to hold back part for themselves and donate the remainder to the church. When Ananias presented his donation to Peter, Peter said, "Why has Satan filled your heart to lie to the Holy Spirit, and to keep back some of the price of the land? . . . You have not lied to men, but to God" (Acts 5:3–4). When Ananias heard these words he fell down dead. Three hours later, his wife came in, unaware of what had happened. Peter asked her if the amount donated represented the total price of the land. She lied and said that it did. She also immediately fell dead at Peter's feet. If you doubt whether lying, breaking a vow, or falling back on a promise is a serious matter to the Lord, reread the story of Ananias and Sapphira in Acts 5:1–11.

Bankruptcy can be either voluntary or involuntary. Voluntary bankruptcy is initiated by the debtor; most debtors seek complete dismissal of all past debts. Voluntary bankruptcy and seeking debt cancellation should not be an option considered by a committed Christian. Sometimes creditors initiate the bankruptcy process as a means of recovering as much as possible and being able to write off the unpaid balance immediately. This is called involuntary bankruptcy, because here the creditors rather than the debtor initiate the process. In most cases the debtor has no choice but to comply. God does not hold you accountable for the actions of others, but you could respond by letting the courts discharge all your debt, then begin a plan to fully repay each lender. That would be honoring your vow and following God's standards rather than man's standards. I know one young man who after his involuntary bankruptcy personally visited each creditor and began to make a payment of $150/month on debts of $65,000 discharged by involuntary bankruptcy. The $150/month payment spread over the eleven creditors would have amounted to slightly less than 20 percent of the interest due on the loans, but the young man persisted and promised to pay more as he received greater income. Four years later, this young man capitalized on a business opportunity, which I feel God brought his way, and he repaid every creditor every penny of both principal and interest due them. Two years later, this young man had become a multi-millionaire, and he credits his success to God who honors those who honor their vows regardless of circumstances. If you are on the fence today, I urge you to be a person of integrity, character, and sound biblical principles. God honors and rewards those whose word is their bond.

## Establishing or Restoring Good Credit

Perhaps you have never established credit and you are thinking of buying a house in the near future. Or a previous foreclosure or other financial troubles have devastated your credit standing. How do you build good credit? Assuming you have paid off any bills you have and reestablished good spending habits, let's look at an inexpensive way to build good credit.

First, deposit your savings, say $1,000, in any bank and simultaneously ask for a loan of $1,000 for one year secured by your savings account. Any lender will accept a 100 percent secure loan, and you will pay only 1 to 3 percent more interest on your loan than you earn on your savings. That's a cost of $10 to $30 for a $1,000 line of credit, assuming you make the required payments on time. Only when you fail to perform on your commitments by being late on payments, making less than the required payment, or skipping payments do you damage your credit. A bad credit report can stay on your record for seven to twelve years, depending on the problem and whether or not the debtor filed for bankruptcy. Good credit is valuable, especially if you travel, rent cars, or use credit cards to keep a record of business purchases. By making the payments on time you are establishing discipline and good credit. If you secure credit, protect your credit rating by honoring your commitments and using credit very carefully and as infrequently as possible.

## THE SIX STEPS TO FREEDOM

Following is a six step plan that will once and forever free you from the bondage of debt and credit.

ONE: Determine exactly where you are: income, outgo, and debt, then eliminate all non-essential spending. Look at every dollar you spend and ask yourself, "Is this necessary?" Is this a need, want, or desire? How can I make do? Do without? Do it less expensively? Vic and Joan used this method to reduce their expenses 50 percent. It works if you plan your work, then work your plan.

TWO: Above all else, commit your plans to the Lord. If you have been a slave to debt, credit, impulse buying, material treasures, or poor stewardship, confess your attitude and ask His forgiveness, help, and guidance. Ask Him to help you discern needs from wants and desires and adopt the habit of patience and prayer before you make any spending decisions. Set some goals for your life: When do you want to be free of credit card debt? When can you be free of installment debt? How long will it be until your car is paid off? Will you commit to make payments to yourself so you can buy your next vehicle in cash? Do you need to replace the credit card in your wallet with a debit card? Now draw up a simple plan to reach your goals and stay with it, one step at a time. Don't be impatient with yourself. It probably took you years to develop wrong thinking and years to accumulate your current bills. You can, however, change your thinking and free yourself of the weight that debt adds to life. It is a choice. My question to you is: *Will you choose to move to a debt-free lifestyle?*

THREE: If you have an outstanding balance on your credit cards, destroy the cards and vow to become debt free as a way of life. If you only put your cards away, they will find a way back into your wallet. Cards have been healed by super glue, so burn rather than cut. I know one woman who froze her cards in ice trays in the freezer to force her to take the time to pray and think as she defrosted them for emergency purchases. If you must have a credit card for travel, business, car rentals, etc., get a debit card which deducts purchases directly from your checking or savings account. Not all debit cards work for plane tickets or car rentals, though, so be sure the one you've acquired will do what you need it to do.

FOUR: Plan your way to freedom like Vic and Joan. Start with your smallest bill (fewest payments remaining) and pay on it until it is gone, then divert its payment to the next shortest bill. Remember that every dollar you pay down on debt has a guaranteed return on your investment of 15 to 18 percent. The only debt with a greater return on investment will be your home mortgage, but since it is your largest and longest debt make it the last entry on your list of debts to pay off.

FIVE: When extra money comes in from gifts, inheritance, bonuses, raises, rebates, or tax refunds, divide the money into three parts. Part one is God's part. Cheerfully give Him the first part and give thanks for your many blessings. You may want to divide what remains in half. Half goes into savings and half is applied to the debt you are currently working to eliminate. At first, it may not seem to make sense for you to save money in an account that pays only 3 to 4 percent interest while credit card and other debt costs 10 to 30 percent interest. But you save half to develop the habit of savings and so that you will have savings (rather than plastic) to draw on if you encounter unplanned expenses, cost overruns, or real emergencies before you are debt free.

SIX: Hold a garage sale and sell all financed, depreciating items you can survive without. Every three or four years we have a garage sale to simplify our lives, reduce the clutter that accumulates, and convert unused and unnecessary items to cash. Eight years ago when we were in Europe I went crazy spending money. I bought Jeanie Baccarat crystal, Christifoli silver, and beautiful china. Jeanie did not desire these, but I thought this was something you had to have as part of a traditional "Beaver Cleaver family." The U.S. dollar was at a fifteen-year high, so I spent $12,000, including import tax and shipping, and rationalized my impulse spending as buying at bargain prices thanks to a strong U.S. dollar. In the next eight years, we used the fancy dinnerware only twice. I learned you don't put crystal and china into the dishwasher and silver has to be hand polished. When I realized I was the one who really wanted the image, not Jeanie, I decided to sell. We are praying for a buyer, but we know that we will only get pennies on the dollars that I spent.

Since almost everything you buy depreciates, consider selling those items you own that are financed and replace them with "make do" items you can buy with cash. Clean out your closets, attic, basement, and garage and donate or sell the items you no longer need or use.

As you go through these six steps, maybe you need to contact one of the three organizations I listed that help people plan and work their way to financial freedom. If your current debts, excluding home and car, exceed 15 percent of your take-home pay, you have a problem you need to address now, with professional help. If your debt load is 5 to 15 percent you can plan your own way to freedom and in a few years know the joy of having more discretionary cash flow than you have now. If your debts are 5 percent or less, pay them off and split the freed cash flow between giving, savings, and spending. Imagine how you will feel when you are completely free and clear of debt. The reward of getting debt free is worth the sacrifice.

I pray that those of you currently in the midst of a financial challenge of reduced or interrupted income will not use credit cards or debt to solve your problem. (See chapter 5 for some things you can do.) The idea sounds logical, but you end up with a load of debt and even less spendable income in the future. Debt is not an asset. Debt is a potential liability that becomes a liability when you use it. Avoid the black hole of debt with its never-ending payments and high interest rates so you can be free to serve the Lord when, where, and how He leads.

## ACTION ITEMS

1. Do you believe credit cards and debt are not wealth but potential liabilities that become real when you use them?

2. Will you choose to free yourself from the bondage of debt starting now?

3. Will you review the ten warnings about debt in this chapter?

4. If you have current debt, what is/are/were the cause(s)?

_____ ignorance of the power of compound interest against you

_____ ignorance of your current financial condition (have you filled out your chart on page 173?)

_____ spiritual problems: discontentment, improper priorities, get rich quick, impatience, laziness, self-indulgence, covetousness, greed, or pride

5. Will you stop comparing what you have with others? Will you avoid the malls? QVC? television? catalogs? Instead, will you choose to count your blessings and give thanks for all God has given you?

6. If you refinance, will you shorten the term of the loan and save interest rather than reducing your payments?

7. Will you commit to paying off your debt by beginning with the smallest bill first?

8. If your debt exceeds 10 to 20 percent of your spendable income, will you seek professional help today?

9. What is your philosophy on cosigning? surety? bankruptcy?

10. Will you begin today to use the six steps to freedom plan?

# CHAPTER 9
# SPENDING PLANS

"A prudent man sees evil and hides himself, the naive proceed and pay the penalty." Proverbs 27:12

## WHY BUDGETS DON'T WORK

Budgets don't work for the same reason diets don't work. Unless you change both your eating habits and your level of physical activity, weight loss from a diet lasts only as long as you are able to stick with your diet. The day you go off your diet, back comes the weight you lost and usually a few extra pounds. In the area of finances, a budget works as long as you stay strictly on the plan, but after a few weeks or months at best, unless you have dealt with the underlying issues of attitudes and habits of spending, the budget ("diet") dies with a pent-up cry of "charge it." That's the reason I do not recommend that you or anyone else goes on a budget. The minute a counselee hears that, he says, "Thank God, I didn't want to spend the time and energy to budget, and I hate to be restricted and confined. I have tried budgets, and they don't work because something keeps coming up time after time to sabotage the plan."

## DEVELOPING BETTER SPENDING HABITS

To deal permanently and effectively with either accumulated weight or financial problems we must begin by correcting the underlying incorrect attitudes and poor habits. Once better financial attitudes and habits are in place, you don't need a budget, and taking care of your finances will require less than one hour a month, including balancing your checkbook. A spending plan differs from a budget by looking deeper—at attitudes and habits of spending, not just at dollar amounts. The foundation of your success formula has five steps; we have already covered four of them.

STEP ONE: Choose to *honor the Lord first from any income* or profit that comes your way. If you skip step number one you are disobeying the clear command of Scripture and you will suffer the consequences rather than reaping the benefits, rewards, and blessing that come with obedience.

STEP TWO: Choose to *pay yourself something* out of every piece of income or profit you receive. You will suffer the consequences of poor decisions until you decide to comply.

STEP THREE: *Pay your taxes*, honestly and in full, when they are due. The Internal Revenue Service is the country's largest, harshest, and most effective collection agency. Comply or suffer the consequences.

STEP FOUR: *Decide now exactly how you will use your next increase in pay, bonus, windfall profit, or inheritance.* Most people don't plan to fail, but by failing to plan they have the same results. You can choose exactly how to divide the increase between: giving, saving, debt reduction (until you are debt free), and spending. Some use a 25 percent allocation to each area until they are debt free, then they put one-third into each of the three remaining categories. Others choose to put one-third each into giving, saving, and debt reduction until they are debt free, then they treat themselves by increasing their spending. What matters is that you have and act on a plan. It doesn't matter where you start; start now, and let Step Four take you toward a balanced life.

I recall a single man I counseled a decade ago when he was struggling to support himself and his daughter. He earned $8.00 per hour, which is about $16,000/year or $1,333/month. He had giving of zero, saving of zero, taxes of $190/month, and no plans as to how he would handle any financial blessing. He owed $3,500 on two credit cards and $4,500 on a three-year-old car. After paying his bills he had absolutely nothing left at the end of the month. Our initial plan was to begin by giving $2.00 a week to his church and saving $2.00 a week. All required taxes were withheld from his paycheck. The most important step was his commitment in writing to put one-third of every blessing, bonus, or unexpected profit toward giving, saving, and debt reduction until he was debt free. The next Sunday when he attended church, he put $2.00 into the offering plate along with a promise to give God one-third of any increase he received. Two days later, his employer paid him a $750 unexpected bonus for a suggestion he had made three weeks prior. Was that a coincidence, or was that the Lord blessing a believer with the right heart? When he got the bonus check, his net pay was $600, so he put $202 into the offering plate the next Sunday, opened a savings account for $204, and paid $100 extra on each of his two credit cards. At the end of the first year, this faithful steward had given $504 to the church, put $404 into savings, and paid off $400 on his credit cards. The second and third years were full of blessings and opportunities, which he handled exactly like he did the first $750 bonus. At the end of year three, he was earning $9.50/hour, giving $994/year, saving $944/year, and adding $800/year to pay off the remainder of his credit card balance which was now down to only $600. His car was completely paid for, but he continued to make car payments to his savings account, which now had a $2,855 balance, so he would never again have to finance an automobile.

At the end of the fifth year his earnings were $12.00 per hour. He was completely debt free, had $8,812 in savings, and was giving more than 10 percent of his annual income to his local church. Today, ten years later, he earns $30,000/year and owns a home with slightly more than ten years remaining on the mortgage. He has a paid-for car, more than $30,000 in savings, and $10,000 built up in his company's profit sharing plan. His giving is almost 20 percent of his gross income to the church, and he is engaged to be married to a lovely Christian woman. They plan to live on his income and split her income four ways after taxes: giving, savings, mortgage reduction, and spending. In less than three years they will have a paid-for home, they will give more of their earnings to the Lord's work than 99 percent of Christians, and he will celebrate his forty-fourth birthday. A lot of individuals earn more than this man, but very, very few can say they handle their income any better. Remember everything he has accomplished came as a result of following step four.

STEP FIVE: *Plan to live on less than your net spendable income* (after giving, saving, taxes, and a margin for error) with an attitude of contentment, thanksgiving, and gratitude. Step five represents the frosting on the cake because 85 percent or more of your financial future and success is determined in steps one to four. To achieve the necessary attitude of contentment and thanksgiving you need to discern needs from wants and desires, then concentrate on being satisfied, content, and grateful when your needs are met. A need is whatever is necessary for you to accomplish God's plan for your life. Needs are not relative to your lifestyle; they are relevant only to God's perfect plan for you. We all need shelter, but our need can be met by: living with family or others; renting or sharing an apartment; or owning a co-op town house, condo, home, or estate. Each of these options meets your need for shelter. The question is which fits His plan for you right now. Wants and desires are insatiable. No matter what you have, it is easy to allow wants and desires to rule your life and leave you in a state of perpetual discontentment. Ask the Lord to help you to clearly understand your true needs, then give thanks to Him as He meets your needs. Choose carefully what you think about, talk about, and spend time and money pursuing. This will determine your attitude and remind you where your real treasury should be. When you choose contentment and start to give thanks right now, you begin an attitudinal metamorphosis as dramatic as the transformation from a caterpillar to a butterfly.

The second half of step five is to *plan your spending within flexible boundaries that you set.* You can view boundaries as restrictive, limiting your choices, and stealing your personal freedom, or you can choose to see boundaries as expanding your freedom, providing you with a wide variety of choices, and being the source of safety, peace, joy, and contentment.

## PROTECTIVE BOUNDARIES

Several years ago we were able to visit Australia and New Zealand on vacation. Our first day there, we got ready to go to the black sand beach at our hotel for wind surfing, snorkeling, and tanning while floating on an air mattress. After breakfast, we came to the beach to find it closed and off limits. We learned there was an epidemic of jellyfish, called box jellyfish, that are extremely poisonous and sometimes fatal to younger children and older adults. The hotel promised us that the next day the beach would be opened, and they invited us to a complimentary buffet dinner where they presented a thirty-minute video on the box jellyfish along with a slide show showing the wonders of down under. The next day when we returned to the beach, we found that an area two hundred yards into the ocean was roped off by a bright orange floating line. The life guard explained that the roped-off area had been seined and was protected from the box jellyfish by nets suspended from the floating orange line. The horrors of the video on the box jellyfish were fresh in my mind, but others in the ocean were wind surfing, rafting, and playing, so we cautiously ventured into the seventy-eight degree water. Being a curious sort, I donned my face mask and swam out to check the net. It was in reality three separate nets, each with a smaller mesh than the one beyond.

Later that afternoon, two new arrivals to our hotel ignored the printed and verbal warnings and swam beyond the boundaries of the net to check out the tropical fish on a breaker reef about three hundred yards off shore. Both the young men were hit by the box jellyfish, and both ended up in the hospital for treatment from the stinging tentacles. I saw one of the men who swam face first into a nine-foot tangle of stinging tentacles, which extends from the box-like body of the box jellyfish. The man was either unconscious or in shock, but his face, neck, and chest looked like he had had a glass of acid thrown right into his face.

The same boundary line from which the nets were suspended were perceived differently by my family and the two young men. The young men saw the boundary as restrictive and limiting their choice to explore the nearby reef. The net was a barrier to their personal freedom, and they chose to ignore it. To me and my family, the boundary provided a safe area, and within its borders we were free to enjoy a number of choices of fun activities. The boundary didn't limit our freedom; it expanded our freedom and enabled us to enjoy and experience the ocean.

The same principle applies to boundaries on your personal spending plan. You are the one who determines and sets the limits. If you don't like them, you are free to change them. How many times have you wondered whether or not you could afford to buy an item or spend money in one way or another? You answer such questions when you look at the big picture and establish self-imposed limits within which you can do as you like. Boundaries, limits, rules, and guidelines are not designed to steal our joy but to protect us from the financial box jellyfish of life. When God set the boundaries for living, it was to protect us from consequences we could not see, not to limit, punish, or restrict our freedom, but to keep us safe. When a parent sets limits such as "Don't play in the street," he does so to keep his child safe. The child is free to do whatever he likes within a predetermined area.

Let's look at the big picture, the ocean of finances, and then examine the component areas which you can choose to divide as you please.

## Record

First, look at the area of total resources and determine exactly where you are right now. Start with your gross income. First, plan to allow for giving, saving, and taxes. What's left is spendable income, which you allocate as you choose, over ten different areas. Begin by studying Form 1 on page 195. As you can see, you begin with gross income from all sources, then subtract what you are currently giving, saving, and paying in taxes. It doesn't matter where you begin, what matters is to record what you are doing right now. We will follow the three R's formula (Record, Review, and Revise) for developing your own unique and personal spending plan. Stop now and to the best of your ability record what you are currently spending within each of the ten areas. Don't worry about being too precise or absolutely accurate, because we will review your first estimate to make it more accurate later. Don't judge or write in what you need to do; simply record where you think you are right now.

## Review

Now you have completed the first "R." You have a record of what you think you are spending. The second "R" is for Review, so let's review. In most cases, our initial estimate of spending is lower than our actual spending, because we forget what we have done or we write in what we should be spending rather than what we actually spend. To review your initial answers, you need to examine the records of actual spending from your check register, your credit card receipts, and any other available written records. If you don't have records, you can either request them from your bank or credit card company or begin to record today everything you spend in some sort of permanent record. Reviewing what you have done will take some effort on your part. If you write checks for most items, look back over the past six months or year to see what you actually spent. Then rerecord your more accurate estimate. To accurately determine what you are spending will require several hours of work as you look at the hundreds of checks you wrote and assign each to the correct category. Then, go through your credit card receipts and try to determine what you spent money for with each transaction. Finally, you probably pay cash for some items and have no records to examine to see exactly where the money went.

For those who can account for 90 percent of their expenses with canceled checks, bank statements, and credit card statements, you have a plan that is at least 90 percent accurate. If you are unable to determine where most of your money went, you need to commit today to record your expenses over the next few months, so you can get an exact record of what, where, and how

### FORM 1: MONTHLY SPENDING PLAN

| | | | | |
|---|---|---|---|---|
| Gross Income | $_____ | 5. | Debts | $_____/___% |
| Salary | $_____ | | Credit cards | $_____ |
| Interest | _____ | | Loans, notes | _____ |
| Dividends | _____ | | Other | _____ |
| Other | _____ | | | |
| Less | | 6. | Entertainment | $_____/___% |
| Giving | $_____ | | Eating out | _____ |
| Saving | _____ | | Baby-sitters | _____ |
| Federal Tax | _____ | | Other | _____ |
| FICA | _____ | | | |
| State Tax | _____ | 7. | Clothing | $_____/___% |
| Net Income | $_____ | | | |
| | | 8. | Medical | $_____/___% |
| 1. Housing | $_____/___% | | Doctors | _____ |
| Payment/rent | _____ | | Medication | _____ |
| Telephone | _____ | | Dentist | _____ |
| Insurance | _____ | | Other | _____ |
| Taxes | _____ | | | |
| Electric | _____ | 9. | School/child care | $_____/___% |
| Water | _____ | | Tuition | _____ |
| Gas | _____ | | Transportation | _____ |
| Sanitation | _____ | | Materials | _____ |
| *Maintenance | _____ | | Day care | _____ |
| *Other | _____ | | | |
| *Improvements | _____ | 10. | Miscellaneous | $_____/___% |
| 2. Auto | $_____/___% | | Lunches | _____ |
| Payments | _____ | | Toiletries | _____ |
| Gas/oil | _____ | | Beauty/Barber | _____ |
| Insurance | _____ | | Cleaners | _____ |
| *Tax/license | _____ | | Allowances | _____ |
| *Repairs | _____ | | *Gifts | _____ |
| *Replacement | _____ | | Subscriptions | _____ |
| 3. Food | $_____/___% | | Other | _____ |
| 4. Insurance | _____/___% | | TOTAL EXPENSES | $_____ |
| Medical | _____ | | LESS NET INCOME | $_____ |
| Disability | _____ | | | |
| Other | _____ | 11. | SURPLUS | $_____ |
| Life | _____ | | THE BOTTOM LINE | |

Chart adapted from the *Family Budget Workbook* by Larry Burkett (Chicago: Northfield, 1993). Used by permission.

*Most planning ignores these items, which will, over time, require some expenditure.

your income is being spent. With every individual or couple I counsel, I recommend getting a small spiral notebook and recording every item purchased over the next month. The information gathering doesn't require much time, but the act of writing down everything you spend will help you begin to evaluate your expenditures more carefully. The process of recording expenses will improve your financial decision-making moment by moment, so even if you can account for 100 percent of your income, try writing down what you spend as you spend it. You will catch yourself asking questions like: Is this a need, or a want, or a desire? Is this item the best use of my income? Can I "make do" or "do without" this expense?

By now you should have a fairly accurate idea of your outgo. Most people are shocked at this stage to see how much they are actually spending. More than nineteen out of twenty people I counsel are spending more than they earn without being aware that they are doing so. If this is the case for you, don't be discouraged or depressed. Be happy and give thanks that you are now aware of your problem. The old saying that a problem well stated is half solved contains a lot of truth. The most common response to a review of a spending plan is, "No wonder I have unpaid balances on my credit cards: I'm spending $300/month more than I make." Give yourself credit for the time and effort you took to figure out what you are spending. You are on the first phase of the journey to becoming a better, more effective steward of the resources that God has provided you. To God your attitude is at least as important as your actions. When your heart is right, your actions will quickly correspond.

## Revise

The third "R" is to Revise the information you Recorded and Reviewed. This revision is your first real spending plan. To help you be realistic and accurate in your plan, below you will find percentage guidelines for spending within each of the ten categories you have recorded. These guidelines are not laws to be obeyed, but a frame of reference for comparison with the spending of a typical family of four. Take a few moments to study the chart of typical expenditures, then compare what you are doing to the guideline in Form 2 on page 197.

You may need to modify the percentages to suit you and your particular circumstances. You can spend more in some categories or less in others, but you can't spend more than 100 percent of your income without accumulating debt, which, as we have seen,

## FORM 2: PERCENTAGE GUIDELINES

| GROSS INCOME | $15,000 | $25,000 | $40,000 | $50,000 | $100,000 |
|---|---|---|---|---|---|
| LESS: | | | | | |
| GIVING | 10% | 10% | 10% | 10% | 10% |
| SAVINGS | 5% | 5% | 5% | 10% | 10% |
| TAXES | 8% | 17% | 18% | 20% | 28% |
| | | | | | |
| NET INCOME | $11,550 | $16,875 | $26,800 | $35,400 | $52,649 |
| | | | | | |
| 1. HOUSING | 38% | 41% | 35% | 35% | 32% |
| 2. TRANSPORTATION | 15% | 15% | 12% | 11% | 8% |
| 3. FOOD | 15% | 12% | 11% | 10% | 6% |
| 4. INSURANCE | 5% | 5% | 5% | 5% | 5% |
| 5. DEBTS | 5% | 5% | 5% | 5% | 5% |
| 6. ENTERTAINMENT | 5% | 5% | 6% | 6% | 7% |
| 7. CLOTHING | 5% | 5% | 5% | 5% | 5% |
| 8. MEDICAL | 5% | 5% | 4% | 4% | 4% |
| 9. SCHOOL/CHILD CARE | 4% | 4% | 6% | 6% | 8% |
| 10. MISCELLANEOUS | 3% | 3% | 4% | 4% | 5% |
| 11. SURPLUS | 1% | 1% | 7% | 9% | 15% |

makes your situation worse in the future. The purpose of a balanced spending plan is to function as a written guideline to help you make daily financial decisions, so over time your current stress is replaced by contentment.

*Our goal is to reduce expenses and create a margin which you intelligently reallocate to move you closer to your objectives.* As you revise your plan you will find both long- and short-term goals begin to emerge. Short-term goals might be reducing expenses so you can:

- Give more to your local church
- Save something for yourself out of each paycheck
- Have a margin left over instead of living to the limit of your income
- Begin to pay off your smallest bill and reverse the debt cycle
- Be realistic in your planning by allowing something for repair and maintenance, clothing, vacations, and gifts

You must be honest with yourself in your planning and consider each and every item. If you skip or ignore expenses that over time will be necessary, you are only creating problems for yourself in the future. Don't worry, you will be able to develop a plan that has room for everything necessary in your life. You are now on the road to financial freedom. The important thing is to start, where you are right now, and plan to move ahead. The numbers aren't as important as the attitude and direction you choose for the future. Developing a spending plan is much like physical conditioning or a weight loss program. Good habits and attitudes over time always produce results. The success you can and will achieve in your financial life will spread to all other areas of your life. Be patient with yourself. Don't expect to lose forty pounds in forty days. Concentrate on the proper attitudes of thanksgiving and contentment, and begin moving in the right direction today. I guarantee you will arrive at your objective as a more effective steward than you may judge yourself to be today.

A balanced, revised spending plan is one characteristic of good stewardship. Don't think of stewardship as an event or a destination; it is a process and a journey toward a moving target. Keep on course, learn to make different and better decisions tomorrow than you made yesterday, and you are on your way to becoming the person God would have you be. Your major assets are time and the choices you make today about how you will allocate your next increase. If all you get out of this chapter is the resolve to intelligently plan where to apply your future increases, you will succeed in managing your financial future.

## LOOKING AT THE FINANCIAL PIECES

Let's look at each category from the spending plan to get a better idea how they fit together and how you can save money on categories where you are at or over wise limits.

### Categories 1 and 2—Housing and Transportation

Combined, housing and transportation will consume 40 to 50 percent of your income. If you have overextended yourself, choose to do what is necessary to reduce your burden so ample money remains to spread over the eight remaining categories. If you aren't overextended in housing or cars then make sure you are considering all the costs so that you eliminate the unpleasant future surprises people receive who don't plan realistically. When you look at housing, your revised spending plan should contain some allowance for: payments, telephone, insurance, taxes, electric, water, gas, sanitation, maintenance, and other improvements.

On Form 1 you will find an asterisk next to maintenance, other, and improvements because most planning ignores these items, which will over time require some expenditure. It is not a matter of incurring the expenses; it is a matter of when they will occur. Your home can either be your castle or your prison; it depends on how much you undercommit or overcommit yourself. See houses for what they really are—shelter. Where you must, choose to cut expense to free up cash flow to be redirected to better uses.

The total cost for transportation includes: payments, gas/oil, insurance, tax/license, repairs, and replacement. Remember why budgets fail? They address symptoms rather than underlying problems. If you are spending more than you should for transportation the payments are not the problem. The problem is either confusing needs (for transportation) with wants and desires (for status) or failure to consider all the costs beyond payments, oil/gas, and insurance. If you don't plan for taxes/license, repairs and maintenance, and building a reserve to replace the car you are driving, you are choosing a future with unpleasant surprises and never-ending car payments.

Don't be legalistic about the 10 to 15 percent guideline for transportation. These guidelines are not absolute rules but suggestions to help you establish a total balance in your overall spending. Maybe your case demands that you exceed the guidelines and reduce other areas. That's fine, as long as you don't rob God or fail to save some of your income for yourself. Remember a balanced spending plan with a positive surplus (category 11) is the goal we are moving toward. Maybe you have overcommitted yourself and for a few months you have no choice but to live with a deficit in other areas until your car is paid off. When you choose today how you will use what you are currently spending for transportation in the future, you are on the path to relief from financial stress. Some people stick it out several years until their payments end; others sell vehicles for less than the payoff to relieve the pressure now. Timing your reduction of expenses isn't the watershed issue; it is the choice to reduce expenses and free up money for better use.

## Category 3—Food

Food costs can be reduced with a few simple ideas and common sense planning. My wife, Jeanie, does all the shopping for our household, so let me show how she reduced our food budget more than $150/month. First, she shops for groceries and household supplies every two weeks by taking inventory of what we have in the pantry and comparing that to her meal plan. She plans what our family will consume in our three daily meals the next fourteen days. Then she goes into the grocery store with a bi-monthly shopping list of what she needs. (Exceptions are bread and milk.) Our goal is good nutrition at minimum cost, so she avoids buying high-priced junk food, expensive labels, or pro-cessed foods. Have you compared the cost of a regular potato with the cost of a family-sized bag of potato chips? Have you read what's on the label, nutritionally, in that two dollar bag of chips? Have you compared store brand prices to nationally advertised brands? Have you ever examined the difference in price between processed foods and the do-it-yourself fresh alternative? Adapt or create a meal plan, and shop with a shopping list so you can re-duce your cost of food 25 percent or more. Not only will you save money, you will also improve your diet, feel better, and become more fit. (See the list of low-cost foods on pages 120–21.)

The other strategy Jeanie uses to save money is to take the time and energy to clip coupons from our local newspaper and integrate them into her planned bi-monthly grocery shopping. Ev-ery Wednesday and Sunday when our local paper arrives, it is filled with food coupons, discounts, sales, and bargains. Jeanie spends one to two hours each week cutting out, organizing, and collecting coupons. Her strategy is to match coupons with items that are on sale. This increases savings tremendously. Last week she showed me the receipt for groceries of $150 which was re-duced $75 for coupons redeemed. That's four hours of effort for $75 return on invested time, $19/hour for her time. Set yourself a goal when beginning to reduce your food bill. Jeanie's first goal was to save enough money to purchase a freezer, and within two and a half months the goal was accomplished. Having the freezer allows her to stock up on sale items, thus reducing the food bill even further. Financial freedom doesn't come from hitting home runs with the bases loaded; it comes from intelligent choices with small amounts of money over long periods of time. All you have to do is start now and move in the direction you want to go, and sooner or later you will arrive.

## Categories 4–6

We will talk about insurance (Category #4) more in the next chapter and we have already discussed debts (Category #5) in a prior chapter, so let's look at Category 6—entertainment—to see a few ideas on cutting expenses so you can have more money avail-able for other areas. In the area of entertainment, people tend to be at one extreme or the other. Some people's plans allow nothing for eating out, baby-sitters, travel, and entertainment, while other individuals really splurge and indulge themselves. My family learned to establish a balance by using the envelope system. Every pay period we allocate a pre-set amount of money to entertainment, and the cash is placed in an envelope labeled "entertainment." We are free to choose how we spend the funds, but we have disciplined my impulse-buying urges by limiting the amount of money allocated to the envelope. Now my challenge becomes how to get maximum mileage out of what we have. For example, when *Jurassic Park* came out, we did not go to the Friday night $6.50 showing; instead we went Saturday afternoon when the cost was $3.25. The lines were actually longer Friday night than Saturday afternoon, and it felt great to go at half-price. Want to rent a video? Tuesday evening we can rent a movie for ninety-nine cents instead of the $3.00 regular price. How about free videos from your local library or church? If you are creative and plan, there are dozens of ideas you can use that are inexpensive and good for family time and relationships such as camping, hiking, fishing, picnics, family board games, high school and college plays, swimming, gardening, travel logs, lectures, and a host of others. It sure beats a trip to Disney World at $200/day plus travel and room cost. Write out a list of inexpensive options for your own family. You will probably have more fun, and you will have money left in your envelope at the end of the month.

## Category 7—Clothing

Now we've come to my favorite category to stretch to the limit. I have learned to stay out of the mall and avoid men's clothing stores. If I went in for a new tie, I would end up with five ties, three shirts, two pair of slacks, a suit, a sport coat, and two new pairs of shoes. I don't set out to spend $1,000; it just kind of happens, if you know what I mean. Guess who doesn't go shopping for clothes for himself? I let Jeanie buy all my clothes for two great reasons. First, the items she buys are all color coordinated, so I get more outfits from fewer clothes. Second, Jeanie is a bargain shopper who buys at sales during the off-season. The first time Jeanie showed me a $30 men's shirt (major label) she bought for $7.00 I though she was putting me on. If you're the impulse buyer, let someone else shop for you or learn how to buy wisely. You can cut your cost of clothing 50 to 75 percent.

There are an array of options to choose that will enable you to cut clothing costs and invest the difference elsewhere. Look in your local phone book for a listing of resale stores, thrift shops, and consignment stores. This could be one of your "free" entertainment options, and it is great fun to hunt for bargains. Another great source of clothing is garage sales, especially if you have small children. Most young children outgrow their clothes before they wear them out.

## Category 8—Medical

Doctors, dentists, medications, orthodontists, and other out-of-pocket medical costs: Depending on your age, health, and insurance coverage these costs can be small or very substantial. Today, costs are coming down some and becoming more competitive, but they are still high. I am not embarrassed or bashful about discussing price with any medical professionals. I ask about options, costs, and ways to reduce the price. All medical professionals give the same good advice to those of us who seek to limit medical costs: Get adequate rest, develop healthy eating habits, exercise four times a week (the dentist says brush after meals and floss daily), and practice preventive health care with a routine periodic check-up and exam. The earlier you detect a problem the less painful and expensive the remedy.

## Category 9—School/Child Care

This category includes tuition, transportation, materials, and day care expenses. As we said earlier, don't assume it is God's plan for all children to attend Christian schools, colleges, and universities, and don't assume it is parents' responsibility to absorb 100 percent of the cost of education. Time after time, I have seen Christian couples unnecessarily burden themselves with private Christian education costs or carry a guilt complex because they were unable to provide their children with the privilege of attending private Christian education. If God has provided you the means for a private Christian education, use it; it is a wonderful resource, but it is a luxury, not a necessity. Day care is an expensive option, but sometimes it is the only available means of caring for your children while you are at work or school. Sometimes, there are other options to consider like swap-care, where parents share the task of day care with other parents and reduce their costs 90 percent or more. Sometimes the only obstacle to grandparent care or family care is pride. Pride is an expensive and deadly sin. Don't tolerate it in any area of life including finance. Evaluate all the alternatives, seek God's guidance and direction, and very often you will find the means to cut costs of school/child care and to free money for other uses.

## Category 10—Miscellaneous

"Miscellaneous" is the catch all, and it is generally the third most abused area for cost overruns. If you economize you can eat lunch out every day for $1,500 to $2,000 a year. If you upgrade you could spend $3,000 to $4,000 a year patronizing an upscale lunch restaurant. Or you can brown bag and spend only $300 per year! If you are married and both of you work, double the figures for all three options and think about a better revised plan for your family.

Next comes toiletries. You can spend from fifty cents to $200 per ounce for perfume, and beauty/barber shops vary in cost from two dollars (barber college) up to $200, depending on who cuts/ styles your hair. At our home we are having a ball introducing friends to a device called the Flowbee. The Flowbee is a do-it-yourself hair-cutting device that attaches to a vacuum cleaner. It sucks hair up into a pair of clippers that cuts hair. It comes with several attachments to produce a professional layered cut from one-half to six inches long. Using the Flowbee has cut our beauty/ barber costs 90 percent. We have had a lot of laughs over our "suck cut," but the best came from an experience with a couple I counseled whose income had dropped 30 percent in one year forcing the wife to give up her weekly manicure. She was accustomed to having her nails done each week at a cost of $40, which adds up to $2,000/year. When Patty Perfect Nails visited our home, her first question was, "Do you really use a Flowbee?" Her husband had told her that our home was paid for, we had two years living expenses in savings, a fully funded retirement plan, no debt or car payments for twenty years, and that we earn an above-average professional income. Her second question was, "I know you are very successful and financially secure, but how can you be so cheap?" I wasn't offended, and I was impressed with her straightforward manner, so I told her the truth. We choose to be frugal (my word for cheap) so we can send the $50/month we used to spend on haircuts to help support a missionary couple currently serving in Albania. Since we have adequate income to meet our basic needs, we invest our excess income and dollars freed by cutting expenses into our church and a few well-selected ministries which build and strengthen His church.

Cleaning costs can be reduced drastically by choosing to buy wash-and-wear clothing. Our total cleaning bill is about $15/month, and that goes for clothes I wear to the office and a few items Jeanie has that require dry cleaning. Look for dry cleaning coupons; they are always available at cleaners who are promoting new business. In cutting miscellaneous costs, or any costs, learn to look at three amounts before you buy: the purchase price, the operational price (to maintain or, in this case, clean) and the expected lifespan of the item. When Jeanie bought her sewing machine she selected a model $150 higher than the basic machine because it will last two to three times as long, making it cheaper to own in the long run. I learned this philosophy from my grandmother who said often enough for me to recall thirty years later, "Don't be penny wise and dollar foolish." Don't forget to consider the cost of operation, because many times the cost of operation is more than your purchase price. Our fifteen-year-old who is a year away from being able to drive has already learned that the cost to insure a truck is about half the cost to insure a car for a male teenage driver living in our town. If you remember the three components of cost in buying, your decisions will improve, you will eliminate unnecessary expenses, and you will have money available for other areas.

## KEEPING COSTS DOWN ON
## YOUR FAMILY'S FAVORITE EXPENSES

Allowances are a favorite subject for our two boys, so let me tell you how we approach an allowance. Since our son John is the only one at home now, we have three tasks for which he is rewarded. First, there are the daily chores like clearing the table and doing dishes after family meals. For his participation in household chores he is rewarded by being included in all family activities. Last year we purchased seats for a series of Broadway shows and musicals that tour the nation, and we ended with a drive to Los Angeles to see "Phantom of the Opera." Both boys were involved in speech, drama, and theater, and the reward was very meaningful to them.

John's second job is to develop good work habits. Receiving his "allowance" is not automatic but contingent on completing his homework, his Bible study, and his exercise plan.

Our third reward is a "bonus" for character development and the acquisition of basic biblical values and attitudes. We do not pay for grades, but we reward effort, discipline, and persistence which are habits the Bible encourages us to develop. Two years ago, John wanted to try to skip a grade in math, his best subject, so he could be in honors/advanced math in high school. Since my first degree was math and physics, I felt comfortable as his personal tutor. We bought the freshman text for Algebra 1–2 and completed the 531-page book in less than four months. We spent the majority of the time on the hardest problems in each unit. John took the final exam with the older freshmen and scored 99 percent, an A + . We rewarded him for his effort, not the grade. We have since completed an English course, two Biology courses, and more than a dozen Bible study programs geared to his interest and ability. John is not a top student for pure intelligence, but he has learned self-discipline, study skills, good work habits, time management, and the value of good, old-fashioned hard work.

What plan you select depends on the goals you set for your child's development. We value contribution to the house, good work habits, developing biblical character and attitude, and learning early and properly how to handle God's money. Next year as a sophomore in high school John will learn how to handle the increase and the value of a spending plan.

I explained earlier our family plan for gift giving. This coming school year we are expanding our plan so John can experience the joy of investing (giving) directly into the kingdom of God. Since he is now responsible for the yardwork his brother J. T. did when J. T. lived at home, next year John will have the privilege of selecting where he will invest a $25/month additional amount. I have explained how I evaluate potential recipients, and he will do his own homework to determine what would be the greatest potential return on investment for his $25/month. John has met several evangelists, ministers, seminary students, and Christian workers as potential recipients. Now, his decision is which one would God have him help support. I am excited to see how John develops and what God teaches and molds out of this experience.

For those of you like me who read 150 books per year, several magazines, technical/trade journals, and who thrive on getting double the CEUs (Continuing Education Units) required, I don't feel we are overspending when we splurge on buying books. (The rest of the world is underspending in that area, and the spending plan guidelines are too low.) When I can't borrow from the eight libraries I have access to, I have learned to wait until I can buy a paperback, rather than a hardback book, for all non-reference material.

I have a long way to go to become the steward, husband, and father God would have me be, but at least I'm moving in the right direction. As we close this segment on cutting expenses, so you have income to use differently, let me give you a short list of cost-cutting ideas that work in all ten areas:

1. Pray before buying and give God the opportunity to provide or re-direct.

2. Buy used for pennies on the dollar of what items cost new.

3. Learn to discern "needs" from wants and desires by prayer and patience.

4. Don't watch QVC or TV; stay out of malls, car dealerships, and new model homes; and avoid reading, watching, or listening to anything that stimulates your material lusts.

5. Be creative and resourceful rather than spending cash or credit.

6. Clip coupons, shop sales, buy bargains, and buy at off-season sales.

7. Decide on a spending plan that will work for you.

8. Make it yourself—you can save a fortune on clothes, for example, and it's fun besides.

9. Try gardening—it's fun, nutritious, saves money, and gives you some exercise.

10. Try do-it-yourself repairs for easy home maintenance and car repairs.

11. If it is a major expenditure, rent it for a while to try it, before you buy it. This is especially important for big ticket items like boats, planes, campers, or second homes.

12. Shop and compare prices on every item, to get the most for His money.

13. Negotiate price, pay cash, and ask for a discount.

14. Learn to buy wholesale, or direct, to save costs that typically go to a middle man.

15. Buy function, not status; pragmatic, not emotional; and utility, not image.

16. Buy in bulk where possible; it will lower your unit cost.

17. Join or form a co-op to save on your major items.

18. Write checks or pay cash rather than using credit cards, debt, and payments.

19. Use the "I want" list.

20. Learn to make do, do without, and consider repairing first before replacement.

## BENEFITS OF A SPENDING PLAN

*A good spending plan will, in worst case, stretch your current income at least 15 percent further.* That's equal to a 25 percent pay hike after giving, saving, and taxes. Better yet, a good spending plan eliminates unpleasant surprises ahead because you have foreseen potential problems and made plans to handle them before they occur. By developing a good spending plan, you also acquire self-discipline, which will generalize and have a positive impact on all areas of your life. My favorite verse for discipline is, "All discipline for the moment seems not to be joyful, but sorrowful; yet to those who have been trained by it, afterwards it yields the peaceful fruit of righteousness" (Hebrews 12:11). The price of your gain is temporary pain that you won't even recall years later as you reap your rewards now and in the life to come. A good spending plan will help you develop the powerful attitudes of contentment, thankfulness, and patience. Two verses that you should memorize and meditate upon for a week each are:

"Not that I speak from want; for I have learned to be content in whatever circumstances I am. I know how to get along with humble means, and I also know how to live in prosperity; in any and every circumstance I have learned the secret of being filled and going hungry, both of having abundance and suffering need. I can do all things through Him who strengthens me." (Philippians 4:11–13)

"Rejoice always; pray without ceasing; in everything give thanks; for this is God's will for you in Christ Jesus." (1 Thessalonians 5:16–18)

Finally, by taking the time and effort to create your revised plan, you have a crystal clear picture of how you want your spending to be. The plan will focus your efforts like a magnifying glass focuses a beam of light. This will add both power and momentum as you accelerate toward your goal. Your spending plan is the next-to-the-last major step required to free yourself forever from your current temporary financial pressure. The spending plan alone will not work magic; neither will any quick fix solution solve years of accumulated bad habits and unbiblical attitudes. The spending plan is only a tool to help you select and develop different attitudes and more effective habits and to keep you on track toward becoming the steward you are capable of being.

## FINAL ROADBLOCKS TO SUCCESS

There are a few reasons that spending plans fail. The most common is that the plans are too complicated and they provide no help in controlling spending. There are dozens of different manual plans that you can use, and a half-dozen good computer programs. All these programs will work if you take the time to learn and use them, but most people grow weary and abandon the plan before it becomes a habit. As explained under entertainment my favorite plan is the envelope system. It takes less than five minutes each week to divide your income into ten or more categories and to place the pre-set amount of money into envelopes labeled for the appropriate category. (Christian Financial Concepts has put together a *Cash Organizer Budgeting System* by Larry Burkett, distributed by Moody Press, 1994.) With the exception of the few payments we make by check, our family puts cash into different envelopes and that is our spending plan. When cash is removed, the amount and purpose is recorded on a three-by-five card within the envelope, and we have a record of our spending. Most important, the envelope system limits our spending. We have resolved never to borrow from one envelope to fund the expenditure from another, so the system continues to work for us. When our clothing envelope is empty, that is it for clothing. In the chapter on debt, you learned that people will spend 27 percent more in credit than they will in cash. Using cash forces us to carefully consider each expenditure. The less effort required, the greater chance you will have of using any plan to help you limit expenses. When you select a plan for you, look for simplicity and ease of use first, and a plan that will help you control your spending.

Unrealistic expectations are another roadblock to succeeding with a spending plan. You can fool yourself and allocate nothing for repair and maintenance, gifts, entertainment, medical expense, or other categories, but very quickly the pressure will mount and will cause you to abandon the plan, because the cure appears worse than the problem. So, be realistic in allocating money, and, just as important, be realistic in estimating the time it will take you to arrive at your goals. To bring your spending plans into balance generally requires a minimum of three months up to a year or more. You don't instantly jump from no giving, no saving, and deficit spending of $300/month to 10 percent giving, 10 percent saving, with a $200/month surplus. Gradual change over a period of months produces new permanent attitudes and habits, while immediate dramatic change tends to be very short-lived. A good spending plan is not a financial crash diet, but a gradual change to new eating habits and attitudes supplemented by exercise and choices. It will always produce a slower but more permanent loss of bad habits and ways of thinking.

*You need to be both flexible and fair in laying your plan.* Starting out you will make some natural errors and oversights that must be faced and corrected for the plan to work. Don't be rigid and inflexible; that will only shorten the time you are willing to work at changing attitudes and years of habits. Once the better habits and attitudes are formed, the plan becomes effortless.

A very common example of unfairness in a plan occurs when one spouse uses the plan to punish another. Remember Vic and Joan with their IRS problem and stack of bills that Vic had created? The first version of their spending plan left Vic with $5/week spending money while Joan got $50/week. Joan's plan would have had Vic pay for the problems he created and left Joan almost exactly where she was. The plan also erred by separating their income into "his" and "her" money, rather than combining their income and sharing the load. Their original plan would have failed, because it was not fair to both, and it created another area of division between them, rather than seeking unity. Fortunately, Joan was flexible, and by learning to approach their problem as one, they began to develop both better communication and more oneness in their marriage. If you are married, your plan should be flexible, fair, and designed to unify, not divide you and your mate.

*Procrastination and impulse spending are two more dangers for any plan.* It never gets easy, so just commit and do it now. The longer you put it off, the smaller the chance you will get around to making it happen, so kill procrastination by developing your plan and acting now. Unfortunately, a plan alone will not eliminate your desires or habits of impulsive spending. You can create a perfect plan but then ignore it or fail to consult it before you splurge, and you only create frustration and guilt for yourself. Now that you have created a financial road map for your future, consult it and allow it to influence your decisions before you choose an afternoon stroll in the mall to window shop. If you must window shop, realize you are stimulating your material lusts and building discontentment. By all means leave your envelopes, cash, checks, and credit cards (if they aren't burned) at home. At first a plan is like any new habit or skill—it feels awkward and unnatural—but after a few weeks, you will feel different, think different, and acquire new tastes, values, and desires.

Sometimes even the best of intentions weaken when birthdays, Christmas, anniversaries, or other special events roll around. Let's say that my plan allowed $100 for Christmas, out of which Jeanie and I exchange gifts, and we purchase a gift each for J. T. and John. What can I buy Jeanie for only $25? John wants a new Genesis game for $250 and J. T. wants six months of guitar lessons at $11/week? I have experienced this dilemma. It is very, very tempting to go ahead and spend $900 more than I planned by telling myself I'll make it up in the coming year and that it was foolish to have committed to such an unrealistically low amount. What I felt was pride, old habits, and years of materialistic brainwashing working against my new attitudes and new habits of spending. Unfortunately, my problem surfaced in November, so my creativity and resourcefulness had to perform under time pressure.

I asked myself what Jeanie valued the most and realized it wasn't a $400 tennis bracelet, but little daily things like love notes, a walk, kind words, my being interested in what was happening in her life each day, a listening ear, and long toe rubs. If you asked Jeanie what she preferred for Christmas it wasn't a material treasure, but love, time, availability, caring, sharing, and toe rubs. So I committed in writing to make showing interest in Jeanie's day a priority. I also gave her coupons for weekly toe rubs and a special night out each week—most of the nights out were inexpensive or free, but she enjoyed just the two of us going out together. The boys were a little harder but I explained the situation, told them I was trying to be a better steward of the assets God had entrusted me with, and asked for their understanding.

Did you know that you can buy four used games for a Nintendo for less than $25? Buying used solved my problem with John, along with giving him coupons he could redeem for six special nights in the coming three months. A special night is whatever John wants to do—just the two of us. Now for J. T.: Did you know most high schools offer guitar courses for only $15 per semester, five days a week, fifty minutes per day for ninety days? Only $15, and he got graduation credit for a fine arts elective at the same time. Any fool can go out and spend money he doesn't have by using his credit cards, but it takes character, creativity, resourcefulness, self-discipline, and commitment to stay with your plan. Unless you earn enough to be sloppy in your spending habits, a spending plan is a tool you need to become the person you can be. When you succeed, you will feel a real sense of accomplishment; with each new habit and skill acquired, it gets easier and easier.

Let me summarize this chapter by reminding you of the four-tiered foundation:

- Honor God first.
- Pay yourself something.
- Pay your taxes.
- Give thanks and be content with what you have.

Next you use the three "R's":

- Record where you are.
- Review and improve your estimate.
- Revise your estimate to create a target spending plan.

Your revised plan will incorporate all the ideas we discussed for eliminating unnecessary expenses to free income for better, more intelligent uses. Revise each of your ten categories, and do what you can do now to take the first step toward your own unique and personal goals. Review the twenty ideas we covered to help you uncover ways to reduce your expenses. You control your financial future. You control it by the choices, attitudes, skills, and habits you choose to develop. One day when you stand before our Lord, imagine the thrill of having Him say to you, "Well done, you are a good and faithful steward. The way you managed the earthly treasures I entrusted to you was a strong and effective witness to many."

## ACTION ITEMS

1. What is the difference between a budget and a spending plan?

2. What is your plan today for:

giving ................................... $_____
saving .................................. $_____
taxes ................................... $_____

3. How will you allocate your next blessing, raise, bonus, or windfall?

giving ................................... _____%
saving .................................. _____%
reducing debt ................. _____%
spending ........................... _____%

4. Will you build a margin (surplus) in your spending plan? Why?

5. Have you:

recorded you initial spending plan?
reviewed your spending plan?
revised your spending plan?
If so, congratulations. If not, when will you start?

6. Is your goal to reduce expenses rather than increase your income?

7. Which ideas will you use to reduce costs for:

food? _____

_____

insurance? _____

_____

debts? _____

_____

entertainment? _____

_____

clothing? _____

_____

medical? _____

_____

school/child care? _____

_____

miscellaneous? _____

_____

Start where you are and do what you can today to free money for better use.

8. Which of the twenty cost-cutting ideas on page 206 will you adapt and use?

9. Will you memorize Philippians 4:11–13 today?

10. Will you learn the roadblocks to success and start now on a plan to stretch your current income at least 15 percent further?

# CHAPTER 10
# YOUR PERSONAL PLAN

". . . work out your salvation with fear and trembling; for it is
God who is at work in you, both to will and to work for His
good pleasure." Philippians 2:12–13

**W**hen Paul wrote these words to the Philippians, he was giving
God's counsel to all of us as we face life's challenges, whether they
be physical, emotional, mental, social, or financial. The word
translated "work out" should remind us that becoming better
stewards or overcoming current or present financial challenges is
a process to enjoy, not a destination to arrive at. We are concerned
with problems and distractions like overdue bills; reduced, interrupted, or inadequate income; car payments, house payments,
lack of savings, and lack of giving. God is concerned with our attitudes, character, testimony, and what we become as we travel toward proper or improper destinations. As you face your financial
challenges, know and believe that if you are a Christian God is
with you, working through you to achieve both His will and His
plan for your life. You are not alone, and there is nothing in heav-
en or earth beyond His power. When you look for His presence,
you will find Him right beside you. When you seek His power and
strength, He will empower and strengthen you. When you seek
Him, His will and His wisdom, He will reveal both Himself and His
wisdom. You will find any financial challenge you face to be opportunity in disguise when you accept your role as co-laborer
with the Almighty God.

Your threefold adversaries (the world system, our sin nature,
and the devil) are formidable, but they are not invulnerable. Jesus
told us that He has overcome the kingdom of darkness, and
through Him we too can become more than conquerors. The

price we pay for victory over materialism, freedom from bondage, and release from financial stress is small. Throughout the pages of this book you have learned the necessary tools and habits to employ to overcome your financial challenges. To be a victor, you must saturate your mind with the truths of Scripture until you can recall them as easily and accurately as you do the multiplication tables you learned years ago in grade school. Unless you have a consistent, persistent daily habit of exposing your mind to the truths of the Bible, your chance of permanent success is small. Memorize the verses this book contains. Better yet, buy a copy of Dr. Gene Getz's *Biblical Theology of Material Possessions*. You will be exposed to everything God has to say about attitudes and use of material possessions. Don't stop there. Ask your pastor for additional resources you can read and study to continually put God's truth into your mind and heart. The price appears high at first, and the effort may be great, but the price is higher and the effort greater if you attack your problems on your own.

The path to victory, freedom, and success also requires eternal vigilance. We are in a spiritual war, and our enemy would love to discredit our testimony, sideline us with injury, or destroy us, so that we pose no threat to his kingdom. When I forgot that the price of victory was eternal vigilance, effort, and standing my ground, I put some black marks on my testimony by using credit cards; splurging on crystal, china, and silver; buying a Rolex; and the worst of all, buying that red convertible Porsche. Such purchases may not be wrong for everybody, but for me they were bad choices that put a potential stumbling block in front of some of my brothers and sisters in Christ, whom I was trying to teach good stewardship. Both eternal vigilance and constant self-evaluation are necessary to keep us on the small, narrow road He calls us to travel.

## REALISTIC TIME LINES

We must be realistic in setting our giving goals. If you set the goal of giving 10 percent, it may take you five years or longer to be able to honor God with a full tithe, but you are successful the moment you take any action toward that goal. The amount you give is not of first importance to God. God looks at our hearts and our attitudes and begins to bless us once we choose to honor Him first, even if it's only an increase of $1.00 per week. You may deem yourself a faithful steward the day you increase your giving to His church. Saving is the same. As long as you are consistently saving something and/or increasing your current saving when blessings come, you are on the path to freedom. If it takes you several years to achieve the saving goals you set in chapter 4, remind yourself that you were successful the day you began, not when you arrive. Reaching your dollar goals for giving or saving is not the objective. The objective is developing proper attitudes and habits that take you where you need to be.

Homes and cars are the hardest goals because of the size of the goals themselves. If you have forty-eight payments left on your car and you choose to grind it out, then to save what used to be your car payment so you can eventually buy a replacement in cash, you are successful the moment you commit to the plan, not eight to ten years later when you arrive. The vast majority of people never escape car or lease payments, so take heart and be encouraged that you choose to free yourself from the bondage of perpetual car payments. I had one forty-year-old client who committed to paying off his home by age fifty-five using the plan of an extra principal payment each month. He asked me if fifteen long years of effort was really worth the reward. I reminded him that the average retiree still owes twenty-three years of house payments.

Plan realistically to pay off your debt: credit cards, installment loans, car loans, and home mortgages. You should feel the thrill of victory with your first step, but maybe it won't occur until you have paid off your smallest loan or you have free income to reallocate as you choose. The longer you persist the greater your momentum. When you make the last payment on your last loan, you will be in the top 2 percent of Americans, and America is still the richest nation on earth. More important, you will be free to serve, give, save, and spend as you choose rather than live with the bondage of never-ending payments and financial pressure.

The purpose of your spending plan is to help you develop good stewardship—new attitudes and habits of spending. When you finally achieve your plan of spending less than you earn, maybe for the first time in your life, the margin left over represents your victory, financial freedom, and growth toward spiritual maturity. You can make the process harder and more painful by looking at how far you have left to travel, or you can concentrate on the fact that you are now on the path to victory and you will arrive at your goal. It's your attitude toward change and tasks that creates your feelings, not the changes and tasks. I pray that you will recall that fact when our three adversaries attempt to discourage you, disillusion you, or cause you to doubt that you are on the correct path.

Setting realistic long-term investment goals is difficult. When you are ready to consider investments, acquire some of the books and resources listed in the bibliography under "investing." We have suggested that you concentrate your efforts first on achieving adequate giving and saving habits, paying off debt, and building adequate savings before you invest. One exception to this sequence may be investing through a qualified retirement plan at your work like a 401K, 403B, or a pension/profit sharing plan. To determine whether or not to put excess money into a retirement plan rather than retire debt, you need to analyze the actual returns and ask yourself these questions: Is my investment deductible? What does the return mean in terms of taxes saved? Is my contribution matched by my employer? If so, what is the return on my investment? Are these funds accessible for an emergency prior to age fifty-nine and a half? by a loan? with or without a nondeductible penalty? Depending on the answer to your unique circumstances, maybe investing into a qualified retirement plan has a better return than paying off your home, but don't do all your savings inside the plan at the expense of reasonable giving and personal savings outside your retirement plan.

## YOUR TESTIMONY

The way you view and use your material resources is a clear testimony to both other believers and nonbelievers. Jesus' half brother put it like this: "Even so faith, if it has no works, is dead, being by itself" (James 2:17). Imagine you are in the following scenario, which I saw when I visited a church on vacation one Sunday: The topic is giving, and the passage is Luke 6:38, "Give, and it will be given to you; good measure, pressed down, shaken together, running over, they will pour into your lap. For by your standard of measure it will be measured to you in return."

After an exposition of the passage, the pastor proceeds to his first illustration. He pulls what appears to be a computer report from under the pulpit and explains that he has had the business office prepare a list of calendar year giving, by member and amount, starting with the greatest givers down to those who have given nothing at all to the church over the last twelve months. He goes on to explain that he had a second list prepared which converts giving to a percentage of annual income for each member. As he explains, he produces another list. He says that he has grouped

givers into groups by both dollar and percentage giving and as-
signed a letter grade from A + to F-, on a bell curve, to every member's name on the list. How would you rank? When the pastor
announces that he is going to publish both lists in the church
newsletter, the congregation comes alive. Several people get up
and walk out, several offer strong verbal protest, but most sink into
their pews like children caught with their hands in the cookie jar.
After a few moments of silence, the pastor says he wants everyone
to silently and prayerfully consider his past commitment, giving to
God's work, and evaluate where he is and where he should be. He
explains that one day each of us will have to stand before Christ
and account for how we have given, spent, and invested all the
resources that He has entrusted to us. Today was only our pre-
test. He explains that the pages of both reports were blank since
he didn't really wish to embarrass, humiliate, or compare one believer to another. The sigh of relief that comes from the pews is
amazing. The pastor closes his message by encouraging each person to evaluate his testimony to the outside world of how we handle God's money.

Does your use of income and assets produce a testimony of
your commitment to God above all else? How do you and I differ
from a nonbeliever in how we give, invest, or spend our incomes?
What kind of testimony is the way we handle our time, talent, and
material possessions?

Whether it is through giving, saving, spending, or investing,
you are choosing the testimony you offer to nonbelievers. You
know that obedience is blessed and disobedience is disciplined,
but *are you living a life of obedience or disobedience?* I know you
believe that what the Bible says about sowing and reaping is true,
but *what are you sowing by your thoughts, attitudes, and actions?*
We know that to live the Christian life we must keep our minds on
the eternal perspective rather than the temporal perspective, but
*what is your general perspective most of the time, eternal or tem-
poral?* We began this book with four fundamental biblical principles: God owns, God provides, God controls, and our proper
identity is in Christ. Are these principles that you merely acknowledge intellectually, or do you practically apply them as you live
your life day by day? The world may choose to ignore our words,
but it cannot argue with the testimony of a life lived by God's principles and precepts. Not only will becoming a more effective
steward revolutionize your life, it may well be the method God
chooses to lead others to the saving knowledge of our Lord and

Savior, Jesus Christ. That, my friends, is a sure way to store up treasures in heaven.

## Failure and Forgiveness

When you are financially challenged by obligations that take every cent you earn, or when your income drops or stops, remember that it is wrong to label yourself as a failure for two reasons. First, God doesn't judge us by the bottom line; He looks at our attitude, our character, and what He seeks to mold us into being. Second, failure is when you quit trying; anything else is temporary defeat. But, since our self-image is often shaped by seeking our identity everywhere else but in Christ, it is common for us to become our own worst critics. If you study the believers in both the Old and New Testaments, you will discover all of them experienced temporary defeats, some of which lasted for a period of years. If you read the biography of great Christian men and women, you will find the same cycle of defeat after defeat, year after year, time after time. What separates Bible heroes and more recent great Christians from the average man or woman is their ability to bounce back and continue to run the race despite past defeats. You may be down today, but you are not out of the race unless you choose to quit trying. If you quit, what was temporary defeat or a setback becomes a failure. Your current condition is neither hopeless nor permanent unless you choose to make it so.

If you set unrealistic standards, you are doomed to failure. If you expect perfection, you are choosing a path that will end in failure. If you refuse to forgive yourself and others for being human, you are imposing non-biblical standards, ideals, and values. Why do you think John wrote: "If we confess our sins, He is faithful and righteous to forgive us our sins and to cleanse us from all unrighteousness" (1 John 1:9)?

Learning to forgive yourself for temporary failure to be perfect sounds simple, but it is a difficult choice when you find yourself flat on your back and all you can see ahead is doom, gloom, and disaster. It is easy to blame God, others, or circumstances for our disaster, but the truth is that we are responsible for our own choices, attitudes, actions, decisions, and their consequences. To move forward, you must confess your sins, bad choices, bad decisions, and bad attitudes to God, then choose to believe that, true to His Word, God forgives and cleanses you. If other people are the target of your hatred, anger, and bitterness, model the Master who spoke these words when nailed to a tree, "Father, forgive them; for they do not know what they are doing" (Luke 23:34). When the disciples asked Jesus to teach them how to pray, three times in three verses Jesus stressed the importance of forgiveness in what people call the Lord's Prayer (Matthew 6:12, 14–15). An unforgiving spirit is not only disastrous to your health, it breaks your fellowship with God and leaves you naked and defenseless to fire from our threefold enemy. I am not asking you to *feel* forgiven—that might be impossible. I do ask you to choose to realize you are forgiven, to forgive others, and to allow your feelings to catch up with your correct thinking.

Forgive yourself and move forward. Separate temporary defeat from failure. Accept the truth that God evaluates you in light of the knowledge you possess at the time of your errors. We looked at Ananias and Sapphira, who were struck dead when they chose to lie to God and break their vows. A little later in Acts we encounter a character named Simon the sorcerer whose sin was as great, if not greater, than Ananias and Sapphira, but God did not strike Simon dead because Simon was ignorant of the truths he was violating. If your problems came from ignorance, don't be unnecessarily harsh in your judgment of yourself. Accept your humanity, confess your sins, accept your forgiveness and cleansing, and begin moving forward. You can't change history, but you can change your future by choosing to forgive yourself and others. Then choose to take the first step in the right direction.

Begin today to fill your mind with God's truth, God's plans, God's values, and God's message to you from His Holy Bible. The goal of any Bible study is not to learn the facts, but to allow yourself to be transformed by the power of the living Word of God.

You can't necessarily control your circumstances, and it may be hard to control how you feel, but you can control how you choose to think. You can choose to dwell on your blessings rather than dwell on your problems. You can choose to develop contentment by practicing the habit of really giving thanks for what you have. You can either choose to search for ways to eliminate your problems, or you can choose to search for reasons and excuses to rationalize away your responsibility. Russell Conwell put it this way in his famous speech "Acres of Diamonds": "As you think so you are—as you continue to think so will you be." Victory begins between your ears, when you choose to practice correct thinking. Once your thoughts are correct, under control, and examined, both your feelings and your attitudes will conform. God gave us both our mind and our emotions. Where the mind leads, the emotions will follow. If I catch myself doubting my own salvation, for example, I allow my mind to lead, and I review the assurances of my salvation found in Scripture. You can overcome financial challenges best by learning to use your mind. Once you've won that battle, you will be pleasantly surprised to see how quickly everything else falls into place.

## Disaster Plans

Thus far we have talked about having living plans for becoming better stewards while we are here on earth. We must also consider a plan to handle our affairs when we die, become disabled, or contract a terminal illness. Good stewards choose to address and solve these problems now rather than leave a mess behind for their loved ones to handle when they die, are disabled, or become terminally ill. The first tool everyone should have in place is a will.

A will is a document that tells how you want your assets distributed at your death. If you have children or other dependents, you should choose who will physically care for them at your death, and you can select who will manage their assets for them until they are of legal age. In a will you also choose your administrator (also called executor or personal representative), who will wrap up the details necessary to finalize your estate. If you don't have a will, I suggest you create one rather than allowing God's assets to be distributed according to your state's law. You should choose your child's guardian (physical care) and custodian (financial care), whether or not they should attend Christian school, and both what they inherit and when they inherit. If you are part of the 80 percent of Americans who have no will, please correct the problem and create one now. The major reason most people don't create a will is that they don't feel they have enough of an estate to bother with. As we have said time after time, God is not as concerned with what you have, as with how you handle it. *A will is a minimum standard of planning for anyone who desires to be a better steward.*

Don't forget about God's work when you write your will. I have reviewed literally thousands of wills for Christian men and women. Fewer than 5 percent leave anything at all to Christian work. Many of these people were faithful givers, but the attorney who wrote the will never bothered to ask about the church or a ministry as potential beneficiary. Result—nothing goes to Christian causes. The vast majority corrected that error when it was brought to their attention and also thought about the best way to leave an inheritance to their children or heirs. Did you know that more than 90 percent of inheritances are totally gone in less than five years? When you add up your home equity, life insurance benefits, retirement plans, and other assets, your estate may represent a substantial sum of money, so plan how to best pass on your inheritance.

One method we recommend and use very frequently is called the give-it-twice (GIT) method. The GIT method spreads an inheritance over time, and it provides for both your children and your church. Thus the name GIT. Let's say on death you leave $111,111. Which would be better—an $11,111 gift to the church and a one time $100,000 lump sum distribution to your child, or a plan that gave your child ten annual payments of $14,238 with the remaining $14,238 ($100,000 plus assumed interest of 7 percent) going to your church? Maybe your heirs are old enough, wise enough, and experienced enough to handle a large lump sum inheritance, but most aren't. Think about what should go to Christian work and what's the best period to spread an inheritance over, then write or have your attorney draft a good will.

*A second type of document everyone should have is a durable power of attorney* (POA). A durable POA lets you determine who can make medical and (in a separate document) financial decisions should you become disabled or unable to act for yourself. A durable POA is not affected by your disability, which voids a general POA, hence the name durable POA. A well-done durable POA should specify at least two people to act for you, a primary and an alternate, to make medical and financial decisions. Every family member, including your children, should have both documents so an emergency can be handled promptly and wisely. Many times having a durable POA represents the difference between life and death in an accident or a medical or financial disaster. You can either have the forms drafted by the attorney who does your will or use one of the many do-it-yourself packets from hospitals or legal supply stores. If you choose the do-it-yourself variety, I strongly suggest you have it reviewed by an attorney specializing in estate planning to eliminate unpleasant surprises and make sure your document will work as you expect when it is needed.

*The third document that we recommend is called a living will, or a medical directive.* In simple English a living will, a separate document from your regular will, says that if you are terminal you do not want your life maintained by artificial life support systems. Both President Richard Nixon and Jackie Kennedy Onassis relied on their living wills to allow them to die natural deaths rather than prolong the inevitable using today's high tech medical procedures. If you believe that a living will is not a biblically acceptable option, that is OK, but most people that I've counseled would prefer to prevent the $93,000 average expense of artificial medical procedures and not force their family through the extra few days that medical science can extend life for terminal patients.

Please don't confuse a living will with Jack Kevorkian's method of accelerating death for those who are in pain, chronically ill, or terminal. I do not believe there is any biblical support for doctor-assisted suicide or removing life support from a patient. Euthanasia stands right beside abortion; neither is an acceptable choice for a Christian who accepts the Bible's authority. A living will does not authorize removal of food or oxygen and introduction of lethal drugs; it states that you do not want artificial measures taken to prolong your life. If you don't have a living will, see your attorney or have an attorney who specializes in the area create one or review the form, or at least use a fill-in-the-blank free document, obtained elsewhere. Legislation state by state is changing very rapidly, so if you have a document more than three or four years old, have it reviewed to make certain it is still valid and effective.

I define good estate planning as: "Leaving what you want, to whom you want, when you want, how you want, at minimal cost and delay." My book *Saving the Best for Last* (Moody, 1994) is an exposition of this definition. For those of you who have more than a $100,000 estate (including life insurance) or who value privacy, an excellent tool to supplement the will, POA, and living will is a trust. Trusts come in many types and forms for various reasons and purposes. There are: living trusts, testamentary trusts, insurance trusts, children's trusts, qualified retirement trusts (e.g., IRA, pension, etc.), charitable trusts, and other trusts. The most common trust is the living trust which can: eliminate probate fees and delays, reduce or eliminate death taxes, provide privacy, and give you seventeen other benefits discussed in *Saving the Best for Last*. If your estate at death will exceed $100,000, do a little study and see if a trust would benefit you more than it will cost to create.

Another type of trust to investigate is a tax qualified, special type of trust, called the Charitable Remainder Trust (CRT). I recently worked with a retiring teacher from a California Christian university whose major asset was her home. She and her husband built their home for $50,000 forty years ago and today it is worth $650,000. The $600,000 profit could be reduced by their one-time $125,000 exemption, but the remaining profit of $475,000 would have cost them $171,000 in federal and state taxes. To solve the problem we created a living trust and a CRT that allowed them to eliminate $171,000 in federal and state taxes. The $171,000 tax savings was invested to pay the couple 8 percent income for the life of both ($13,680/year) or a period of twenty years. This amounts to a total return of $273,600 on what otherwise would have been paid in taxes. At the end of twenty years, what remains in their trusts will be divided between their two children and the university where she taught. When given the choice of selling their home and paying $171,000 in taxes, or planning, which eliminated their federal income tax and gave them $273,000 more income over twenty years and still left over $100,000 to God's work, they chose to plan. There are dozens of ways with and without trusts to maximize the efficiency of your estate. If you are one of the many whom God has blessed and allowed to steward a large estate, I pray you will choose to plan rather than allow His assets to be unnecessarily dissipated.

## THE INGREDIENTS

You now have 99 percent of the ideas and tools you need to overcome your financial challenges when they occur. To really understand and use these principles will take some additional effort and review of the material, but over your remaining years these ideas will literally be worth hundreds of thousands or even millions of dollars. The time to begin is now. You are a better steward the moment you choose to take that first step in a new direction. I wish I could invest time with each of you as you develop the biblical attitudes and use the ideas we have discussed that you need to put into action today. Since that is physically impossible, let me leave you with a ten-step game plan that I use with those I have financially discipled and counseled.

ONE: You need another, preferably a mature Christian, to whom you can be accountable over time as you turn these concepts and ideas into habits. Without an accountability partner, good intentions and plans die before they have a chance to mature and bear fruit. The ideal solution is a mentor who has had the experience of walking the path that lies ahead for you, but if there is no one like that in your life today, select someone who is available and begin now. Who will you pick as your accountability partner? _____ When will you start? _____

TWO: Choose an existing plan of study that will expose you to what the Bible says about the topic of money. Out of the more than one hundred Christian books I have read on this topic the best for me was Gene Getz's *Biblical Theology of Material Possessions*. If the size, title, or cost intimidate you, begin with the condensed version, "Real Prosperity." You might enjoy studying my other three books. Books written by Larry Burkett, Ron Blue, Howard Dayton, or other fine Christian authors are also excellent resources to acquire. (See the bibliography for more resources.) There are also a few good books in the secular market on finance, but most do not teach biblical attitudes and values. Many give unscriptural advice, and some merely use books as a tool to market other products such as newsletters, investments, seminars, etc. Be careful what you read and be discerning. If you go through one good book or study each year over the next ten years you will be a well-grounded mature Christian who has mastered both the attitude and the applications of finances.

How will you begin? _____ What will you (and your spouse if you are married) begin with to study? _____

THREE: Split your learning between both attitude and application. To get the correct attitude there is no substitute for Scripture, memory, and meditation. Once the truth is programmed into your permanent long-term memory, the application is easy and almost automatic. My current program is to memorize all 126 principles contained in the *Biblical Theology of Material Possessions* and the verse or verses from which the principles come. At the rate of only one principle per week memorized, I will have mastered all the principles in less than thirty months. I pray you choose to conform your attitude to God's standards. What will be your plan for Scripture memory? _____
What will you study for attitude? _____
What will you study for application? _____

FOUR: Choose to invest some time each week to develop excellence at whatever is your current job. In addition to being excellent insurance against layoff or pay cuts, it will make you more marketable if you must change jobs. Most important, choose and commit how you will allocate the next windfall, bonus, raise, or unplanned blessing between: giving __%, saving __%, debt reduction __%, and spending __%. This simple commitment will transform your future. If you have not done so earlier in the book, please stop now and fill in the blank percentages above.

FIVE: Be obedient to Proverbs 3:9–10: "Honor the Lord from your wealth, and from the first of all your produce; so your barns will be filled with plenty, and your vats will overflow with new wine." How much per week will you increase your current giving? $_____. Please fill in this blank. In those thousands that I have counseled, I have never heard one say that their decision to give was a bad investment. No one ever said to me, "I wish I had back the money I gave to God." Giving is the only area of investing where that is a true statement.

SIX: Commit and begin today to pay yourself first something from every piece of income that you receive. If you are already saving, consider increasing your commitment. How much will you pay yourself out of your next check? $_____. Anything in the blank besides a zero is a wise decision. Please fill in the blank.

SEVEN: Carefully and prayerfully examine your existing commitment to both housing and transportation. If you are over the guidelines, look at your options and reduce your expenses as soon as possible so you will be able to achieve your balanced overall, revised plan including a surplus. How much is your existing commitment to housing ____%? How much is your existing commitment to transportation ____%? Is either category over the guideline for the area (housing 32 to 40 percent of spendable income, transportation 12 to 15 percent)? Once you are under the guidelines, most of your past problems and financial pressure will be behind you. If you haven't yet done so, please complete Form 1 (page 195) and then fill in the blanks above.

EIGHT: You filled out your list of existing debts in chapter 7. Now, rank that list from your shortest term loan, to the longest, and begin to pay on your smallest debt until it is paid off. Decide now how you will divide the freed payment, when all the loans are paid off, between: giving ____%, saving ____%, debt reduction ____%, and spending ____%. Please fill in the percentages for your choices above.

NINE: Begin your spending plan with the bottom line. How much surplus do you want to build into your plan? $_____. Now, work out the other expenses with the money that remains. For 85 percent of you this will be your first plan ever that has a surplus, which is your margin for error. You will appreciate this step the most the next time you are able to pay an emergency, unplanned expense, or cost overrun from your surplus rather than adding to your debt or credit cards. So start with the surplus (after giving, saving, and taxes) and use what's left to divide wisely over the remaining categories.

TEN: In six months or a year, recycle these ten steps with someone who needs or could benefit from the process. Ask your pastor or Sunday school teacher who is struggling with finances. You will have more than a few names to pick from. Nothing will help you discipline yourself better than serving as someone else's mentor. Maybe a nonbeliever or friend will be your first to disciple.

Last, but most important of all, don't forget your own family as candidates for discipling in the area of finance. Your children will probably not be exposed to these principles in Christian schools, universities, or seminaries. If you don't disciple and model good stewardship to each member of your family, you are overlooking a major area, leaving an incomplete legacy, and leaving your family and children vulnerable to financial bondage. My dream is to see these ideas a mandatory part of all Christian education from secondary school through seminary. If that were accomplished, giving to churches, ministries, missions, and other areas of the Lord's work would triple or quadruple in one generation. Do your part and start now to master these principles, then model and disciple your own children and family. In Bible days parents discipled their children because the children were the parents' "retirement plan." Two good opportunities and goals I encourage and challenge you to begin now: Become a better steward, and disciple a steward yourself.

## ACTION ITEMS

1. Will you ask your mate or a mature Christian if you are realistic in both your goals and the time to accomplish your goals?

2. After completing this book, here is a question I promised I would ask you at the end: To what extent are you infected with the disease of materialism and discontentment?

3. Do you see how your attitude, view, and use of material possessions is your testimony?

4. How much of what you know are you living? How will you develop habits that will aid you in your goal of excellence in stewardship?

5. Have you failed or are you just temporarily defeated (or redirected)? Will you choose now to forgive yourself and others?

6. Do you need to create disaster plans? i.e.
   - will—which acknowledges God and provides for your family
   - power of attorney—medical and financial—to solve problems if you are disabled

- living will/medical directive—if or when you are terminally ill
- trust—of various types to accomplish your goals

7. Will you follow the ten steps used in counseling and discipleship?

- finding an accountability partner
- starting a topical plan of Bible study
- dividing your study between attitudes and application
- pursuing excellence and wisely allocating God's blessing
- honoring God first, foremost, and always
- beginning now to pay yourself something from each check
- carefully and prayerfully examining your financial commitments (especially homes and cars)
- listing, ranking order, and systematically eliminating debt
- beginning your spending plan with an entry into category eleven—surplus
- recycling the process with a financial disciple of your own

# BIBLIOGRAPHY

## Financial Pressure

Larry Burkett, *The Coming Economic Earthquake*, revised and expanded edition. Chicago: Moody, 1994. This national best-seller discusses the impact of government spending and national debt and projects a clear parallel between today's economy and the great crash of 1929.

_____. *Whatever Happened to the American Dream?* Chicago: Moody, 1993. The American Dream of life, liberty, and the pursuit of happiness, as well as freedom of religion, freedom from government oppression, and the freedom to build a better future for our families, is dying. This volume explores the reasons and the cure.

## Proper Attitudes

Neil Anderson, *The Bondage Breaker*. Eugene, Ore.: Harvest House, 1990. Learn how to get out of the bondage most people have to faulty thinking.

_____. *Freedom in Christ*. Eugene, Ore.: Harvest House, 1993. Once we understand the problem, the phrase "freedom in Christ" takes on new meaning. This book explores how we are "in Christ" and the revolutionary power of our identity in Christ.

Charles Colson, *Kingdoms in Conflict*. Grand Rapids: Zondervan, 1990. To get a proper perspective on the battlefield of life we must understand that we live in a war zone. Although the outcome is certain, the battle between the kingdom of God and the kingdom of Satan has a substantial effect on each attitude and decision we choose to accept and act upon.

Charles Swindoll, *Laugh Again*. Waco, Tex.: Word, 1993. This excellent commentary on the book of Philippians is a perfect blend of sound doctrine and practical applications. Our attitudes determine both our results and our joy or lack of joy during our daily walk. Learn how to make joy your permanent companion with this two-thousand-year-old letter packed with timeless truths.

Jack Taylor, *The Hallelujah Factor*. Nashville: Broadman, 1983. Drawing from thirty-five years of pastoral and teaching experience, the author tells simply and clearly how to develop contentment. The value of thanksgiving and praise are clearly demonstrated and applied in this small but powerful book.

## Your Career and Your Income

Chap Clark, *The Performance Illusion*. Colorado Springs: NavPress, 1993. Most men are trained to focus on performance and now, rather than godliness and eternity. Learn how to recognize and correct wrong thinking; watch your life change as you begin to view things His way.

Stephen R. Covey, *Seven Habits of Highly Effective People*. New York: Simon & Schuster, 1989. Although the writer is not a Christian, the seven fundamental principles of success are all scriptural. This book continues to be a best-seller because it helps people recognize and use tools to survive and thrive in daily life.

James Dobson, *Holding on to your Faith When God Doesn't Make Sense*. Wheaton, Ill.: Tyndale, 1993. If you are currently waist-deep in problems, pressure, and stress, this book will help. No quick fixes or easy answers are offered, but what is presented —biblical truths and principles—work all the time with God's people.

Brenda Hunter, *Home by Choice*. Grand Rapids: Zondervan, 1990. If you are struggling with the question of being a full- or part-time employee or a stay-at-home mom, I suggest you read this one. Despite the impressive amount of research presented, the text is clear, straightforward language.

Leland Ryken, *Work & Leisure in Christian Perspective*. Portland, Ore.: Multnomah, 1987. This book helped me to see a difference between my job and my career. Both are a calling from

God, not just a product of circumstances. It demolishes the lie that some jobs are more sacred and important to God than others.

## Giving

Gene A. Getz, *Real Prosperity.* Chicago: Moody, 1990. Of all the books on finances available, this one is, in my opinion, the absolute best. You will learn how to study Scripture and learn 126 principles from the Bible and how to put them to work in your life.

Charles Swindoll, *Hand Me Another Brick* (1986), *Improving Your Serve* (1982), and *Strengthening Your Grip* (1990): Waco, Tex.: Word. This trilogy by master pastor-teacher Swindoll looks at various aspects of Christian life and service. Nobody can tell stories that superglue principles into your life like Swindoll.

## Your Reserves

Ron Blue, *Master Your Money.* Nashville: Thomas Nelson, 1986. If you are detail-oriented, the author is speaking your language. Not only will you learn biblical financial principles, you will learn the systems and procedures that professionals have used for years.

Howard L. Dayton, Jr., *Your Money—Frustration or Freedom.* Wheaton, Ill.: Tyndale, 1985. If you are a conceptual, creative type who detests details and are not math-oriented, this book has the same principles as the book above, written in your language.

## Living on a Reduced Income

Mary Hunt, *The Best of the Cheapskate Monthly—Simple Tips for Living Lean in the 90's.* New York: St. Martin's Press, 1993. This practical book is a compilation of tips from the author's newsletter.

Rhonda Barfield, *Eat Well for Fifty Dollars a Week.* St. Charles, Mo.: Rhonda Barfield, 1993. Learn from someone who has been there; the author tells in detail how she feeds her family of six on less than $50/week!

Three good newsletters will give you cost-cutting tips:
*The Cheapskate Monthly,* P.O. Box 2135, Paramount, CA 90723-

8135; *The Tightwad Gazette*, Rural Rt. 1, Box 3570, Leeds, ME 04263; *Thrifty Times*, P.O. Box 6164, Scottsdale, AZ 85261-6164.

## Buying and Financing Your Home and Car

Wilson J. Humber, *Dollars & Sense.* Colorado Springs: NavPress, 1993. This practical Bible-based book gives you 108 principles that will help you put your life back on solid financial ground.

Gary Smalley, *His Needs, Her Needs.* Grand Rapids: Zondervan, 1978. Understanding your spouse's needs can help you both when you are planning to make major purchases and you want to be sure both of you are happy with what is bought. By learning to focus first on God, then on the spouse, partners find the majority of sources of tension removed. If more men would read this book, dormant marriages would be revived.

## Emerging from Debt—The Black Hole

Ron Blue, *The Debt Squeeze.* Colorado Springs: Focus on the Family, 1989. Simple, straighforward, and practical, this book will get you out of debt in three years or less.

Larry Burkett, *Debt-Free Living.* Chicago: Moody, 1989. Everything you want to know about getting out of debt once and for all. There are more than 200,000 copies in print of this book written by a Christian author/broadcaster who identifies then illustrates most common methods of getting debt free.

## Creating Spending Plans

Larry Burkett, *Financial Planning Workshop.* Chicago: Moody, 1979. This simple, practical program is available in paperback or for your home computer.

"QUICKEN" from Intuit. This is the country's most popular financial planning software. Available for most home computers, this powerful package does budgets, investment, tax plans, and more.

## Insurance & Investing

Wilson J. Humber, *Buying Insurance: Maximum Protection at Minimum Cost*. Chicago: Moody, 1994. If you want to cut the cost of insurance (medical, disability, home, auto, and life) 25 percent or more, this small book will tell you how.

_____. *Saving the Best for Last*. Chicago: Moody, 1994. If you want to learn tax, investment, and estate planning from a Christian perspective, this book is your best resource. It covers small to large incomes and estates.

Austin Pryor, *Sound Mind Investing*. Chicago: Moody, 1992. This reference book on investing is full of valuable information on investing, particularly into mutual funds.

## Perfecting Your Personal Plan

Larry Crabb, *Finding God*. Grand Rapids: Zondervan, 1993. This work is the story of facing and solving personal challenges of life. The same principles will apply to finances or any area of life.

Howard and William Hendricks, *Living by the Book*. Chicago: Moody, 1991. If your personal Bible study is non-existent, shallow, or mundane, allow "the prof" to tell you three simple but powerful methods to help you master effective Bible study.

J. I. Packer, *Knowing God*. Downers Grove: InterVarsity Press, 1973. I read this Christian classic biannually to keep my attitude and actions in proper balance. Besides deepening your mental concept of our Creator, Dr. Packer stresses personal relationship with God.